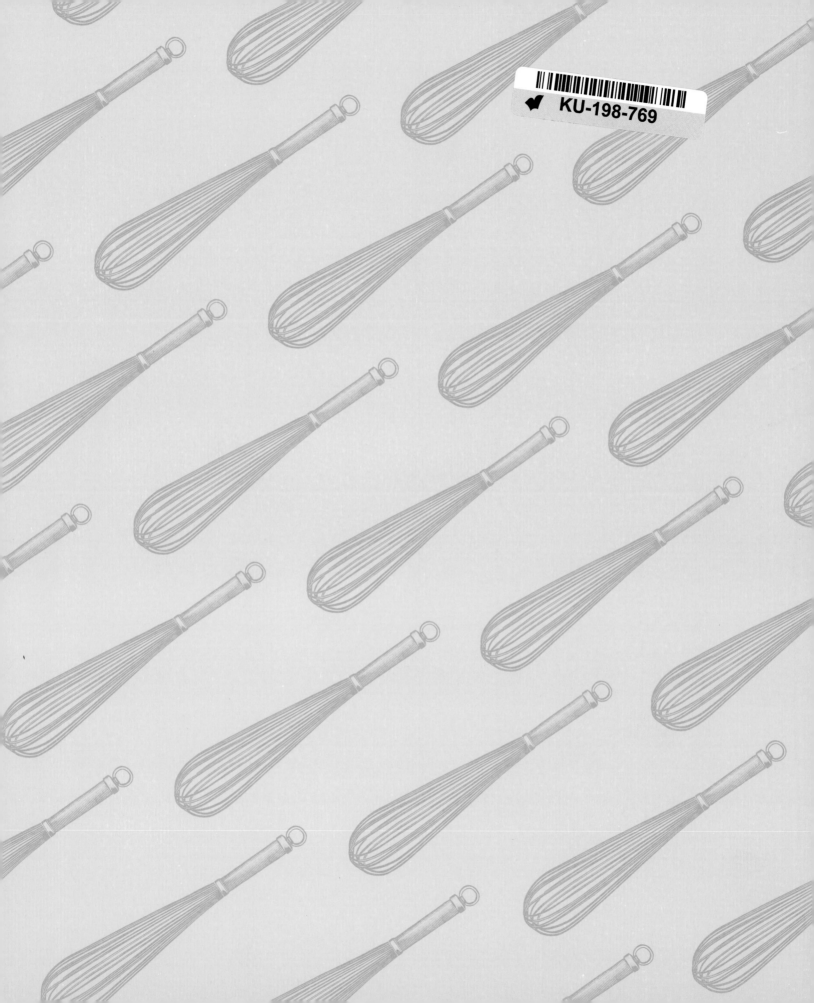

Patisserie

by
THE EDITORS OF TIME-LIFE BOOKS

TIME-LIFE BOOKS·AMSTERDAM

TIME-LIFE BOOKS
EUROPEAN EDITOR: Kit van Tulleken
Design Director: Louis Klein
Photography Director: Pamela Marke
Planning Director: Alan Lothian
Chief of Research: Vanessa Kramer
Chief Sub-Editor: Ilse Gray

THE GOOD COOK
Series Editor: Ellen Galford
Series Co-ordinators: Liz Timothy, Debbie Litton

Editorial Staff for *Patisserie*
Text Editor: Nicoletta Flessati
Anthology Editor: Anne Jackson
Staff Writers: Sally Crawford (principal), Alexandra Carlier, Tim Fraser, Thom Henvey
Researchers: Joy Davies (principal), Nora Carey
Designers: Michael Morey, Mary Staples
Sub-Editors: Kate Cann, Frances Dixon, Charles Boyle, Sally Rowland
Anthology Researchers: Stephanie Lee, Debra Raad
Anthology Assistant: Aquila Kegan
Design Assistant: David Mackersey
Proofreader: Judith Heaton
Editorial Assistant: Molly Sutherland

EDITORIAL PRODUCTION FOR THE SERIES
Chief: Ellen Brush
Quality Control: Douglas Whitworth
Traffic Co-ordinators: Jane Lillicrap, Linda Mallett
Picture Co-ordinators: Sarah Dawson, Ros Smith
Art Department: Janet Matthew
Editorial Department: Lesley Kinahan, Debra Lelliott, Sylvia Osborne

TIME LIFE BOOKS

PEOPLES OF THE WILD
THE EPIC OF FLIGHT
THE SEAFARERS
WORLD WAR II
THE GOOD COOK
THE TIME-LIFE ENCYCLOPAEDIA OF GARDENING
HUMAN BEHAVIOUR
THE GREAT CITIES
THE ART OF SEWING
THE OLD WEST
THE WORLD'S WILD PLACES
THE EMERGENCE OF MAN
LIFE LIBRARY OF PHOTOGRAPHY
THIS FABULOUS CENTURY
TIME-LIFE LIBRARY OF ART
FOODS OF THE WORLD
GREAT AGES OF MAN
LIFE SCIENCE LIBRARY
LIFE NATURE LIBRARY
YOUNG READERS LIBRARY
LIFE WORLD LIBRARY
THE TIME-LIFE BOOK OF BOATING
TECHNIQUES OF PHOTOGRAPHY
LIFE AT WAR
LIFE GOES TO THE MOVIES
BEST OF LIFE

Cover: Resplendent in silken coatings of white and pastel-tinted fondant, iced petits fours lie enticingly displayed on a silver platter. The cakes began as sheets of sponge that were sandwiched with apricot glaze and cut into a variety of little shapes—each of which was then individually iced and decorated (*page 44*).

THE CHIEF CONSULTANT:
Richard Olney, an American, has lived and worked since 1951 in France, where he is a highly regarded authority on food and wine. He is the author of *The French Menu Cookbook* and the award-winning *Simple French Food,* and has contributed to numerous gastronomic magazines in France and the United States, including the influential journals *Cuisine et Vins de France* and *La Revue du Vin de France.* He has directed cooking courses in France and the United States and is a member of several distinguished gastronomic and oenological societies, including *L'Académie Internationale du Vin, La Confrérie des Chevaliers du Tastevin* and *La Commanderie du Bontemps de Médoc et des Graves.*

THE STUDIO CONSULTANT:
Pat Alburey is a Member of the Association of Home Economists of Great Britain. H wide experience includes preparing foods for photography, teaching cookery a creating recipes. She was responsible for the majority of the step-by-step demonstr tions in this volume.

THE PHOTOGRAPHERS:
John Elliott, based in London, trained at the Regent Street Polytechnic. He has extensi experience in photographing a wide range of subjects for advertising and magazi assignments. His special interest is food photography.
John Cook, born in London, trained as a photographer with the Royal Air Force a with the Regent Street Polytechnic. He specializes in food and still-life photography both advertising and editorial use.

THE INTERNATIONAL CONSULTANTS:
Great Britain: *Jane Grigson* was born in Gloucester and brought up in the north England. She is a graduate of Cambridge University. Her first book on food, *Charc terie and French Pork Cookery*, was published in 1967; since then, she has published number of cookery books, including *Good Things, English Food* and *Jane Grigso Vegetable Book.* She became cookery correspondent for the colour magazine of t London *Observer* in 1968. *Alan Davidson* is the author of *Fish and Fish Dishes of La Mediterranean Seafood* and *North Atlantic Seafood.* He is the founder of Prospe Books, which specializes in scholarly publications on food and cookery. **Franc** *Michel Lemonnier* was born in Normandy. He began contributing to the magazi *Cuisine et Vins de France* in 1960, and also writes for several other important Fren food and wine periodicals. The co-founder and vice-president of the society *L Amitiés Gastronomiques Internationales,* he is a frequent lecturer on wine and member of most of the vinicultural confraternities and academies in France. **German** *Jochen Kuchenbecker* trained as a chef, but worked for 10 years as a food photogr pher in many European countries before opening his own restaurant in Hamburg. *An Brakemeier,* who also lives in Hamburg, has published articles on food and cooking many German periodicals. She is the co-author of three cookery books. **Italy:** *Massir Alberini* divides his time between Milan and Venice. He is a well-known food writer a journalist, with a particular interest in culinary history. Among his 14 books are *Storia Pranzo all'Italiana, 4000 Anni a Tavola* and *100 Ricette Storiche.* **The Netherlan** *Hugh Jans,* a resident of Amsterdam, has been translating cookery books and artic for more than 25 years. He has also published several books of his own, including *Bis Koken* and *Sla, Slaatjes, Snacks,* and his recipes are published in many Dut magazines. **The United States:** *Carol Cutler,* who lives in Washington, DC, is the auth of three cookery books, including the award-winning *The Six-Minute Soufflé and Ot Culinary Delights. Judith Olney* received her culinary training in England and Fran and has written two cookery books.

Valuable help was given in the preparation of this volume by the following members Time-Life Books: *Maria Vincenza Aloisi, Joséphine du Brusle* (Paris); *Janny Hoving* (Amsterdam); *Elisabeth Kraemer* (Bonn); *Ann Natanson, Mimi Murphy* (Rome); *Bo Schmid* (Milan).

CONTENTS

Glories of the Baker's Art

Of all the branches of culinary enterprise, patisserie is the most fanciful. Included in its realm are such tempting morsels as snowy meringue swirls, rum-soaked babas and tiny sponge cakes swathed in fondant, as well as plump, jam-filled doughnuts and choux rings laden with cream and raspberries. Much of the delight in making such cakes lies in the design and fashioning of decorations. These can be as straightforward as a lattice of piped meringue or a coating of jam and coconut, or they can be as whimsical as delicately wrought chocolate tracery and rosebuds moulded from icing. When the great 17th-century French painter Claude Lorrain conceded that the only two arts were "painting and ornamental pastry" he knew what he was talking about—he had been apprenticed to a pastry-cook when young.

In this volume, due emphasis is given to the art of decoration without neglecting the careful preparation of ingredients and the assembly of the cakes themselves. Thus, the introductory section contains a guide to garnishes for patisserie and detailed demonstrations of piping techniques, as well as information on how to cook sugar syrups and beat meringues. The four chapters that follow describe the basic techniques for assembling, baking and embellishing meringues, cakes, pastries and yeast cakes. The final chapter illustrates cooking methods other than baking, including how to deep fry doughnuts, poach fruit-filled dumplings and use a heated iron to produce waffles. An anthology of international recipes completes the book.

All over the world, decorative confections are the stuff of celebration. Into this category fall the fruit-filled pastries known as Hamantaschen (recipes, pages 124 and 125) that are eaten for the Jewish festival of Purim. In many parts of Christendom, Lent is marked by the serving of waffles, small yeast cakes, pastries or fritters, such as the semlor or Shrove Tuesday buns of Sweden (recipe, page 136). In Andalusia in Spain, cooks make almond-flavoured tarts called hornazos (recipe, page 119) for Easter, while in parts of England spicy yeast buns known as wigs (recipe, page 136) are fare for Ascension Day and at Christmas time.

There is no need, of course, to limit the enjoyment of patisserie to special days; it is food to be appreciated at any time. A homely yeast bun is just as welcome at breakfast as a tray of miniature éclairs is admired at the finale of a formal dinner. Even so, many devotees of patisserie believe it is best appreciated at its own hour—mid-morning or in the afternoon—and for its own sake, in quiet and leisurely fashion. Accompanied by a cup of coffee or tea or a glass of wine, the occasion becomes a calming respite from the day's distractions, permitting the small self-indulgence of a tartlet, iced sponge cake or nut-flavoured meringue.

The forerunners of such delicacies were probably no more than coarse flatbreads, sweetened with honey and fruit and enlivened with spices. Although the flour available today is a good deal more refined than that used in the ancient world, the unleavened Greek cakes known as melomacarona (recipe, page 107) have changed surprisingly little over the centuries. The ancient world's major contribution to patisserie, however, was the discovery of leavened bread. By flavouring this, the Egyptians were able to make the first yeast cakes.

Throughout the Middle East, cooks continued to develop the nascent art of patisserie, making use of cloves, nutmeg, ginger, walnuts and almonds. The Italians introduced these delicate Arabian pastries to European tables. From Beirut and Alexandria, Venetian trading ships brought not only spices, but also treatises on the theory and application of Arabian cuisine. The impact of Arab pastry-making on Italian cooking was revealed when Bartolomeo Scappi, chef to Popes Pius IV and V, published his Opera in 1570, which contained over 200 recipes for pastries.

These new ideas soon travelled to France and, some 85 years later, the first French book devoted entirely to pastry-making was published—Le Pastissier François by La Varenne. Hitherto, pastries and cakes had been baked as a kind of afterthought in the large ovens used for making bread, but La Varenne is the first to mention small ovens expressly for the pastry-maker's use. These ovens—petits fours in French—may have given their name to the tiny, exquisitely decorated cakes.

Patisserie was now an established art. Throughout the 18th century, cooks created new confections. During this period, millers discovered that by sieving flour through finely woven silk, they could extract most of the husk. Pastry-cooks no longer had to rely on yeast to leaven their cakes; eggs alone would raise the more refined flour, producing airy sponges. The new developments were not confined to flour-based confections; in 1720, a Swiss pastry-cook from the town of Mehrinyghen beat egg whites and sugar together to create meringues.

In the early 19th century, patisserie reached new heights of elaboration at the hands of the legendary chef Antonin Carême. It was then that the most fantastic creations of patisserie were made—the ornate and colourful centre-pieces that decorated the tables of the rich. As replicas of temples, windmills and castles, these towering structures were inspired more by architecture than cookery. Such flamboyant displays are no longer fashionable but, happily, the tradition of fine baking continues in pastry shop and café. And, through the pages of this volume, the age-old arts of patisserie find their way to your own oven and table.

Concentrating Sweetness: from Syrups to Caramel

Syrups and caramels are solutions of sugar and water that have been boiled to high temperatures. A light sugar syrup, made with 500 g (1 lb) sugar and 60 cl (1 pint) water, is often used in patisserie for moistening sponge cake and for thinning fillings and icings. The syrup is boiled for only a minute or two and it remains liquid when cooled. Longer boiling causes water to evaporate, which increases the sugar concentration. At various stages of concentration, the syrup takes on distinct qualities that makes it suitable for a range of different purposes. The most important stages for patisserie (*boxes, below*) take their names from the way a few drops of syrup look and feel when tested.

Thread syrup is used to make buttercream (*page 16*). At the soft-ball stage, syrup can be transformed, by beating, into fondant (*page 16*). Hard-ball syrup, whisked into beaten egg whites, produces Italian meringue (*page 8*). Caramel will function decoratively as an amber glaze (*page 59*) and is valued for its rich flavour.

Because sugar syrup reaches a high temperature, you should use a heavy pan that will conduct heat efficiently—a copper pan is ideal. A sugar thermometer is invaluable for giving accurate readings of the syrup's temperature and therefore of its degree of concentration. Before use, test the accuracy of your thermometer by placing it in a pan of water and bringing the water to the boil. When the water is boiling, the thermometer should read 100°C (212°F); if the reading is a few degrees higher or lower, your readings for all the syrups' stages should be increased or decreased accordingly.

How long you need to boil the syrup before it reaches the stage you want will depend on the amount of water you have added. The proportions used here for more concentrated syrups—500 g (1 lb) sugar to 15 cl (¼ pint) water—are recommended for maximum convenience: the sugar will dissolve easily and you will not need to boil the syrup for so long.

When you begin to cook the syrup, stir the mixture gently so that all the sugar dissolves completely. Crystals left undissolved once the mixture begins to boil may spoil the syrup by causing it to crystallize.

1 **Adding sugar.** Put water into a pan and pour in granulated sugar (*above*)—here, the proportions are 500 g (1 lb) sugar to 15 cl (¼ pint) water. Set over a medium heat and stir the mixture gently with a wooden spoon to dissolve the sugar.

Thread 106°-113°C (223°-236°F)

A fine filament. When the syrup has reached the temperature appropriate for the thread stage, remove the pan from the heat and put it in a bowl of iced water. Dip a spoon in the syrup, then raise the spoon and allow the syrup to fall back into the pan. The syrup should form a fine, short thread (*above*).

Soft Ball 112°-116°C (234°-240°F)

1 **Testing syrup.** When the syrup has reached the temperature appropriate for the soft-ball stage, arrest cooking by dipping the pan in iced water. Drop a little of the sugar syrup—about half a teaspoonful—from a spoon into a bowl of ice and water (*above*).

2 **A pliable shape.** With your fingers, mould the syrup into a ball. Remove the ball from the water and hold it between your fingers. It should begin to lose its shape immediately (*above*). The syrup has no resistance when squeezed and feels sticky to the touch.

2 **Removing crystals.** Stir the syrup until the sugar has dissolved completely. If any sugar has splashed on to the sides of the pan, brush down the sides with a pastry brush dipped in warm water (*above*). Alternatively, place a lid on the pan so that condensing steam will wash any sugar down the sides of the pan.

3 **Boiling the sugar syrup.** Stop stirring and increase the heat slightly. Warm a sugar thermometer in a jug of hot water and place the thermometer in the pan of syrup. Bring the syrup to the boil and boil it rapidly until the thermometer registers the temperature corresponding to the stage of syrup you want (*boxes, below*).

4 **Arresting cooking.** Remove the sugar thermometer to a jug of hot water. Take the pan off the heat and immediately put it into a bowl of ice cubes and water to prevent further cooking (*above*). Here, the syrup—a rich amber colour—has reached the dark-caramel stage. □

Hard Ball 121°-130°C (250°-266°F)

A firm sphere. Continue boiling the syrup until the hard-ball stage is reached, then arrest cooking. Pour some syrup from a spoon into a bowl of ice cubes and water (*opposite page, below, Step 1*). With your fingers, mould the syrup into a ball. Remove the ball from the water—it will feel sticky but should keep its shape and be resistant to pressure.

Light Caramel 160°-170°C (320°-338°F)

Honey-gold syrup. Boil the sugar syrup until the temperature is appropriate for light caramel; arrest the cooking. Pour a spoonful of syrup on to a white plate; the syrup should be a pale honey colour.

Dark Caramel 165°-177°C (330°-350°F)

Reddish-amber syrup. Dip the pan of sugar syrup into iced water when the temperature is correct for dark caramel. Pour a spoonful of syrup on to a white plate. If the syrup is reddish-amber in colour, it has become dark caramel (*above*). Do not boil the syrup any more or it will taste bitter.

Whisking Egg White for a Foamy Foundation

When egg whites are beaten, they trap air and mount into a stiff, foamy mass. The addition of sugar stiffens the egg whites further, enough for them to retain their shape when piped or spooned on to baking sheets. This light, airy mixture, known as meringue, is usually baked very slowly until it is dry and crisp.

The texture of the meringue, which largely determines its uses, depends on the way the egg whites and sugar are combined. Each of the three types of meringue shown here—French, Swiss and Italian (*recipes, pages 164-165*)—has its own particular advantages.

French meringue is the simplest to prepare. It is made by whisking the whites and then gradually beating in the sugar (*right, above*). The result is best suited for spooning or piping simple shapes that, after baking, make delicate meringues for filling and decorating (*pages 28-31*).

For Italian meringue, the sugar is added to the whites in the form of a boiling syrup (*right, below*). This method partly cooks the ingredients, producing a stable meringue that can be used, without any further baking, to lighten mousses and buttercreams (*page 17*). Italian meringue is also ideal for decorative toppings that only require the briefest time in the oven to colour them (*page 56*).

The third type of meringue—Swiss—is made by beating egg whites and sugar over boiling water (*box, opposite page*). This produces a dense mixture that holds its shape well and bakes to a particularly firm meringue. It is suitable for piping into complex shapes (*page 26*), and is the best choice for ornate decorations.

Whichever mixture you are making, the whites must be free from any trace of egg yolk, which would prevent the whites from mounting fully. The mixing bowl should be made of a material that does not retain grease, such as glass, porcelain or stainless steel. Best of all is copper, which reacts chemically with egg whites to produce a very stable foam.

French meringue should be shaped and baked immediately after you have prepared it, as it easily absorbs moisture and starts to separate. Italian and Swiss mixtures will keep for a few hours before use, provided they are covered.

1 **Separating eggs.** Over a small bowl, crack an egg sharply and prise apart the two halves of the shell. Pass the yolk from one half shell to the other, letting the white fall into the bowl. Put the yolk in a second bowl and transfer the white to a large mixing bowl. Separate the remaining eggs in the same way. Reserve the yolks for use in other preparations.

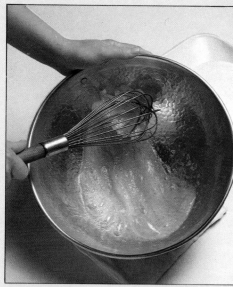

2 **Beating the whites.** Using a balloon whisk, beat the egg whites slowly and regularly with a figure-of-eight motion. When the egg whites have formed a translucent froth, whisk more rapidly with a circular motion, lifting the whites to incorporate the maximum amount of air.

An Adaptable Meringue Made with Boiling Syrup

1 **Adding sugar syrup.** Prepare a sugar syrup and cook it to the hard-ball stage (*page 6*). Separate eggs and whisk the whites until they form stiff peaks (*above, Steps 1 and 2*). Whisking all the time, pour the boiling syrup into the whites in a thin, steady stream (*above*); this operation is easier with the help of another person.

2 **Finishing the meringue.** When all the syrup has been beaten into the whites, continue to whisk the meringue mixture vigorously while it cools. Once cool, the meringue will be very thick and glossy and ready for use (*above*).

3 **Adding sugar.** Continue whisking the whites until a stiff peak is formed on the whisk when you lift it from the bowl. Sprinkle a little castor sugar over the whites (*above*). Beat the sugar into the whites until the mixture is stiff and shiny.

4 **Finishing the meringue.** Sprinkle the rest of the castor sugar over the beaten egg whites, a little at a time, beating well after each addition until the mixture has regained its stiff texture and shiny appearance. When all the sugar has been incorporated, the meringue will be very stiff and glossy (*above*). □

A Stable Meringue Formed Over Heat

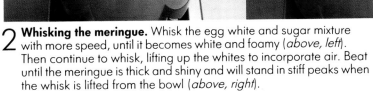

1 **Beating egg whites and sugar.** Bring a pan of water to a gentle simmer over low heat. Separate egg whites and put them into a large mixing bowl; add sugar. Set the bowl over the pan, making sure that the bottom of the bowl does not touch the water. Whisk the mixture gently until the sugar has melted (*above*).

2 **Whisking the meringue.** Whisk the egg white and sugar mixture with more speed, until it becomes white and foamy (*above, left*). Then continue to whisk, lifting up the whites to incorporate air. Beat until the meringue is thick and shiny and will stand in stiff peaks when the whisk is lifted from the bowl (*above, right*).

A Chocolate Compendium

Chocolate serves patisserie in numerous guises. Melted to satin smoothness, it blends readily into fillings and batters, conferring dramatic colour and seductive flavour. It can also be poured or brushed over cakes and pastries to provide glossy coatings and frostings. And because it is malleable when warm, firm when cool, chocolate can be shaped and moulded into an array of charming decorations.

Chocolate is a blend of cocoa solids and cocoa butter, to which manufacturers may add other vegetable fats, milk and sugar. The higher the proportion of other fats incorporated during manufacture, the softer the chocolate will be. If no milk is added the chocolate is termed plain; its degree of sweetness depends, of course, on how much sugar is added. For patisserie, a soft dipping chocolate and a hard, plain eating chocolate—either bitter or semi-sweet according to preference—are the varieties most widely used.

The outstanding virtue of soft chocolate is its fluidity. It melts to a flowing consistency that is ideal for dipping or coating cakes and meringues. It can also be poured in a thin layer (*right, below*), allowed to set, and then formed into decorative frills and garnishes. On its own, chocolate easily scorches if it is exposed to direct heat, so it is best to melt it in a bowl set over a pan of hot water (*right*).

For the majority of preparations, hard chocolate is chosen; it contains more cocoa butter and has a better flavour than soft chocolate. It chops and grates well (*right, above*) to furnish simple decorations such as chocolate chips and feathery curls.

Melted on its own, hard chocolate can be poured and left to set (*opposite page, below*) for shaping into decorations that contribute greatly to a cake's flavour.

For the most luxurious fillings and coatings of all, hard chocolate is mixed with ingredients such as double cream and butter. Blended with butter, icing sugar, flavourings and milk, it becomes a glossy frosting (*opposite page, above; recipe, page 165*). Heating chocolate with double cream yields another sumptuous covering; the same mixture chilled and whisked to airy lightness constitutes the classic filling known as *ganache* (*opposite page, centre; recipe, page 167*).

Slivering with a Sharp Knife

Chopping chocolate. Break a block of hard chocolate into pieces. Using a large, sharp knife, press on the tip of the blade with one hand. Pivot the blade in an arc and slice up and down to make slivers.

Grating Feathery Curls

Grating chocolate. Break a block of hard chocolate into large pieces. Rub the chocolate against the coarse side of a grater, using long strokes to form curls.

Smooth Melting Over Steam

1 **Cutting soft chocolate.** Using a large knife, cut a block of dipping chocolate into slices (*above*). Place the slices of chocolate in a heatproof bowl that will fit snugly over a pan.

2 **Melting the chocolate.** Quarter-fill the pan with water and heat until almost boiling. Set the pan on a trivet. Place the bowl over the pan and stir the chocolate until it melts to a smooth liquid.

Fashioning Delicate Frills

1 **Spreading melted chocolate.** Melt soft chocolate (*box, above*) and pour it on to a marble slab or baking sheet. Using a metal spatula, spread the chocolate in a thin layer (*above*); leave to cool and set.

2 **Shaping frills.** Line a tray with wax paper. Position a small metal spatula at a low angle against the chocolate. As you push the blade tip, a thin layer of chocolate will curl into a frill. Transfer the frill to the tray.

A Fudge Frosting Beaten Over Ice

1 **Melting chocolate and butter.** Break hard chocolate into small equal-sized pieces. Put them in a pan with cubes of butter and set over gentle heat. Stir with a wooden spoon until the chocolate melts.

2 **Adding milk.** Stir icing sugar, salt and vanilla extract into the mixture. Pour in milk (*above*) and beat over low heat until the ingredients blend to a smooth paste. Remove the pan from the heat.

3 **Thickening the frosting.** Partly fill a large bowl with water and ice cubes. Set the pan in the bowl. Beat the icing with a wooden spoon for about 5 minutes, until it is thick enough to coat the spoon.

Blending in Cream for a Touch of Luxury

1 **Heating the ingredients.** Chop hard chocolate—here, semi-sweet is used. Pour double cream into a pan set over a low heat; add the chocolate. Melt the chocolate and stir for about 10 minutes.

2 **Whisking the mixture.** Pour the mixture into a bowl, cover with plastic film and refrigerate it for at least an hour, or overnight. Steady the bowl on a damp cloth and whisk the mixture thoroughly.

3 **Completing the ganache.** Continue to whisk until the mixture doubles in volume and becomes fluffy—10 to 15 minutes of whisking by hand, or 5 to 10 minutes using an electric mixer.

Precision Cutting for Paper-Thin Squares

1 **Smoothing chocolate.** Butter a Swiss roll tin; line it with wax paper. Melt hard chocolate over hot water; pour it into the tin 3 mm (⅛ inch) deep. Rap the tin on the work surface. Smooth with a spatula.

2 **Unmoulding the chocolate sheet.** Leave the chocolate to set in a cool place— about 30 minutes. Place a sheet of wax paper on the surface; invert the tin over it. Lift the tin and peel away the lining paper.

3 **Making shapes.** Using a long, sharp knife or a decorative cutter, cut the sheet of chocolate into shapes. To make squares, slice the sheet lengthwise into strips, then cut the strips crosswise (*above*).

Preparing Nuts to Play Their Part

Nuts are an indispensable ally in sweet cookery. They can be used to decorate anything from a petit four to a dumpling. Chopped, grated or finely ground, they add flavour and texture to fillings, cake batters, meringues and pastry doughs. Nuts can also be combined with sugar to make marzipan (*opposite page, centre; recipe, page 166*)—or to make praline, a brittle confection (*boxes, below; recipes, page 167*) that adds a crunchy texture to buttercreams and meringues.

After shelling, nuts are usually peeled to rid them of their bitter inner coat. Almonds and pistachio nuts are easier to peel if they are parboiled first (*right, above*). Most other nuts respond to dry roasting, after which their skins can be rubbed off (*opposite page, above, left*). The tight, inner skin of coconut can be peeled off with a knife (*right*).

Nuts should be chopped with a heavy knife (*opposite page, above, middle*), or ground in a food processor (*opposite page, above, right*). Ground nuts—usually almonds—are mixed with icing sugar and bound with egg white to form marzipan. Kneaded into a small ball, the mixture can be rolled out and cut into decorative shapes or used as a cake filling or topping.

Whole or finely ground nuts can be combined with sugar and caramelized to make praline, or mixed with sugar syrup to make white praline. Both mixtures are cooled, then crushed to a powder.

Blanching to Loosen Skins

1 **Loosening the skins.** Tip shelled nuts—here, almonds are used—into a pan of boiling water (*above*); parboil them for about a minute. Drain the nuts.

2 **Rubbing off the skins.** Spread out a towel and tip the parboiled nuts on to it; fold the towel over them (*above*). Rub the nuts vigorously in the folded towel until they have all shed their skins.

Opening and Grating a Coconut

1 **Cracking the coconut.** Remove the tuft to expose the eyes; pierce them with a skewer and drain the liquid. Use the back of a cleaver to crack the seam near the nut's base; it will open along the seam.

2 **Grating the flesh.** Use a knife to divide the flesh inside the nut into sections. Insert the knife behind each section to prise it loose from the shell. Cut away the brown outer skin. Finely grate the flesh (*above*).

Praline: a Brittle Amalgam of Nuts and Caramel

1 **Caramelizing the nuts.** Put blanched almonds and sugar into a heavy pan. Using a wooden spoon, stir over a low heat until the sugar melts and turns a pale amber. Remove from the heat.

2 **Cooling the mixture.** Pour the mixture on to an oiled marble slab or baking sheet. While still hot, quickly spread it out with the spoon; leave to cool and harden.

3 **Crushing the praline.** Break the cooled praline into pieces and put in a strong plastic bag. Holding the bag closed with one hand, use a rolling pin to crush the praline until it forms coarse crumbs.

Parching Off Papery Skins

Peeling roasted nuts. Tip nuts—here, hazelnuts—on to a baking sheet; roast in a preheated 170°C (325°F or Mark 3) oven for about 10 minutes. Transfer the nuts to a towel; rub off the skins.

A Neat Method of Chopping

Pivoting a knife. Using a heavy knife, coarsely chop nuts—here, pecan nuts. Press on the tip with one hand and pivot the blade in an arc while moving it up and down to chop the nuts more finely.

Pulverizing in a Processor

Grinding the nuts. Put peeled nuts— here, almonds—into a food processor. Grind in short bursts, using a spatula to push down nuts that cling to the sides, until a coarse-textured flour results.

A Firm Paste from Ground Almonds

1 **Mixing nuts and sugar.** Squeeze lemon juice and lightly beat egg whites. Blanch almonds, grind them in a processor and place them in a bowl. Stir sifted icing sugar into the ground nuts (*above*).

2 **Adding egg white.** To prevent sticking, use a knife to stir the lemon juice and a little egg white into the almond mixture. Add more egg, a little at a time, mixing it in by hand to make a stiff paste.

3 **Kneading the paste.** Lightly sprinkle a work surface—here, marble—with icing sugar. Gather the paste into a ball and knead it lightly—do not overwork the paste or it will become oily.

4 **Sieving the praline.** Put the praline in a coarse-meshed metal sieve set over a bowl. Use your fingertips to force the praline through the sieve. Return large pieces to the bag and crush them again.

White Praline: a Soft Variation

1 **Adding nuts.** Cook a sugar syrup to the hard-ball stage (*page 6*). Off the heat, add finely ground almonds and stir them in. Pour the mixture on to an oiled marble slab, spread it out and let cool.

2 **Sieving the white praline.** Break the cooled praline into pieces with your hands. Using a wooden spoon, press the praline through a metal sieve (*above*).

13

Fruit Glazes in a Rainbow of Hues

Fruit purées, syrups and glazes provide flavour, colour and gloss to little cakes and pastries and often act as edible adhesives for different parts of an assembly.

Purées are easily made from fresh soft fruit such as raspberries or strawberries (*right*), or from lightly cooked apples, apricots or peaches. Purées can be blended with whipped cream for use as a filling or a decorative finish. A fruit purée can also be combined with a light sugar syrup (*page 6*) for flavouring meringue.

Fruit syrups are made by adding fruit juice, such as the passion fruit juice shown here (*right, centre*), to a light sugar syrup. Syrups are brushed on to sponge cakes to moisten and flavour them.

A fruit glaze contains a higher concentration of sugar than fruit syrup. A glaze is fluid when warm, becoming stiff and glossy as it cools. Its sheen provides eye-catching coatings for tarts or savarins (*page 72*). A glaze will also seal crumbly surfaces of cake and sponge.

The simplest fruit glaze is made by warming jam, then sieving it to remove solids (*far right, above*). Apricot jam has a mild taste and is suitable when a pale colour is required; use seedless raspberry or strawberry jam for a warmer tone.

Other glazes are made by cooking fresh fruit in a sugar syrup, then reducing the syrup to concentrate its flavour and thicken it. Fresh redcurrants produce a fine rosy-hued glaze when treated in this way (*below*); the poached fruit itself can be used in a tart.

A Crushed Strawberry Purée

Sieving strawberries. Remove leaves and hulls from ripe strawberries; put the fruit in a nylon sieve set over a bowl. Using a wooden spoon or pestle, rub the strawberries through the sieve (*above*).

An Apricot Glaze

Sieving the jam. In a pan set over low heat, warm apricot jam until it is liquid. To remove any solids, press the liquid jam through a fine-meshed sieve (*above*). Warm the glaze before use.

A Tropical Glow from Passion Fruit

1 **Extracting pulp.** Cut passion fruit in half. Using a teaspoon, scoop the seed-laden pulp into a nylon sieve set over a bowl (*above*); discard the skins. Press the pulp through the sieve; discard the seeds.

2 **Finishing the syrup.** Put the sieved juice into a measuring jug. Stir in an equal volume of sugar syrup. Pour the mixture into a pan (*above*) and stir over very low heat until the liquids are well blended.

A Ruby Syrup from Redcurrants

1 **Removing stems.** Rinse redcurrants and drain them in a colander. Place the stem of a spray of redcurrants between the prongs of a fork. Pull gently on the stem, allowing the berries to fall into a bowl.

2 **Poaching the berries.** Add the berries to a wide pan of simmering sugar syrup and poach them—without stirring—for about 2 minutes. Using a slotted spoon, transfer the berries to a bowl (*above*).

3 **Straining the syrup.** Boil the syrup until it reduces to a thickened glaze. To remove any solids, strain the glaze through a nylon sieve into a bowl (*above*).

Primer of Icings and Fillings

uch of the charm of patisserie lies in the
ings and fillings that so often adorn it.
ings are basically sugar pastes, often
pplemented with lemon juice or some
her flavouring, and fluid enough to be
ured or spread in a thin layer. Fillings
e usually more substantial than icings.
hey range from a simple layer of fruit or
m to creams and mousses flavoured in a
ide variety of ways.

The simplest icing is glacé (*right; rec-
e, page 166*), a paste of icing sugar and
arm water or fruit juice that forms a
anslucent, semi-hard glaze. A stiffer,
ore opaque icing can be made by mixing
e sugar with egg whites (*right, below;
cipe, page 166*); this icing—known as
yal icing—spreads easily and sets hard.

A third icing, fondant (*page 16, above;
cipe, page 165*) starts as a sugar syrup
hich is worked until crystals form. Set
ide to mature, the fondant gradually
ftens and acquires its characteristical-
silken texture. Before use, the fondant
warmed and diluted with water or a
ght sugar syrup for a glossier effect.

Two particularly versatile fillings—
uttercream and pastry cream—are dem-
nstrated overleaf. Buttercream (*page
6, centre; recipe, page 166*) consists of
eaten egg yolks, sweetened with a hot
gar syrup, then mixed with butter. You
n flavour the buttercream with melted
ocolate, a little orange or lemon zest,
nely chopped nuts or praline. An espe-
ally light buttercream combines Italian
eringue with softened butter (*page 17,
entre, left; recipe, page 167*).

Pastry cream (*page 16, below; recipe,
age 166*) also contains beaten egg yolks
nd sugar, but in this case the ingredients
re cooked with flour and milk to produce
thick custard. Pastry cream will with-
tand further cooking: it can be cut into
hapes and deep fried in hot oil (*page 90*)
r combined with choux and baked as an
nusual pastry filling (*page 62*).

Another adaptable patisserie filling is
ruit mousse—in the demonstration here,
is flavoured with passion fruit juice
age 17, right; recipe, page 167). The
ice is first mixed with a little gelatine,
en combined with meringue to lighten
and with double cream to enrich it.

Glacé: a Simple Coating From Icing Sugar

1 **Adding liquid.** Sift icing sugar into a bowl to eliminate any lumps. Make a well in the centre of the sugar. In a pan, heat water until it is warm to the touch. Pour the water—a spoonful at a time—into the well (*above*), stirring after each addition.

2 **Beating the icing.** Mix in enough water to make a fairly loose paste. Beat the icing to blend it thoroughly (*above*). Check the consistency, adding a little more water if necessary, until the icing is thin enough to coat the spoon; use immediately.

Royal: a Stiff Paste of Sugar and Egg White

1 **Stirring in sugar.** Separate eggs; reserve the whites and set the yolks aside for another use. Sift icing sugar into another bowl. Squeeze lemon juice. Gradually stir a little of the sugar into the egg whites (*above*), then add the lemon juice.

2 **Completing the icing.** Using a spoon, whisk or electric mixer, beat the mixture vigorously until it is light and smooth. Gradually stir in the remaining sugar and continue to beat the mixture until it is stiff—about 15 minutes by hand or 7 minutes with an electric mixer. Use the icing immediately or cover it with a damp cloth to prevent it from drying out.

Fondant: Syrup Kneaded to Satin Smoothness

1 **Pouring syrup.** Lightly coat a marble slab or a large baking sheet with water. Cook a sugar syrup to the soft-ball stage (*page 6*); pour the syrup on to the marble (*above*). Allow to cool for a few minutes.

2 **Working the syrup.** Use a dampened spatula or a metal scraper to lift the edges of the syrup repeatedly and fold them into the centre (*above, left*). As the syrup becomes more viscous, work it in a figure-of-eight (*above, right*). The syrup will turn opaque; continue to work it until coarse-textured and stiff—about 10 minutes.

Buttercream: a Classic Blend of Eggs and Butter

1 **Adding sugar syrup.** Separate eggs and whisk the yolks. Gradually whisk in a hot sugar syrup cooked to the thread stage (*page 6*). Continue to whisk until the mixture is thick and fluffy.

2 **Blending butter.** Soften butter at room temperature, then beat it until smooth and creamy. Add the egg yolk and syrup mixture gradually (*above*); stir until the ingredients are evenly mixed.

3 **Finishing the cream.** Continue to beat the mixture until it is smooth and shiny. Use the buttercream immediately or put it in an airtight container and refrigerate it for up to one week.

Pastry Cream: a Versatile Cooked Filling

1 **Mixing the ingredients.** Sift flour and salt into a small bowl. Put sugar and egg yolks in a mixing bowl and beat the yolks with a wooden spoon until pale and fluffy (*above*). Add the flour and stir it in.

2 **Adding hot milk.** In a large pan, bring milk to the boil. Gradually add the milk to the flour mixture, pouring it in a thin stream and stirring at the same time to incorporate it smoothly into the mixture.

3 **Cooking the cream.** Pour the mixture into a pan and place it over a medium heat. Stirring constantly, bring the mixture to the boil. Cook the mixture, stirring, for a further 2 minutes.

3 Kneading the fondant. Moisten your hands and gather the fondant into a ball. Push it out with the heel of one hand; gather it back and repeat. Knead until the fondant feels smooth—5 to 10 minutes.

4 Ripening the fondant. Put the ball of fondant into a bowl. To prevent the fondant from drying out, cover the bowl with a damp cloth. Leave in a cool place to ripen for at least 24 hours.

5 Melting the fondant. Place the bowl of fondant over a pan half filled with hot water. Over low heat, melt the fondant; dilute it to the consistency of thick cream with sugar syrup, as here, or water.

Meringue Buttercream

Adding meringue. Prepare an Italian meringue (*page 8*)—here, using a syrup made with vanilla sugar. Cream butter. Gradually stir in the meringue, then beat the mixture until smooth and fluffy.

Sieving the cream. To ensure that the cream is perfectly smooth, sieve it into a bowl. Cool the cream and use it at once, or press plastic film against its surface and refrigerate for up to two days.

Fruit Mousse: Subtle Support from Gelatine and Cream

1 Softening the gelatine. Prepare fruit juice —here, passion fruit juice (*page 14*). Put a little of the juice into a pan; sprinkle on powdered gelatine. Leave the gelatine to absorb the liquid—about 15 minutes.

2 Adding the remaining juice. Place the pan over a low heat. Stir the mixture until it is clear. Remove the pan from the heat. Warm the rest of the fruit juice and add it to the gelatine mixture (*above*); let it cool.

3 Incorporating meringue. Make Italian meringue (*page 8*). Whip double cream. Gradually add the fruit juice and gelatine mixture to the meringue, folding it in gently with a spatula (*above*).

4 Finishing the mousse. Continue to fold in the fruit juice mixture until it has all been incorporated. To finish the mousse filling, use the same gentle folding action to incorporate the whipped cream (*above*).

Piping Decorations: Tools and Techniques

In the realm of fine cake decoration, the piping bag stands supreme. The device itself could scarcely be simpler: a conical bag filled with icing, with a hole or a shaped metal nozzle in its tip. But with this rudimentary equipment and a little practice, you can produce the exquisite array of adornments shown here and on the following pages.

Commercially produced piping bags are easy to obtain; it is even easier, though, to make your own from paper (*right*). Home-made piping bags take moments to prepare and work well with the small amounts of icing needed for little cakes. If you are piping icing of different colours, make as many bags as you need and throw them away after use.

The pattern of the piping will depend on the size and shape of the hole in the bag. For lines and dots, snip off the tip of the bag; the less paper you cut away, the finer your piping will be. For fluted piping and for petals and leaves, make V-shaped cuts in the bag; for more intricate patterns still, insert a shaped commercial nozzle.

Simple lines and borders are applied directly to the cake; more intricate decorations, such as flowers, are best made separately and fixed in place once they have dried completely. Use royal icing, which sets rock-hard, for these delicate structures. Because intricate shapes are difficult to form on a stationary surface, professional decorators pipe flowers on to a small platform called a flower nail, which can be turned to the most convenient position. You can buy flower nails in specialist shops but a good substitute can be made easily from a cork and a skewer (*right, centre*).

Delicate decorations known as lacework (*right*) are best made with the aid of a carefully drawn design. Icing—here, chocolate—is piped on to silicon paper placed over the drawing, which serves as a template for further decorations.

Both flowers and lacework should be allowed to dry completely before they are disturbed. If you are making them in advance, store them without removing them from their paper; they will be less likely to suffer damage. They will keep well in an airtight container but chocolate decorations are best used within a week.

Making a Paper Piping Bag

1 **Cutting triangles.** Cut out a rectangle of greaseproof paper about 25 by 20 cm (10 by 8 inches). Fold the rectangle in half diagonally, then cut along the crease (*above*); reserve one triangle.

2 **Folding paper.** With the right angle of the triangle at the bottom left-hand side and the shortest edge near you, take the top corner in your right hand and the bottom right-hand corner in your left hand.

Piping a Narcissus on a Flower Nail

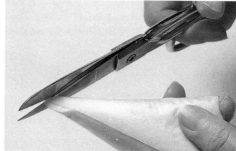

1 **Making a flower nail.** Stick a small skewer into the base of a cork (*above*). Cut a sheet of wax paper into little squares. Fix a square of paper to the top of the cork with a dab of icing.

2 **Cutting a petal nozzle.** Fill a paper piping bag two-thirds full with royal icing. Fold over the top of the bag to secure it. Flatten the tip; cut diagonally from each side to make a V-shape (*above*).

Tracing Chocolate Filigree

1 **Drawing a design.** Draw a design on a strip of card or paper. Place silicon paper over the card. Melt dipping chocolate (*page 10*); thicken it with sugar syrup. Fill a piping bag with the chocolate.

2 **Piping decorations.** Cut a tiny hole in the tip of the bag. Hold the bag above the paper and, squeezing gently, follow the lines of the drawing (*above*). Slide the paper along; pipe another decoration.

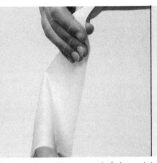

3 Making a cone. Bring your right hand under your left hand (*above, left*). Wrap the paper round your left hand to form a cone (*above, centre*). Pull the paper in your right hand towards you to make a very sharp point to the cone (*above, right*).

4 Securing the cone. Tuck the corner held in your right hand inside the cone. To prevent the cone unwinding, make two small tears in the folded edge and press down the paper between them (*above*).

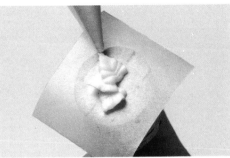
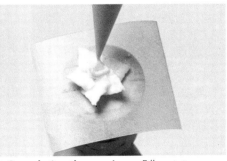

3 Piping the first petal. Hold the flower nail upright. Begin at the centre of the paper, holding the bag at a 45-degree angle to the cork. Squeeze the bag gently, moving it back and forth slightly to ripple the icing.

4 Piping more petals. When the petal is about 5 mm (¼ inch) long, pull the bag away to create a point. Continue piping petals round the flower nail, overlapping the petals slightly (*above*).

5 Completing the narcissus. Fill a piping bag with royal icing of a contrasting colour. Cut across the tip to make a tiny hole. Hold the bag perpendicular to the flower; pipe a coil in its centre.

Forming a Rose with a Petal Nozzle

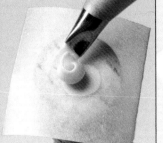

1 Fitting a metal nozzle. Make a paper piping bag; cut straight across the bag 1 cm (½ inch) from the tip. Drop a metal petal nozzle into position. Make a flower nail (*opposite page, centre*).

2 Piping a rose. Fill the bag with royal icing. With the wide end of the nozzle tip nearest the flower nail, pipe a central scroll, rotating the nail anti-clockwise as you work (*above, left*). Lower the nozzle to the scroll's base (*above, centre*). Starting and finishing at the base each time, pipe overlapping petals round the scroll (*above, right*).

Piping Decorations: the Star Nozzle

The star is the most versatile of all commercially available nozzles. It produces a fluted cylinder of icing which, by manipulating the piping bag and varying the pressure you apply, you can turn into such diverse shapes as ropes, rosettes, shells and scallops. And the star nozzle will work equally well with royal icing, buttercream, whipped cream or meringue, provided the mixture to be piped is fairly stiff and free of lumps.

The simplest straight lines of fluted piping (*right, above*) can be criss-crossed to give a lattice effect. Rosettes make attractive single motifs (*right, centre*) or they can be piped in rows on a petit four. By moving the piping bag from side to side in a zigzag motion you can create a wide rope border (*right, below*). By bringing the nozzle round in a series of arcs you can produce a flowing shell design (*opposite page, above*) that makes an interesting shape for meringues as well as for small-scale ornaments. A raised flourish is achieved by varying the pressure you apply as you make the stroke (*opposite page, centre*); by altering the direction and the pressure you can pipe a pretty curvilinear scallop (*opposite page, below*).

Before you attempt to pipe any of these decorations directly on to a cake, it is a good idea to practise first on a work surface or on an upturned tray or plate. Hold the piping bag in one hand and squeeze from the top with your thumb. To steady the bag, support it from underneath with your other hand. Squeeze gently at first, then apply more pressure to the bag if you want a thicker line. For a clean break, stop squeezing and pull the bag away sharply at the end of the line of icing.

Releasing a Rope of Icing

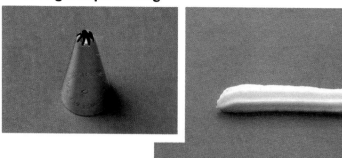

Piping a fluted line. Hold a paper piping bag with a star nozzle at a 45-degree angle and 5 mm (¼ inch) above the surface. Pipe towards yourself, raising the bag slightly as the icing falls on the surface. To finish, lower the nozzle and pull it away sharply.

A Single Action for a Neat Rosette

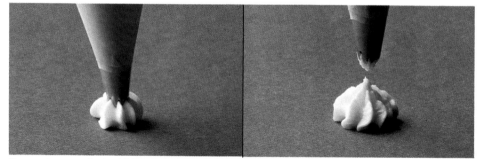

Squeezing gently. Hold the piping bag so that it is perpendicular to the work surface and just above it. Squeeze the piping bag gently to make a rosette (*above, left*). When it is the size that you want, stop squeezing and lift the bag away (*above, right*).

A Tightly Woven Cable

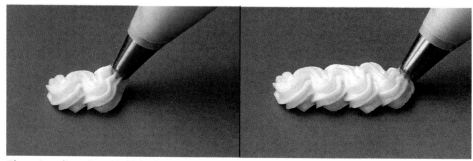

Changing direction. Hold the bag at a 45-degree angle about 5 mm (¼ inch) above the surface. Pipe a short line to the left; reverse direction and pipe a second short line to the right, close to the first. Continue piping from left to right to form a thick zigzag of icing.

A Continuous Spiral

Building up overlapping lines. Hold the bag at a 45-degree angle. Pipe a short line towards yourself, then move the bag a little to your left. Lift the bag up and over the previous line (*above, left*). Continue piping in arcs that increase in size towards the middle, then decrease towards the end (*above, centre and right*).

An Undulating Band of Shells

Varying pressure. Hold the bag at a 45-degree angle to the work surface. Squeeze a small mound, then move the bag up (*above, left*). Reduce pressure and bring the bag down to the surface and towards yourself (*above, centre*). Pull away sharply. Pipe another shell over the end of the previous one (*above, right*).

A Border of Interlocking Shells

Forming curves. Hold the bag almost perpendicular and pipe a small mound. Reduce pressure, move the bag to the right (*above, left*) in a half circle round the mound. Draw the nozzle downwards to form a tail (*above, centre*). Begin the next scallop by piping another mound over the tail of the previous one (*above, right*).

Piping Decorations: a Sampler of Possibilities

Once you have learnt the basic techniques of piping (*pages 18-21*), you are ready to experiment with some of the many metal nozzles available. A selection of these is illustrated here; beneath each nozzle are some of the patterns it produces. If you treat these examples as starting points, and then give free rein to your imagination, you will discover that the range of piped decorations is almost limitless.

Before selecting a decoration, consider the scale of the cake: a wide icing ruffle may fit comfortably on a *japonais* meringue (*page 32*), but a daintier flourish is more appropriate for a tiny petit four (*page 44*). Also, bear in mind that for any cake, large or small, the best decoration is usually simple; too much ornamentation would overpower the cake.

On the whole, any fairly stiff icing will pipe successfully. Royal icing, fondant icing, buttercream, and melted chocolate that has been thickened with a spoonful of sugar syrup (*page 6*), will all produce good results with any nozzle.

The tips of nozzles vary not only in shape but also in size. Thus, plain and fine plain nozzles are both circles, but of different diameters. Either of these will shape icing into a cylinder that can be piped into scrolls, dots, flourishes, S-shapes, coils and zigzags. You can decorate a fondant-coated profiterole with a spiral of plain piping (*page 60*), or you can pipe a lattice of straight lines to complete a buttercream tartlet (*page 54*). Rows of parallel lines or dots are made simple with double and triple plain nozzles.

Nozzles with wide, flat ends fashion icing into ribbons and, if the tip of the nozzle is also serrated, it will add an elegant, fluted effect. With other nozzles, you can fashion more complex ribbons that will resemble frills or ruffles; to produce these patterns, just hold the bag on the surface and pipe a straight line. The leaf nozzle is used for piping the petals of icing flowers and—as its name implies—for making single leaf shapes.

A serrated, semi-circular nozzle will mould icing into ridged shells that can be twisted into ropes and snails. Flower nozzles can be used to pipe swirling borders, shooting stars or, if held perpendicular to the surface, perfect single blossoms.

Plain

Fine plain

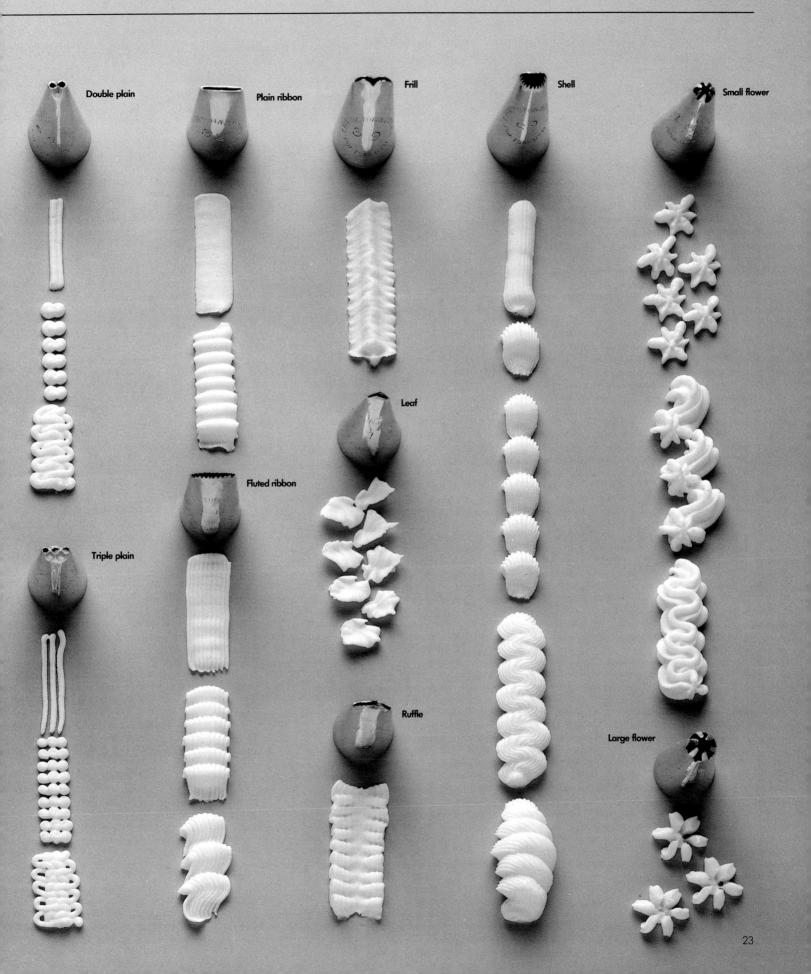

Double plain

Plain ribbon

Frill

Shell

Small flower

Leaf

Fluted ribbon

Triple plain

Ruffle

Large flower

Meringue Assemblies
Delicate Confections
Conjured from Air

The starting-point for meringues—one of the most decorative branches of patisserie—is no more than a bowl of egg whites, beaten to a snowy foam with sugar (*page 8*). But with shaping and cooking, meringue becomes the stuff of fantasy: an ethereal substance that is a perfect foil for almost any filling and topping. Just two examples from an infinite range are the chocolate-dipped assemblies filled with coffee-flavoured cream on page 26 and the twin shells adorned with strawberry-tinted cream and white fondant icing shown opposite and on page 28.

Whether the final effect is to be simple or complex, the first step is to shape the raw material. The most straightforward method is to spoon small portions of the mixture on to a lined baking sheet. Most shapes, however, require the use of a piping bag. This allows you more control and, by using nozzles of different patterns, you can make fingers and shells—plain and fluted—or elaborate whirls and curlicues.

Meringues are cooked in the slowest of ovens. The moisture in the egg whites gradually evaporates, leaving a characteristically light, crisp shell without a trace of browning. The method, in fact, is closer to drying than baking—some cooks even leave the meringues overnight in an oven heated only by its pilot light.

After the meringues are cooked, creative assembly can begin. Pairs of meringues sandwiched together with whipped cream or buttercream (*page 16*) are as simple as they are delightful. On page 30, two hemispheres of orange-flavoured meringue are hollowed out and bonded with a filling of orange mousse to make meringue "oranges". Filled meringues can receive any number of embellishments: a lustrous coating of fondant, for instance, or a thicker creamy finish such as the chocolate buttercream sprinkled with grated chocolate shown on page 28.

Meringue mixtures that incorporate chopped or ground nuts form a special sub-group known as *japonais* (*page 32*). The nut-flavoured meringue is usually baked flat at a slightly higher temperature than ordinary meringue, producing thin, crisp cakes with a hint of chewiness at their heart. Stacked with alternating layers of buttercream, *japonais* is the basis of some of the most impressive assemblies in patisserie.

eringue shells sandwiched with strawberry eam are arranged for serving. The uncooked eringue was shaped, baked at a very low mperature, then coated with fondant. To ɔmplete each assembly, cream blended with ɔréed strawberries was piped on to the base one meringue shell and topped with another.

Fluted Shells with a Contrasting Filling

Light-textured meringue is the perfect medium for creating sumptuous little cakes. Simple to make (*page 8*), meringue is supple enough to form into decorative shapes that become dry and crisp when baked in the gentlest oven heat. Sandwiching pairs of cooked meringues with a creamy filling provides a mouthwatering contrast of tastes and textures (*right; recipes, pages 92-94*).

You can spoon uncooked meringue on to a baking sheet lined with silicon paper, or you can pipe it with a plain nozzle or a star nozzle (*page 20*). Since silicon paper is non-stick, you should not have any difficulty detaching the meringues after baking. Gently lift each meringue and pull the paper away from under it.

When they are completely cool, pairs of meringues can be bound together with whipped double cream or with buttercream (*page 16*), flavoured, if you like, with ground nuts, a liqueur or a fruit purée (*page 14*). If using a liquid flavouring it is a good idea to add it to cream before you whip it, to avoid over-whipping. When adding a flavouring to butter-

cream, on the other hand, stir it into the finished mixture. Buttercream will be easier to spread if you remove it from the refrigerator about 30 minutes before use.

Coatings can be applied to the meringues either before or after they are filled. Dipping the flat bases of meringues in melted chocolate (*page 10*) provides a striking colour contrast. After the chocolate has set, you can sandwich the meringues with coffee-tinted whipped cream for a pleasing trio of flavours.

For a more delicate effect, meringues can be coated with fondant (*page 16*). A filling of whipped cream combined with a strawberry purée completes the pastel ensemble (*page 28, below*).

Alternatively, meringues can be completely masked by rich coatings (*page 28, above*). Pairs are bound with chocolate-flavoured buttercream, then spread with the same mixture and sprinkled with chocolate flakes or flaked almonds. For these assemblies, it is important to refrigerate the meringues after they have been filled with buttercream so that they do not slide about when the coating is applied.

1 Drawing guidelines. Line a baking sheet with silicon paper. Using an oval metal cutter to guide you, trace shapes on to the paper with a pencil; leave about 2.5 cm (1 inch) between each oval. To avoid marking the meringues with pencil, turn the paper over and stick the corners to the baking sheet with small dots of the uncooked meringue.

5 Flavouring a filling. Make a cup of very strong filtered coffee and let it cool. Put double cream into a bowl and add about 2 tablespoons of coffee, a spoonful at a time (*above*). Whisk the cream and coffee together until a soft peak forms on the whisk when it is lifted out of the bowl.

6 Filling the meringues. With your fingers, gently lift a meringue from the tray, pulling it off the wax paper. Take care not to mark the white surface of the meringue with chocolate. Using a metal spatula, spread the cream evenly over the chocolate base (*above, left*). Press the flat base of another meringue against the cream to form a sandwich (*above, right*). Place each assembly on its side in a paper case to display the contrasting stripes of coffee and chocolate.

2 Filling the piping bag. Prepare meringue (*page 8*)—here, Swiss meringue. Insert a medium-sized star nozzle into a large piping bag. Holding the bag two-thirds of the way from the nozzle end, pull the sleeve back over your wrist and spoon in the meringue mixture (*above*) until the bag is full. To close the piping bag, fold back the bag and twist the top.

3 Piping oval shapes. Pipe the meringue mixture on to the baking sheet, moving the piping bag in arcs (*page 21, top*) within the pencil lines (*above*). Bake the meringues until dry to the touch—about 3 to 4 hours in a preheated 115°C (240°F or Mark ¼) oven. Cool the meringues for about 30 minutes.

4 Dipping in melted chocolate. Melt some dipping chocolate (*page 10*). Keep it liquid over a pan of hot water. Line a tray with wax paper. With your fingers, lift up one meringue at a time and dip the flat base in the melted chocolate. Place each meringue, dipped side down, on to the wax paper. Allow the chocolate to set— this will take about 30 minutes.

7 Serving. Continue to sandwich pairs of meringues together with the coffee cream until all the meringues have been used up. Serve the assemblies in their paper cases on a plate (*right*). Once filled, meringues should be served within a few hours but unfilled meringues can be stored after baking in an airtight tin for two to three weeks.☐

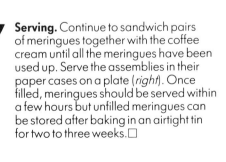

Crisp Spheres Masked in Chocolate Flakes

1 **Piping mounds.** Line a baking sheet and draw circular guidelines using a round metal cutter (*page 26, Step 1*). Prepare the meringue (*page 8*)—here, French meringue—and spoon it into a piping bag fitted with a large, plain nozzle. Pipe out mounds, finishing each with a twist. Flatten any sharp peaks with a knife.

2 **Sandwiching the meringues.** Bake the meringues and let them cool. Prepare buttercream (*page 16*); add melted chocolate to it. With a metal spatula, spread the base of one meringue with the cream. Join a second meringue to the base of the first (*above*) and then place the sandwiched meringues on a tray.

3 **Coating with buttercream.** Refrigerate the meringues for 15 minutes to firm the buttercream and bond the meringues. Grate chocolate coarsely (*page 10*). Have ready paper cases. Spear one sandwiched meringue on the tip of a small, sharp knife; using the spatula, spread buttercream over its surface.

Graceful Whirls of Strawberries and Cream

1 **Piping coils.** Prepare a baking sheet (*Step 1, above*). Spoon meringue—in this case, French meringue—into a piping bag fitted with a large plain nozzle. Pipe the meringue in a spiral from the outside in, making the mound slightly higher in the middle and finishing with a peak.

2 **Coating with melted fondant.** Bake the meringues, let them cool and transfer them to a wire rack placed over a tray. Melt fondant (*page 16*) to a coating consistency and keep it liquid over a pan of hot water. Spoon the fondant over the meringues. Any drips of fondant on the tray can be melted again for re-use.

3 **Mixing a filling.** Leave the coatings to set: the fondant will harden to a glossy finish. Meanwhile, prepare a fruit purée (*page 14*)—here, strawberry is used. Pour double cream into a bowl and add the purée to the cream. Whisk the two together (*above*) until thick.

4 Covering with grated chocolate. When the meringue assembly is coated with buttercream, hold it over the bowl of chocolate flakes and sprinkle them over the surface; the chocolate will adhere to the buttercream. Put the meringue in a paper case resting on the base where it was speared by the knife.

5 Serving the meringues. Coat the remaining meringues first with the buttercream and then with the chocolate flakes until all have been covered. Serve the meringue assemblies the same day, keeping them in a cool place before serving.

4 Piping the filling. Loosen the meringues from the wire rack and trim off any fondant drips with a small, sharp knife. Spoon the strawberry cream into a large piping bag—fitted with a medium-sized star nozzle. Pipe the cream in a spiral on the base of one meringue and press a second, flat side down, on to the first.

5 Serving the meringues. Continue to sandwich pairs of fondant-coated meringues together, putting each one into a paper case as you finish. Serve the meringues arranged on a cake stand and present one serving on an individual plate garnished, if you like, with a single fresh strawberry.

Sculpted Fruit with a Surprise Filling

For a spectacular *trompe-l'oeil*, meringues can be flavoured, shaped, filled and coated to resemble delectable little fruits. Replicas of citrus fruits are particularly successful—the flavours are easy to extract and they add a refreshing edge to the meringue. Miniature oranges are shown here (*recipe, page 92*), but tangerines, limes or lemons are all possible.

To build up layer upon layer of complementary flavouring and colouring, the meringue mixture itself is first flavoured with grated citrus rind from the appropriate fruit. For an Italian meringue mixture, the sugar syrup can be flavoured with fruit juice or a thin fruit purée.

The orange-flavoured meringue mixture is then piped in rounds and lightly sprinkled with sugar to give the domes a thin crust. Scooping out the centre of the cooked meringues creates space for a filling of creamy orange mousse. The shells are sandwiched in pairs and coated with orange-flavoured fondant. A clove serves as the stem of each orange, to complete the delicate illusion.

1 Dusting with sugar. Make meringue—here, French meringue (*page 8*). Grate orange rind finely and fold it into the meringue. Line a baking sheet (*page 26, Step 1*) and, using a large piping bag and a large plain nozzle, pipe out the meringue in rounds. Dust the rounds with icing sugar (*above*). Bake the meringues (*page 27, Step 3*) and leave to cool.

2 Adding syrup. Put sugar and orange juice into a pan set over medium heat; s˙ until the sugar has dissolved. Boil the syrup to the thread stage (*page 6*) and set it aside. Whisk egg yolks in a large bowl set over a pan of hot water on a lo˘ heat. When the yolks thicken and their colour lightens, slowly pour on the syrup whisking constantly (*above*).

6 Filling the shells. Remove the mousse from the refrigerator or freezer. Using a teaspoon, fill the hollows of two scooped-out shells with mousse (*above, left*). Level the surface of the filling using the back of the teaspoon, then sandwich the two shells together (*above, right*). Put the sandwiched meringue on a wire rack set over a tray. Fill and sandwich the rest of the shells in the same way. Refrigerate the meringues to prevent the mousse from melting.

7 Melting fondant. Prepare fondant (*pag˙ 16, Steps 1 to 4*) and set the bowl over a pan of hot water on a low heat. Prepare sugar syrup (*page 6*) using orange juice instead of water, and add it to the fondant. Stir the mixture until it coats the back of a wooden spoon. If the mixture i˙ too thick, add more syrup. Stir in grated orange rind (*above*).

3 **Whisking the mousse.** Continue to whisk the egg and syrup mixture until it is very pale in colour and its volume has almost doubled (*above*). Sprinkle finely grated orange rind on to the mousse and stir it in. Remove the bowl from the heat and whisk the mousse until it is cool.

4 **Blending in cream.** Whisk double cream until it forms soft peaks; transfer the cream to the bowl of mousse (*above*) and gently fold it in. Place the mousse, in a plastic container, in the ice-making compartment of the refrigerator, or in the freezer, for about 2 hours, until it is firm. To prevent ice crystals from forming, stir the mousse several times while it is freezing.

5 **Scooping out the meringues.** To hollow out each meringue, hold it over a plate and gently work the tip of a teaspoon into the centre of the flat base. Twist the spoon to crumble the meringue at the centre (*above*), then tip out the loose meringue. Put the meringues on a tray with their hollowed-out bases uppermost.

8 **Coating with fondant.** Remove the bowl and pan from the heat and put them on a trivet. Remove the meringues from the refrigerator; make sure they are steady on the rack. Ladle fondant over each meringue (*above*). To prevent a skin from forming on its surface, stir the bowl of fondant frequently. Leave the meringues on the rack until their coating sets.

9 **Serving the meringues.** To attenuate the strong flavour of dried cloves, remove the centre from the top of each clove with your fingertips. Stick a clove into each of the meringues (*above*). Then remove the meringues from the rack, trimming away any drips of fondant, and place them in paper cases. Arrange them on a cake stand (*right*) and serve.□

Transforming Textures with Nuts

When ground nuts are added to a basic meringue mixture they contribute more than flavour: the nuts transform the texture of the finished product. After baking, nut meringues—often known by their French name *japonais*—are crisp and firm on the outside with a distinctive, chewy interior (*recipe, page 92*).

The best nuts for mixing into the uncooked meringue are those with a delicate flavour. Almonds and hazelnuts are the most common choices; if you like, you can combine the two. Once mixed, the meringue should be piped out quickly; oil from the nuts will soon cause the foam of egg whites and sugar to subside.

Since *japonais* is denser than other meringues, it is piped in thin, flat shapes which cook through evenly. When they are baked, the flat shapes—usually discs or ovals—lend themselves well to being stacked two or three deep and interspersed with layers of filling.

Nut-flavoured fillings complement *japonais* perfectly. You can use whipped cream—plain or liqueur-flavoured—and stir in ground or chopped nuts. Walnuts, hazelnuts, pistachio nuts or blanched almonds are all suitable. Nuts in any form also blend well with buttercream (*page 16*). For a particularly light effect use the meringue buttercream used in this demonstration—here, mixed with praline.

When the layers have been stacked, the assembly can be decorated with a topping of chocolate frosting or fondant icing (*pages 11 and 16*). A traditional finish for nut-flavoured meringues is a coating of chopped nuts or praline, pressed into a layer of buttercream. The buttercream will be easier to apply to the top and sides of the meringues if the assemblies are chilled first. Praline gives the cakes a crunchy amber-coloured exterior; for a softer coating, use white praline (*box, right*). Finally, add a simple garnish such as chocolate frills (*page 10*) or use a knife to press decorative ridges into the soft surfaces of the cakes, as shown right.

1 **Adding almonds.** Line a baking sheet and draw oval guidelines (*page 26, Step 1*). Grind almonds (*page 13*) and sieve them into a small bowl; mix in two-thirds of the sugar. In a large bowl, beat egg whites until they form soft peaks. Add the remaining sugar, a little at a time, and whisk until the peaks are stiff. Fold in the almond mixture (*above*).

2 **Piping the meringue.** Insert a plain 5 mm (¼ inch) nozzle into a piping bag and fill it two-thirds full with meringue. Working from the outside of each oval inwards, pipe spirals of meringue (*above*). Bake the ovals in a 170°C (325°F or Mark 3) oven until they turn a pale gold—about 50 minutes—then cool them.

A Fluffy Effect from White Praline

1 **Making round cakes.** Pipe *japonais*—here, into 5 cm (2 inch) rounds. Bake them (*Steps 1 and 2, above*). Sandwich them in pairs with meringue buttercream (*page 17*). Refrigerate the meringues, then coat them with the buttercream. Prepare white praline (*page 13*); press it on to the surfaces. Press three lines into the top.

2 **Serving the meringues.** When you have decorated all the meringues, transfer them to a serving plate lined with a napkin. Arrange the finished meringues in a single layer so that their patterned upper surfaces are clearly displayed.

3 **Preparing a filling.** In a large bowl, make buttercream—here, made with Italian meringue (*page 17*). Prepare praline, crushed and sieved until fine (*page 12*). Reserve two-thirds of the praline to coat the cakes, and add the rest to the bowl of buttercream (*above*). Using a wooden spoon, beat the two together.

4 **Assembling the cakes.** Free the meringues from the paper; if they have spread unevenly during baking, trim the edges with a small, sharp knife. Using a metal spatula, spread the upper surface of a meringue with the buttercream, then press another meringue gently on top; place the sandwiched meringues on a tray. Refrigerate them for about 20 minutes to firm the filling. Hold each assembly in your hand and spread first the sides and then the top with the buttercream (*above, left*). Hold the cake over the reserved praline and gently press it on to the surfaces (*above, right*).

5 **Finishing the meringues.** If you like, you can decorate the meringues with small chocolate shapes, such as the frills used here. Since chocolate frills are fragile, use a small spatula or a knife to transfer them to the cakes (*above*). Use a cake slice to serve the meringues (*right*). □

2
Creamed, Melted and Whisked Cakes
From the Simple to the Sublime

All cakes—from buttery madeleines and spicy honey cakes to the layered slices shown opposite—stem from a very few ingredients: flour, butter, eggs, and a sweetener such as sugar or honey. The great variety in taste, texture and appearance is largely the result of varying the proportions of these basic elements, and judiciously adding flavourings and decoration.

Changes in proportions lead to corresponding changes in the techniques used to mix the ingredients. A cake batter that includes a large amount of butter, for instance, is made by the creaming method: the butter is thoroughly beaten with the sugar, ensuring smoothness and at the same time capturing air that will guarantee lightness (*page 36*). For cakes made with generous amounts of honey, treacle or molasses, the melting method is the most appropriate. First melted with the butter, the sweet ingredients are easy to blend with the eggs and flour (*page 38*). The lightest cakes of all—the sponges—have the highest proportion of eggs. These are usually whisked with sugar over heat, yielding an airy batter and giving the cake its springy texture (*pages 40-47*).

Like mixing techniques, the flavourings should suit the style of cake. Finely ground nuts, fruit purées or cocoa will flavour a sponge without weighing it down. A sturdier batter can support more substantial additions—chopped nuts and dried fruit, for example, or crystallized peel.

How a cake is shaped depends largely on the consistency of its batter. From a fairly firm dough-like blend, such as the honey cake mixture on page 38, you can stamp out shapes before baking. A more fluid batter, such as a sponge cake mixture, must be cooked first. Moulds will give a precise shape to any batter, forming individual cakes from darioles or fluted tartlets tins, and, from large tins, flat sheets of cake ready for thick layers of topping (*opposite*), or for curling into a Swiss roll.

Whatever their ingredients, small cakes invite embellishment—and in patisserie, decoration can be as important to the finished product as the flour from which the cake was made. The art of decoration encompasses simple garnishes, as well as elaborate toppings. But perhaps the most exquisite example of its application is in the miniature sponge cakes known as iced petits fours (*page 44*), where carefully selected icing, piping and ornament combine to produce jewel-like perfection.

Bands of velvety mousse and translucent jelly—both flavoured with tropical passion fruit—rest on a bed of sponge. The cake was assembled layer upon layer in a deep tin, then unmoulded and sliced into individual servings (*page 40*).

Shapely Results from a Creamed Batter

Individual moulds will shape a batter as it bakes, producing little cakes of perfect symmetry. Fluted moulds—circles, ovals or diamonds—yield shapes which are decorative in themselves. You can place a simple garnish, such as chopped nuts, on the cakes before they are baked (*right*) or you can ice them afterwards. Plain deep tins, such as dariole moulds, produce cakes with smooth surfaces for more elaborate coatings—here, raspberry jam and freshly grated coconut (*right, below*).

An ideal batter for these little cakes includes generous amounts of butter and eggs, so that the texture will be moist and tender. To make such a batter (*recipe, page 164*), butter is beaten on its own, then beaten a second time with sugar. This creaming process forces air into the butter, which lightens the mixture. To achieve a homogeneous blend, eggs are incorporated one at a time. Finally, flour is folded in, together with baking powder, which helps to raise the batter.

For a selection of cakes, you can divide the batter into batches and add a different flavouring to each. Cocoa, sifted with the flour, will add colour and flavour, or you can stir chopped nuts, dried fruit or crystallized peel into the finished batter.

To ensure that the batter does not stick, cake moulds should be carefully prepared each time you use them. Each mould must be thoroughly buttered, then coated with flour. Alternatively, you can stand paper cases—which do not require buttering or flouring—inside bun tins. The cases are removed when the cakes are eaten. You can spoon batter into small moulds or cases, but a piping bag is the best way of filling deep, narrow tins. The batter will expand during baking, so the moulds or cases should be only two-thirds full.

When the baked cakes have been unmoulded and allowed to cool, they are ready for the decoration of your choice. Choose an icing or buttercream topping to match or contrast with the flavour of the batter. Another method of decorating moulded cakes—especially those baked in shallow round tins—is to slice the tops off the cakes and pipe on fresh cream or buttercream. The cake tops, cut in half, are set into the cream to resemble butterfly wings (*recipe, page 95*).

Decorative Moulds for a Simple Finish

1 Adding eggs. Put soft butter in a mixing bowl and beat with a wooden spoon until the butter is pale. Add sugar and beat until the mixture is light and fluffy. Break an egg into the mixture and beat it well (*above*). Add the rest of the eggs, one by one, beating well after each addition.

2 Adding flour. Sift together flour and baking powder—for maximum aeration, sift the flour mixture several times. With a metal spoon, fold a little of the flour mixture into the creamed batter (*above*). Fold in the remaining flour mixture a little at a time to combine it evenly.

Miniature Towers with a Coconut Coating

1 Filling moulds. Coat the inside of dariole moulds with butter; sprinkle them with flour. Set the moulds on a baking sheet. Prepare a creamed batter (*Steps 1 and 2, above*); spoon the batter into a piping bag fitted with a plain, medium-sized nozzle. Fill the moulds two-thirds full. Tap the moulds to settle the mixture.

2 Trimming the cakes. Bake the cakes in a preheated 190°C (375°F or Mark 5) oven for 15 minutes, or until golden-brown. When they are cool enough to handle, unmould on to a wire rack. Let them cool completely, then place one in a clean mould. Using the rim of the mould as a guide, slice off the top of the cake.

3 **Filling moulds.** Brush the inside of little fluted moulds with softened butter using a pastry brush. Sprinkle flour over the butter and tip out the excess flour. Place the moulds on a baking sheet. Take a teaspoonful of batter and, with another spoon, push the batter into a mould until it is two-thirds full (*above*). Fill the rest of the moulds in the same way.

4 **Adding nuts.** Tap each mould lightly on the baking sheet to settle the batter. To create a crunchy surface, sprinkle sugar over the batter. Place a few chopped nuts—here, flaked almonds—on the top of each cake (*above*).

5 **Unmoulding the cakes.** Bake the cakes in a preheated 190°C (375°F or Mark 5) oven for 15 minutes, or until they are golden-brown. Remove them from the oven and leave them until they are cool enough to handle—about 10 minutes. Unmould the cakes on to your hand (*above*) and place right side up on a wire rack. Leave to cool before serving. □

3 **Decorating the cakes.** Gently brush the cakes to remove loose crumbs. Grate coconut (*page 12*). Warm jam—here, seedless raspberry—over a low heat. Spear the base of a cake on a fork. Using a pastry brush, paint the top and sides of the cake with jam, then roll it in the coconut. Coat the remaining cakes.

4 **Serving the cakes.** Arrange the cakes on a serving dish and garnish with halved glacé cherries, shapes cut out of marzipan (*page 13*) or angelica. To remove surface sugar from the angelica, plunge it into boiling water and leave for a minute or two. Dry the angelica on a cloth and cut it into shapes—here, diamonds. Serve the cakes. □

Molten Blends of Honey and Chocolate

Small cakes containing high proportions of honey, treacle, molasses or chocolate are usually made by means of the melting method. Such viscous sweet substances are much easier to incorporate into dry ingredients if they are first melted with butter. In the demonstrations here, the melting method is used to make golden-brown honey cakes (*right; recipe, page 106*) and to capture the flavour of melted chocolate in traditional American brownies (*box, opposite page; recipe, page 104*).

To make honey cakes, the molten mixture of honey and butter is allowed to cool, then eggs are added to lighten the cakes. Sugar and flour are folded in, together with bicarbonate of soda to help leaven the dough. The sweetness of the honey dough is often complemented by a generous sprinkling of ground spices—ginger, cinnamon, nutmeg, cardamom or cloves.

The honey dough shown here is firm enough to roll out and shape with cutters. Before baking, the cakes are glazed to give them a shining surface and to help any decorations to adhere. You can use beaten egg yolks for the glaze, or a mixture of yolks and cream; soured cream lends a subtle flavour to honey cakes redolent of their East European provenance. Here, the decorative flower pattern is achieved by combining nuts and fruits.

After baking, the cakes have a firm, chewy texture; they can be eaten at once or kept for two to three days, after which time they will be moister and their flavours will have developed.

Brownies, flavoured with chocolate and chopped pecan nuts or walnuts, are also made by the melting method. The chocolate is melted with butter, the mixture left to cool and eggs, sugar and flour added. Here, the relatively small quantity of egg stirred into the batter gives the cakes a pleasingly fudge-like consistency. If you prefer a texture similar to sponge cake, you can add more eggs.

Since the brownie batter is more fluid than the honey cake dough, it is baked in a tin rather than rolled out for cutting. When it has cooled, the slab of cake can be left plain or spread with a chocolate frosting (*page 11*), then sliced into squares or oblongs for serving.

1 **Melting honey and butter.** Put butter and honey—here, acacia honey—in a pan. Using a wooden spoon, stir over a gentle heat until the butter melts and mixes with the honey. Remove the pan from the heat and leave the mixture to cool slightly.

2 **Adding eggs.** Sift bicarbonate of soda and flour into a bowl; add flavourings—in this case, grated lemon rind, ground cinnamon and ground cloves. Measure sugar into another bowl. Add eggs—here, one whole egg and two yolks—to the pan; stir the eggs into the melted butter and honey mixture (*above*).

3 **Blending the dough.** Add the sugar to the other ingredients in the pan and stir it in thoroughly. Then add the flour mixed with the flavourings; as you stir it in, the dough will become very stiff (*above*).

4 **Rolling out the dough.** Lightly flour a work surface. Transfer the dough to the surface. With floured hands, knead the dough into a ball. Sprinkle it with flour and roll it out about 1 cm (½ inch) thick.

Fudge Brownies: a Celebrated Speciality

1 **Mixing the batter.** Melt chocolate and butter over a gentle heat; leave to cool. Stir in eggs, then add sugar and flour sifted with baking powder and salt. Mix in chopped nuts—in this instance, pecan nuts. Butter a rectangular tin—about 4 cm (1½ inches) deep. Pour the chocolate batter into the tin (*above*).

2 **Applying frosting.** Bake the batter in a preheated 180°C (350°F or Mark 4) oven for about 30 minutes or until the cake starts to leave the sides of the tin. Allow to cool. Prepare chocolate frosting (*page 11*). Use a metal spatula to spread the frosting over the cake; if you like, swirl the surface of the frosting with the end of the spatula. Leave the frosting to set.

3 **Slicing and serving.** With a sharp knife, cut the slab lengthwise and widthwise into small oblongs about 5 cm (2 inches) long and half as wide. Serve the cakes piled on a platter (*above*).

5 **Shaping cakes.** Lightly butter a baking sheet. With a pastry cutter—here, a 5 cm (2 inch) circular cutter—cut the dough into rounds and place them on the sheet. Gather the trimmings into a ball, roll the ball out and cut more rounds.

6 **Glazing and garnishing.** Lightly whisk egg yolks and soured cream. Using a pastry brush, coat each cake with this glaze, then add a decoration, if desired. Here, quartered glacé cherries, halved, blanched almonds and triangles of citron peel are arranged in a flower pattern.

7 **Baking and serving.** Bake the cakes in a preheated 190°C (375°F or Mark 5) oven until golden-brown; rounds of this size will take about 10 minutes. Place the cakes on a rack to cool before serving them. If you prefer moister cakes, store the rounds in a tin for up to three days before serving them (*above*). □

A Springy Platform for a Sumptuous Mousse

A whisked egg sponge has a particularly light texture and a resilience that makes it an excellent base for a great variety of luxurious toppings. These range from deep layers of mousse and jelly (*right*) or a creamy ganache filling (*page 43*) to the delicate petits fours on pages 44-46.

The strength and flexibility of sponge is derived from the high proportion of eggs in the batter; the characteristic airiness is achieved by first whisking air into the eggs. Beating over a saucepan of hot water speeds this process: the gentle heat sets proteins in the eggs, trapping the air. Sugar, beaten with the eggs, dissolves in the liquid ensuring a smooth mixture.

To yield a sheet of sponge, the batter is baked in a large, shallow tin, which requires some preliminary preparation. To prevent the sponge from sticking to the tin and breaking when you unmould it, butter the tin, line it with greaseproof paper and butter it again (*box, below*).

When the sponge has cooled, it is ready for its filling or topping. Liquid toppings based on gelatine need special treatment if they are to set into clearly defined layers. First, jelly—made by dissolving gelatine and adding it to fruit syrup—is poured into a deep tin approximately the same size as the tin used to bake the sponge. The jelly sets as it cools so that when the mousse is poured on top the two layers will not mix.

Here, the mousse is flavoured with passion fruit, but sieved soft fruit such as redcurrants or blackberries, or the juice of citrus fruits, can be used instead. The mousse is refrigerated to firm it, and the sponge, brushed with fruit syrup, is then placed on top of the mousse. The assembly is inverted and the tin lifted off, revealing the finished cake (*recipe, page 109*).

A much simpler technique can be used to apply fairly stiff fillings such as ganache. In the demonstration on page 43, ganache is spread between two layers of chocolate-flavoured sponge (*recipe, page 164*) and the assembly finished with a smooth chocolate and butter icing.

Cakes that are assembled in slab form are best presented as individual servings. Each slice or piece will then display neat bands of tempting filling.

1 **Whisking eggs and sugar.** Quarter-fill a saucepan with hot water and set it over a low heat. Put eggs and sugar in a large bowl and place it over the pan, making sure that the bowl does not touch the water. Whisk the mixture until it is pale, foamy, and falls from the whisk in a thick ribbon which leaves a trail on the surface (*above*)—about 15 minutes.

Lining a Rectangular Tin

Cutting paper. Position a rectangular baking tin on a sheet of greaseproof paper large enough to cover the base and sides of the tin. Using scissors, make diagonal cuts from the corners of the paper to the corners of the tin. Brush the inside of the tin with melted butter. Place the paper in the tin; press it neatly against the sides. Brush the paper with butter.

5 **Softening gelatine.** Put a few spoonfuls of cold water in a small saucepan and sprinkle powdered gelatine into the pan (*above*). Leave it until the water has been absorbed—about 5 minutes. Place the pan over a low heat and stir the mixture until the gelatine dissolves.

6 **Dissolving sugar.** Put sugar in another saucepan. Add fruit juice (*above*)—here juice extracted from passion fruit (*page 14*). Using a wooden spoon, stir the ingredients over a low heat until the sugar has dissolved.

2 Adding butter. Remove the bowl from the pan and whisk the mixture until it is cool. Melt butter and allow it to cool. Measure out flour and sift a third of it into the whisked mixture; fold it in gently with a spoon. Pour in a third of the butter and fold it into the mixture (*above*). Continue to fold in the flour and butter alternately.

3 Filling the baking tin. Line a shallow baking tin (*box, opposite page*). Pour the batter into the tin and spread it with the spoon. Bang the tin on the work surface to even out the mixture. Bake it in a preheated 220°C (425°F or Mark 7) oven for 7 minutes, until the sponge is light golden and springs back when pressed gently with a finger.

4 Cooling the sponge. When the tin is cool enough to handle, place a sheet of silicon paper over the top. Place a wire rack over the paper. Holding the rack and the tin together, turn them both over quickly. Lift off the tin and peel away the greaseproof paper from the base of the sponge. Let the sponge cool on the rack.

7 Skimming the syrup. Increase the heat and bring the fruit juice syrup to the boil. Set the pan on one side of the heat and simmer the syrup. As scum from the fruit rises to the cooler side of the pan, remove it with a metal spoon (*above*). Continue skimming the syrup until no more scum appears—about 5 minutes.

8 Adding the melted gelatine. Remove the pan of syrup from the heat and place it on a trivet. Pour the melted gelatine into the syrup while stirring the mixture with a wooden spoon (*above*).

9 Pouring a layer of jelly. Take a large, rectangular tin approximately the same size as the tin used to make the sponge, and 5 cm (2 inches) deep; brush the inside surfaces of the tin with almond oil. Pour enough jelly into the tin (*above*) to make a layer about 3 mm ($\frac{1}{8}$ inch) thick. Let the jelly cool; refrigerate the tin until the jelly has set—about 30 minutes. ▶

10 **Adding a fruit mousse.** Prepare a fruit mousse—here, passion fruit is the flavouring (*page 17*). Pour a layer of the mousse about 2.5 cm (1 inch) thick over the set jelly in the tin (*above*). Smooth the surface of the mousse and then put it in the refrigerator while you trim and glaze the sponge.

11 **Adding the sponge.** Trim the sponge to the same size as the tin containing the mousse. Make a sugar syrup (*page 6*), let it cool, and add passion fruit juice. Brush the underside of the sponge with the syrup. Lay the sponge—syrup side down—on top of the mousse (*above*). Refrigerate the cake until firm enough to unmould—at least 2 hours or overnight.

12 **Unmoulding the cake.** Remove the t from the refrigerator. To loosen the jelly, dip the base of the tin in hot wat for a few seconds. To unmould the cake without disturbing the layers, cover the sponge with a large sheet stiff card. Holding the card and the ti together, invert the whole assembly (*above*). Lift off the tin.

13 **Cutting the cake.** Dip a long, sharp knife in hot water; cakes containing fruit are best cut with a stainless steel knife to avoid imparting a metallic taste. Trim the edges of the cake (*above*); divide it in two lengthwise, then cut each half into slices about 2.5 cm (1 inch) wide (*right*), dipping the knife in hot water after each cut. □

Chocolate Mirrored in Multiple Layers

1 **Adding cocoa.** Whisk eggs and sugar (*page 40, Step 1*). Melt butter and let it cool. Put flour and cocoa into a sieve. Fold the cocoa mixture and the butter, alternately, into the eggs and sugar. Line a shallow baking tin with greaseproof paper (*page 40, box*). Pour the batter into the tin and bake it in a preheated 220°C (425°F or Mark 7) oven for 7 minutes.

2 **Spreading a filling.** Turn out the sponge and cool it on a wire rack lined with silicon paper. Prepare ganache (*page 11*). Cut across the rectangle of sponge to divide it in two. Slide a large piece of card under one half of the sponge. Using a metal spatula, spread the ganache filling over the top of the sponge to a thickness of about 2.5 cm (1 inch) (*above*).

3 **Sandwiching the filling.** Place the other piece of sponge, underside up, on top of the filling (*above*). Press gently on the sponge to level it. Smooth the sides of the cake with a metal spatula. Refrigerate the cake to firm the filling—about 1 hour. Place the cake on a rack set over a tray.

4 **Icing.** Stir 6 tablespoons of water and 9 oz (275 g) hard chocolate over low heat until the chocolate melts. Remove from heat; stir in 3 oz (90 g) butter cubes until well blended. Spread the icing over the top of the sponge (*above*); refrigerate to set the icing. Trim the edges of the cake with a long, sharp knife dipped in hot water; cut into squares (*right*).

Gleaming Gems of Cake and Fondant

Beneath the elegant exterior of an iced petit four lies a simple sponge cake. These miniatures are assembled in quantity from sheets of sponge cake which are layered with sweet fillings and then cut into bite-sized pieces. Individually iced in delicate shades of pastel, the petits fours lend themselves to exquisite decoration.

Sponge cake, light but firm, is the perfect foundation for these tiny shapes; it can be cut into neat morsels without crumbling. The sponge batter can be left plain, or enlivened with any one of a variety of flavourings—sieved raspberries, orange-flower water, grated lemon rind or ground nuts are a few examples.

After baking, you can sandwich the sponge cake with jam or buttercream before cutting it into shapes. From a single batch of baked sponge cake you can create a variety of petits fours. Simple straight-sided shapes—squares, rectangles, triangles and diamonds—can be accurately cut with a knife; ovals, rounds and stars are more easily stamped out with cutters.

To provide a smooth foundation for an icing, the cakes are coated with jam glaze. If you like, you can add a decoration at this stage by placing a marzipan ball, a nut or small piece of crystallized fruit on top of the cake before it is iced.

Fondant is a particularly good icing to use as it provides a smooth, even coating and a satiny sheen (*recipe, page 165*). You can tint the icing delicately with tiny amounts of food colourings. Spinach extract will tinge it green; cochineal, pink; and saffron, yellow. Very strong coffee will both flavour the fondant and colour it a pale *café au lait*. Judicious mixing can produce interesting results: for a peach-coloured fondant, add a blend of cochineal and saffron. Any excess icing that drips off the cakes need not be wasted—it can be reheated and used again.

You can garnish the petits fours with crystallized flowers or fruit, marzipan shapes, nuts, or with delicately piped lines and flourishes (*pages 20-23*). Carefully applied motifs, such as chocolate lacework or delicate icing flowers (*page 18*), are also appropriate.

1 Cutting sponge. Make a sponge batter (*recipe, page 164*); pour it into a lined, deep tin to a depth of 1 cm ($\frac{1}{2}$ inch) and bake in an oven preheated to 180°C (350°F or Mark 4) for 20 to 25 minutes. Turn out the sponge and cool it on a rack. Make buttercream (*page 16*) or apricot glaze (*page 14*) as here. With a long knife, halve the sponge horizontally.

2 Filling the sponge. Set the top half of the sponge aside. Using a metal spatula, spread a thin layer of apricot glaze over the bottom half of the sponge. Place the top half of the sponge over the filling (*above*). Using a long, sharp knife, trim the edges of the cake.

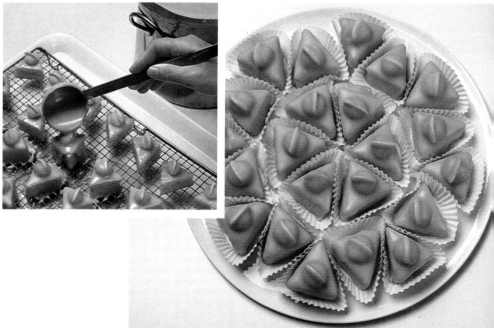

6 Icing the cakes. Set the rack over a tray. Prepare coffee-flavoured fondant (*page 16*). Pour a ladleful of fondant over each cake to coat the top and sides (*inset*). Using the tip of a small knife, quickly cover any bare areas. From time to time, stir the bowl of fondant to prevent a skin from forming. When the icing is dry, trim the bases of the cakes and serve them in paper cases (*above*). □

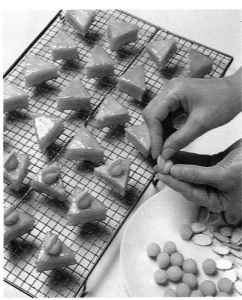

3 **Shaping triangles.** Cut the cake into strips 4 cm (1½ inches) wide, then slice diagonally across the strips in alternate directions to form little triangles (*above*). With a pastry brush, gently brush the triangles to remove loose crumbs.

4 **Coating with jam.** Spear the base of a cake on the prongs of a fork. Paint the sides and top of the cake sparingly with apricot glaze (*above*). Place the triangle on a wire rack. Paint the remaining cakes with the apricot glaze.

5 **Adding marzipan and almonds.** Make marzipan paste (*page 13*); break off small lumps and roll them one at a time between your palms to make balls of about 1 cm (½ inch) in diameter. Press half a blanched almond into each ball of marzipan (*above*). Place a marzipan ball and almond on top of each cake.

A Final Flourish for Pearly Triangles

Piping lines of fondant. Cut a sheet of sponge in small rectangles, then halve them to make triangles; coat them with fondant (*Step 6*). Fill a paper piping bag (*page 18*) with fondant. Cut a fine end in the bag. Begin piping at one corner of a cake; hold the bag vertically and move your hand across the cake. Pipe slightly beyond the edge of the cake to form a loop on the side. Continue piping backwards and forwards. Trim the decorated cakes and serve in paper cases.

Ovals Topped with Chocolate Lace

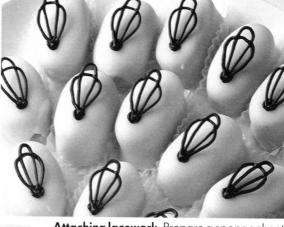

Attaching lacework. Prepare a sponge sheet layered with apricot glaze (*page 44, Steps 1 and 2*); stamp ovals with a 4 cm (1½ inch) cutter. Coat the cakes with apricot glaze and fondant (*page 44, Steps 4 and 6*)—here, peach-coloured fondant. Prepare chocolate lacework (*page 18*). Cut a fine end in a paper piping bag (*page 18*); fill the bag with melted chocolate (*page 10*). Pipe a dot on a cake and place one end of the lacework on the dot, at a slight angle. Hold with a knife until set.

Narcissi on a Snowy Ground

Attaching icing flowers. Make royal icing (*recipe, page 166*) and pipe little flowers (*page 18*)—here, narcissi. Leave them to set. Prepare a sponge sheet layered with apricot glaze. Stamp out 2.5 cm (1 inch) rounds of sponge with a cutter. Coat them with apricot glaze and white fondant. Pipe a dot of fondant on top of a cake, and place a flower on it. Decorate all the cakes with icing flowers. When the fondant has set, trim the bases and serve the cakes in paper cases.

vish Adornments for Little Sponge Cakes

nge cakes of any size are versatile
es for decoration; their light texture
l mild flavour provide a fine foil for
st sweet toppings and garnishes. Two
ssic ways of ornamenting sponges are
wn here, but by referring to the decor-
g techniques demonstrated on pages
21 you will be able to create countless
iations of your own.

n the demonstration on the right, a
ck of sponge is iced with lines of pink,
en, and pale yellow buttercream—
ing-time colours that give the cakes
ir French name of *printaniers*. In this
nonstration, the three buttercreams
flavoured with vanilla extract and
nge liqueur, but you can vary the fla-
ring, and the colouring, as you like.
Below, chocolate squares pressed to the
es of little sponges form neat boxes,
ving space on the top of the sponge for a
er of flavoured cream. A decoration of
stallized flowers, icing flowers or pis-
hio nuts completes the assembly.

Buttercream Stripes in the Colours of Spring

1 **Piping lines.** Prepare sponge (*page 44, Step 1*). Make buttercream (*recipe, page 166*); layer the sponge with a third of it. Divide the rest into four; leave two batches plain, colour one pink and one green. Using a paper piping bag and a small star nozzle, pipe plain lines on the cake, leaving spaces between; fill the spaces with lines of pink and green.

2 **Serving the cakes.** Chill the cake for about 30 minutes. Dip a long, sharp knife in hot water. Cut the cake into strips 4 cm (1½ inches) wide in the same direction as the buttercream lines; cut diagonally across the strips at intervals of 2.5 cm (1 inch) to give slices about 4 to 5 cm (1½ to 2 inches) long. Arrange the slices on a plate and serve (*above*).☐

ocolate Boxes: Showcases for Cream and Flowers

Assembling boxes. Prepare 4 cm (1½ inch) squares of chocolate (*page 11*) and place them on a sheet of wax paper. Make a sheet of sponge and cut it into 4 cm (1½ inch) squares. Brush the sides with apricot glaze (*page 14*). Place a cake on a square of wax paper and, using a knife, press the chocolate squares to the sides of the cakes; trim the corners to fit neatly.

2 **Filling the boxes.** To crystallize flowers, mix a quantity of gum arabic with twice the amount of rose-water; brush over freshly picked flowers—here, borage. Sprinkle the flowers with castor sugar, set on a wire rack and dry in a warm place. Whip double cream with vanilla sugar and rum. Spoon or pipe the cream into the chocolate boxes (*above*).

3 **Serving the chocolate boxes.** Decorate each cake with one or two crystallized flowers. Using a cake slice or a metal spatula, arrange the chocolate boxes on a plate, and serve (*above*).☐

3
Pastries
Crisp Containers for a Multitude of Fillings

ady for serving, choux rings—crowned with
monds and icing sugar—partially reveal a
ng of whipped cream and fresh raspberries
age 60). The assembly demonstrates one of
e principal virtues of choux dough, which can
e piped into well-defined shapes and then
ed and decorated after baking.

Not surprisingly, some of the best-loved products of the pastry-maker's art are the pastries themselves. Among pastry doughs, shortcrust and choux are justly celebrated: they have inspired pastries as homely as the custard tart and as sophisticated as the choux rings filled with whipped cream and raspberries (*opposite*).

Basic shortcrust consists of butter and flour—about half as much butter as flour—blended together, then bound with a little water. In richer variations, the proportion of butter can be increased or you can replace the water with eggs. Some versions also include sugar, finely ground almonds or hazelnuts (*page 50*). Whatever the ingredients, shortcrust bakes to a crisp, compact pastry. It makes smooth linings for open-faced tartlets that might display simple fillings of fruit or more elaborate arrangements of buttercream and icing (*page 54*); furthermore, it provides a sturdy base for a large layered assembly (*page 56*).

A ball of shortcrust dough is also the starting-point for rough-puff pastry. Repeated rolling and folding creates layers in the shortcrust dough; on baking, the layers rise to form crisp, buttery flakes. Although shortcrust and rough-puff can be treated as interchangeable, rough-puff comes into its own in patisserie that reveals its complex texture. There is little purpose in using it for a filled tartlet where it will have no opportunity to rise; in a turnover, though, it will bake to a fine, layered crust.

Choux pastry has quite different properties. The dough contains butter, flour and a lavish proportion of eggs and water; mixed over heat, these ingredients form a moist, airy paste soft enough to be piped into shapes such as fingers, rings or little balls. In the oven, the moisture in the dough turns to steam and the choux expands into shells that are crisp on the outside and hollow within. Filled and decorated in many fanciful ways, choux appears in a multiplicity of presentations; a selection of these is demonstrated on pages 58-61.

Other assemblies use choux and shortcrust together, exploiting the advantages of both. Polkas, for instance (*page 62*), have a crisp shortcrust base, and walls of choux containing a smooth filling of pastry cream.

Basic Steps to Perfect Pastries

Shortcrust is not one pastry, but several. The basic dough is simply a mixture of flour and fat—usually butter—with just enough liquid to make a cohesive paste. But variations, both in the ingredients and in the method used to mix them, yield pastries with very different textures.

For a standard shortcrust (*recipe, page 163*), butter is cut or rubbed into about twice its weight of flour; to prevent the butter from melting—a mishap that produces tough pastry—both the ingredients and the utensils should be cold, and the mixture must be worked quickly, with minimum handling. The resulting dough bakes to a crisp, general-purpose pastry.

A higher proportion of butter—equal to the weight of flour—produces a richer, more tender pastry. The cutting method demonstrated on the right is the most convenient way to make it: by cutting small chunks of butter into the flour, using two knives in a criss-cross movement, you can work in a large quantity without overhandling the pastry. A little water provides the necessary binding. Because the butter is distributed unevenly throughout the dough, the finished pastry has a distinctive, flaky texture.

Such a shortcrust dough invites yet further transformation. Rolled out into a rectangle, folded and rolled again, the dough becomes layered with butter and air; in the oven, the layers open out forming crisp leaves of pastry. For an even more flaky effect you can repeat the rolling and folding several times more to produce rough-puff dough (*recipe, page 163*).

Here, 350 g (12 oz) of butter-rich shortcrust dough is rolled and folded once to make *chaussons*—pastry turnovers with an almond filling. Other possible fillings include curd cheese, puréed apples or other soft fruit, jam or pastry cream.

Extra butter is not the only source of enrichment for shortcrust. Eggs may replace the water, and sugar can be added to the flour. One interesting variation (*box, below; recipe, page 163*) includes ground hazelnuts in the dough; these produce a delicately flavoured pastry particularly well suited to tarts where you can use complementary fillings such as coffee, chocolate or nut-flavoured buttercreams.

1 Cutting in the butter. Put cold water into a jug and set it aside. Sift flour and a pinch of salt into a large mixing bowl. Cut chilled butter into 1 cm (½ inch) cubes and add them to the dry ingredients. Using two table knives, cut the butter into the flour with a rapid criss-cross movement (*above*). Continue cutting until the cubes of butter are about the size of peas.

A Rubbed Shortcrust Enhanced with Nuts

1 Rubbing butter into flour. In a bowl, mix sifted flour, salt, ground nuts—here, roasted hazelnuts—and sugar. Add the cubes of butter. With your fingertips and thumbs, lift up small amounts of the ingredients and rub them lightly together, then let them fall back into the bowl (*above*). Continue until the mixture has the consistency of coarse breadcrumbs.

2 Adding eggs. Make a well in the centre of the crumbs. Add whole eggs and stir the mixture quickly and thoroughly with a fork (*above*), until the eggs are evenly distributed throughout and the dough starts to cling together.

3 Gathering the dough. With your hands, gather the dough together (*above*) and press it into a ball. If the dough feels very sticky, knead it lightly on a floured work surface with the heel of your hand, until the dough has absorbed enough flour to be workable. Wrap the dough in plastic film and chill it in the refrigerator for at least 30 minutes before rolling it out.

2 **Mixing the dough.** Pour a little of the cold water into the centre of the ingredients and, using a fork, lightly stir in the liquid, gradually drawing in the mixture from the sides of the bowl. Stir the ingredients until the water is absorbed and the dampened mixture starts to cling together (*above, left*). If necessary, add a little more water to help the dough cohere. Gather the mixture together (*above, right*), and press it into a ball. Refrigerate the dough for at least 30 minutes to relax it; to prevent a skin from forming, wrap the dough in plastic film.

3 **Preparing the filling.** In a bowl, blend 125 g (4 oz) each of ground almonds, castor sugar and softened butter with your fingertips. Add a whole egg, an egg yolk, and a generous dash of rum; use a fork to stir in the liquids (*above*). Stir until smooth, then cover and refrigerate it for about 30 minutes until it is firm enough to work with. Flour the work surface.

4 **Filling the pastries.** Roll the dough into a rectangle, then fold over the ends to meet in the centre. Fold the dough in half to align the folded edges, then fold in half again to make a square package. Turn through 90 degrees and roll out 3 mm (⅛ inch) thick. Use a plain 9 cm (3½ inch) cutter to cut out rounds. Spoon a little filling into the middle of each circle.

5 **Sealing the pastries.** Fold each circle in half to create a crescent shape. To seal in the filling and make a fluted edge, pinch the curved sides with a floured thumb (*above*). Transfer the pastries to a baking sheet; since the dough contains a large quantity of butter there is no need to grease the sheet. Glaze each pastry with egg yolk mixed with water.

6 **Baking and serving.** Put the baking sheet in a preheated 200°C (400°F or Mark 6) oven. After 5 minutes, reduce the heat to 190°C (375°F or Mark 5) and bake the pastries for another 10 minutes, or until they are golden-brown. Cool them on a wire rack. Arrange the pastries on a plate for serving (*above*).□

Blind-Baking for Crisp Cases

Pastry dough baked in daintily shaped tartlet moulds will yield crisp, fragile shells that make ideal show-cases for fillings. By varying the filling, the pastry and the mould, you can produce a vast range of attractive tarts that can be served both hot and cold. Lightly cooked apples or a softly set custard are just two of many possible fillings; here, these ingredients are combined in apple custard tarts (*recipe, page 111*).

Whatever filling you intend to use, choose dough you can roll out thinly—a plain or an enriched shortcrust, or a rough-puff. For the mould, choose whatever shape takes your fancy—fluted ovals or rounds, or boat shapes.

You can cut the dough by one of two methods, according to the type of mould used. For moulds with blunt or irregular edges, dough linings must be stamped individually with a cutter. For moulds with sharp edges, you can lay a sheet of dough over a group of moulds, then roll the pin over them (*box, below*).

Pastry cases are -often pre-cooked—

baked "blind"—either partially or fully, depending on the filling to be used. When a moist filling such as custard is to be cooked inside the tartlet, the cases are partially baked first to firm the raw dough and to prevent it from becoming soggy when the filling is added. Once filled, the tartlets are returned to the oven, so that the various elements will finish cooking simultaneously.

For fillings that require no cooking—fresh, glazed strawberries, for example, or buttercream (*page 54*)—the cases must first be completely baked.

Simple precautions will prevent the dough from losing shape as it bakes blind. When shortcrust is baked in very small moulds, as here, pricking the uncooked dough with a fork should keep the dough from buckling and the sides from shrinking unevenly. Rough-puff should always be weighted down, otherwise it will tend to expand too much. To do this, you can stack three or four dough-lined moulds on top of one another, then top the stack with an empty mould filled with weights.

1 **Lining the tins.** Roll the dough—here, butter-rich shortcrust—to a thickness of 3 mm (⅛ inch). Using a cutter that is about 2.5 cm (1 inch) larger in diameter than the moulds, stamp out circles. Gently press each circle into a mould (*above*). Stack the lined moulds in threes. Place an empty mould on top; weight it with dried beans, or metal baking beans as here.

A Rapid Method for Filling Moulds

1 **Covering the moulds.** Arrange straight-edged tartlet moulds close together on a work surface. Roll out the dough—here, egg-enriched shortcrust—to a thickness of 3 mm (⅛ inch). To lift it, roll it loosely round the rolling pin. Unroll it over the moulds (*above*). Lightly indent the dough over each mould with your fingertips.

2 **Lining the moulds.** Roll the pin gently over the moulds (*above*), so that their sharp edges cut through the dough. Lift away the trimmings. Take each mould and, with your thumbs, lightly press the dough into the base and sides, easing the dough upwards to about 3 mm (⅛ inch) above the top of each mould.

3 **Pricking the dough.** Taking one mould at a time, prick the base and sides of the dough thoroughly with the prongs of a fork (*above*); transfer the mould to a baking sheet. Bake the prepared cases in a preheated 190°C (375°F or Mark 5) oven for about 15 minutes, or until the pastry is firm and lightly coloured.

2 **Slicing apples.** Put the stacked moulds on a baking sheet in a preheated 190°C (375°F or Mark 5) oven. After 10 minutes, unstack the moulds and bake for a further 5 minutes to firm the pastry bases. Meanwhile, quarter, peel and core the apples. With a sharp knife, cut each quarter into thin slices (*above*).

3 **Tossing the apples.** Melt butter in a large sauté pan over low heat. Add the apple slices and sauté them for 4 to 5 minutes over a fairly high heat. Shake the pan constantly to toss the slices and colour them evenly (*above*).

4 **Preparing custard.** Crack whole eggs into a bowl and pour in double cream (*above*); add sugar. Using a fork or a whisk, beat the ingredients until they form a smooth custard mixture.

5 **Filling the cases.** Remove the baking sheet from the oven and allow the tartlet cases to cool. To unmould them, pick up each mould and turn it over, shaking the case on to your empty hand; transfer the case back to the baking sheet. Spoon a few apple slices into each case (*above*).

6 **Adding the custard.** If you like, sprinkle the apples with a little spice, such as ground cinnamon or grated nutmeg. Spoon the custard mixture into the shells so as to barely cover the apples. Bake the tartlets in a preheated 190°C (375°F or Mark 5) oven for 10 to 12 minutes, or until the custard is just set.

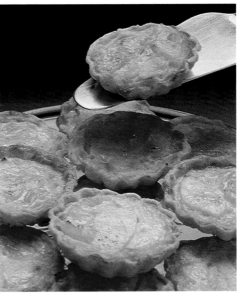

7 **Serving the tartlets.** Before handling the tartlets, let them cool slightly. Slide a cake slice underneath each tartlet and transfer it to a serving dish. Apple custard tarts are delicious either warm or cold.□

Luxurious Fillings for Elegant Tartlets

Some of the most decorative tartlets can be made by using smooth fillings that are firm enough to permit embellishments to their upper surface. Such fillings include flavoured buttercream, ganache or chestnut purée; they can be spread into the contours of a pastry case, or mounded high above it, and then coated with fondant, icing or chocolate.

On the right, meringue buttercream, flavoured with lemon, is mounded into boat-shaped cases. The sloping sides of the filling are coated with pale green and yellow royal icing—colours that reflect the flavour of the filling. Similarly, you could use pink icing for a raspberry or strawberry-flavoured buttercream.

Pastry shells can be enhanced by a coating of chocolate; below, hazelnut tartlet shells are enrobed in dipping chocolate, filled with a coffee buttercream and topped with coffee-flavoured glacé icing. The tartlets could have been further decorated in a number of ways (*pages 18-23*); here, some simple lines of piped chocolate complete the assembly.

Boats Laden with Iced Buttercream

1 **Filling shells.** Prepare dough—here, egg-enriched shortcrust (*page 50*)—and fully blind-bake it in boat-shaped moulds (*page 52*); unmould and cool the cases. Make meringue buttercream (*page 17*) flavoured with a little lemon juice and zest; use a small metal spatula to mound it into each shell; smooth the sides into a sharp crest (*above*), then chill.

2 **Coating with icing.** Make royal icing (*page 15*) and divide it into two batches. Colour one green with spinach extract, and the other one yellow by adding powdered saffron dissolved in a little hot water. Using the spatula, coat one side of each mound with the green icing; to prevent sticking, dip the spatula in hot water occasionally.

Chocolate-Dipped Coffee Cups

1 **Brushing with chocolate.** Fully blind-bake dough—here, hazelnut shortcrust (*page 52*)—in tartlet moulds; unmould the shells and cool them. Melt dipping chocolate (*page 10*). Brush it over the base and sides of each shell; start at the centre and brush outwards (*above*). Put each shell, chocolate side up, on a wire rack set over a tray.

2 **Filling with buttercream.** Leave the chocolate coatings to set—about 30 minutes. Meanwhile, make a meringue buttercream filling and flavour it with strong coffee (*page 17*). Using a metal spatula, fill each shell with buttercream, smoothing the surface level with the top of the pastry case (*above*). Refrigerate for 30 minutes to firm the buttercream.

3 **Coating with icing.** Prepare icing—here glacé (*page 15*)—flavoured with coffee. Remove the tartlets from the refrigerator and, holding one in your hand, spoon a little icing into the centre. Using a metal spatula, gently draw the icing outwards to the rim (*above*), until the filling is smoothly and evenly covered. Ice the remaining tartlets in the same way.

3 **Completing the decoration.** Spread the yellow icing over the uncoated side of each mound (*above*), making a neat edge along the crest. Using a bag fitted with a fine plain nozzle or a star nozzle, pipe a line of icing in either colour along the crest. When the icing has set—about 30 minutes—place the tartlets in paper cases for serving (*right*).□

4 **Finishing the tartlets.** Let the icing set. Make a paper piping bag (*page 18*); fill it with melted dipping chocolate thickened with a little sugar syrup (*page 6*). Pipe a design, holding the bag just above the tartlet. Trim any drips from the edges before the chocolate sets.□

Splendid Arrays of Fruits and Toppings

Spectacular effects can be achieved by building colourful layers of fruit and topping on a platform of pastry. The large surface area of the pastry enables you to introduce fragile ingredients—meringue and sponge batter, for instance—that would be very difficult to apply neatly to individual pastries.

Soft, juicy fruit, which is a fine partner for crisp pastry, is used in both of the assemblies here. For the first (*right; recipe, page 113*), lightly poached redcurrants are spread over a baked pastry base, then topped with a lattice of piped meringue, which colours slightly when it is briefly baked. Striking results could be achieved with blackcurrants or blackberries.

In the more substantial construction below (*recipe, page 116*), a topping of sponge batter seeps into the hollows that are created by a layer of halved, stoned plums supported by pastry. Other large stoned fruits such as apricots or peaches could be used instead. The pastry base will crisp in the oven while the batter firms into a springy topping.

Redcurrants Viewed Through a Lattice of Meringue

1 **Fitting the pastry base.** Prepare the dough—in this case, an egg-enriched shortcrust—and roll it out 5 mm (¼ inch) thick to fit a Swiss roll tin. With your fingers, press the dough firmly into the tin (*above*). Prick the dough all over with a fork, then bake it in a preheated 190°C (375°F or Mark 5) oven, until it is lightly golden—15 to 20 minutes.

2 **Arranging the redcurrants.** Poach the redcurrants in sugar syrup for about 2 minutes, then, using a slotted spoon, transfer them to a bowl. Boil the syrup to reduce it, then strain it (*page 14*). Allow syrup to cool slightly, then brush it over the pastry base. Arrange the redcurrants in a single layer on top (*above*).

Triple Textures in a Single Slice

1 **Stoning the plums.** Wash plums in cold water. Using a sharp knife, make an incision round the circumference of each plum. Gently twist the plum to prise apart the two halves of the fruit. Remove the stone (*above*). When all the plums are stoned, sprinkle them with lemon juice to prevent discoloration, then set aside.

2 **Arranging the plums.** Prepare an egg-enriched shortcrust dough. Roll it out, press it into the base of a tin about 5 mm (¼ inch) deep and prick the dough all over. Partially bake the dough in a preheated 190°C (375°F or Mark 5) oven for 10 to 15 minutes, or until it is pale gold. Arrange the halved plums, cut-side up, in neat rows on top of the pastry (*above*).

3 **Topping with sponge batter.** Make a sponge batter and pour it over the layer of plums (*above*). Spread the batter out gently, letting it seep into the cavities; it will eventually form a smooth and even surface. Lower the oven temperature to 180°C (350°F or Mark 4) and bake the assembly for about 25 minutes.

3 **Piping a lattice of meringue.** Prepare meringue—here, Italian meringue (*page 8*). Preheat the oven to 220°C (425°F or Mark 7). Fit a large piping bag with a nozzle—here, a star nozzle. Fill the bag with meringue. Pipe the meringue in criss-cross lines over the redcurrants (*above*).

4 **Serving.** Bake the tart for 5 minutes or until the meringue is slightly coloured (*above*). Use a long, sharp knife to divide the tart into individual servings; dip the knife in hot water before each cut. Divide the tart into 4 to 5 cm (1½ to 2 inch) slices, and serve them either hot or cold (*inset*).□

4 **Finishing and serving.** The tart is done when a skewer inserted into the sponge comes out clean. When the tart has cooled slightly, sprinkle it with sugar—here sifted icing sugar (*above*). Cut the tart into slices, each about 2.5 cm (1 inch) wide and 7.5 cm (3 inches) long (*right*). Serve the slices warm or cold.□

Choux: a Mellow Mixture Soft Enough to Pipe

Choux dough is a culinary phenomenon; it is soft enough to be piped into shapes that puff up on baking into crisp, hollow shells. Just dusted with sugar, the shells alone are delicious. The hollow centres, though, seem made for filling and the golden crust invites a topping; for most cooks, baked choux is only the starting point. Here, choux fingers filled with pastry cream and covered with caramel become éclairs; overleaf, the same dough produces fondant-covered buns and sandwiched pastry rings filled with whipped cream and fresh raspberries.

Choux is made by bringing butter and water to the boil and then stirring in flour to form a thick, cohesive paste. Lastly, eggs are beaten into the dough, giving it its characteristic lightness. You will need about one egg to every 30 g (1 oz) of flour; because flours vary in absorbency (and eggs in size), it is best to add the last egg gradually until the mixture is just firm enough to hold small peaks—a sign that the dough has reached the right consistency for piping into the required shape.

Towards the end of baking, the choux shapes are pierced with a knife to release trapped steam. A final few minutes in the oven allows the interiors to dry out while the outsides become firm and golden.

The combination of shapes, fillings and toppings is largely a matter of taste: almost any form of icing, cream or pastry cream will suit. A few simple precautions should be observed, however. In the case of the éclairs demonstrated here, the caramel coating is applied and then allowed to set before the shapes are filled; liquid caramel is so hot that it would melt the cream filling. If the choux pastries are given a fondant coating—as used for the buns demonstrated on page 60—it is a good idea to fill the pastries before coating them to avoid disturbing the icing.

1 Melting butter. Sift flour and salt on to a piece of greaseproof paper and set it aside. Pour a little water into a heavy pan set over low heat. Add butter (*above*). Increase the heat so that the butter melts and the liquid comes to the boil at the same time. Turn off the heat immediately.

2 Adding flour. Slide the flour and salt from the greaseproof paper into the hot liquid all at once (*above*); if the flour is added gradually, lumps may form. Once you have added the flour, stir the mixture with a wooden spoon. Continue stirring until the ingredients are thoroughly mixed.

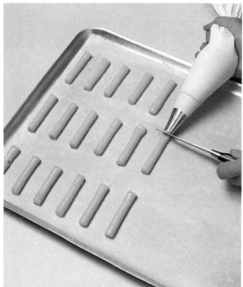

6 Piping the dough. Line a baking tray with silicon paper. Fit a 1 cm (½ inch) plain nozzle to a piping bag, and fill the bag two-thirds full with the dough. Pipe the dough in strips about 6 cm (2½ inches) long, cutting off each length with a knife (*above*). To allow room for expansion during baking, leave 4 cm (1½ inches) space between the strips.

7 Piercing the choux. Bake the shapes in an oven preheated to 220°C (425°F or Mark 7). After 15 minutes, remove them from the oven and use a small sharp knife to pierce the ends of each shell (*above*). Return the pastries to the oven and bake them for a further 5 minutes. Cool them on a wire rack. If necessary, trim their bases so that they will lie flat.

3 **Beating the mixture.** Beat the mixture vigorously over a medium heat. After about a minute, when the dough forms a solid mass that comes away cleanly from the sides of the pan, remove the pan from the heat and set it aside.

4 **Adding eggs.** Let the dough cool for a few minutes or the heat of the dough might curdle the eggs. Break eggs, one by one, into the pan and, with a wooden spoon, beat the dough until the egg is thoroughly incorporated (*above*). Beat the last egg before adding it, and then add it a little at a time, until the dough holds a small peak.

5 **Finishing the dough.** Continue beating the dough with the wooden spoon until the ingredients are well blended and the dough forms a smooth, firm mass that will drop very slowly from the spoon. Use the dough immediately; if it is allowed to stand, it will stiffen.

8 **Dipping the éclairs.** In a heavy pan, prepare caramel—here, dark caramel (*page 7*). Hold the base of each éclair between finger and thumb and dip the éclair's upper surface into the caramel, removing it quickly and allowing excess caramel to drip off (*above*). Carefully place each éclair, base-down, on a wire rack set over a tray.

9 **Filling the éclairs.** Leave the coating to set—about 5 minutes. Make a filling— here, pastry cream (*page 16*) mixed with praline (*page 12*) and whipped cream— and spoon it into a piping bag fitted with a star nozzle. Slit each éclair lengthwise, open it out, and pipe the filling into the opening (*above*); close the éclair and transfer it to a tray.

10 **Serving.** When you have filled all the éclairs, arrange them on a serving dish. The éclairs are best eaten immediately, but they can be kept in a cool place for a few hours before serving. □

Feather-Light Buns Glossed with Fondant

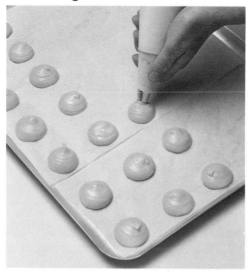

1 **Piping the dough.** Prepare choux dough (*page 58, Steps 1 to 5*). Spoon it into a piping bag fitted with a 1 cm (½ inch) plain nozzle. On a baking tray lined with silicon paper, squeeze the bag to pipe out small mounds—making each one about 2.5 cm (1 inch) in diameter. Twist the piping bag as you lift it away to give each mound a smooth surface (*above*).

2 **Filling the buns.** Bake the buns in a preheated 220°C (425°F or Mark 7) oven. After 20 minutes, pierce a small hole in their bases with a small, sharp knife. Bake for a further 5 minutes, then cool. Fit a small plain nozzle to a piping bag and fill it with pastry cream (*page 16*)—here, flavoured with rum. Pipe the cream into the hole in each bun (*above*).

3 **Dipping the buns.** Make fondant (*page 16*) and flavour it with melted chocolate (*page 10*). To keep the mixture smooth and fluid, put it in a bowl set over a pan of hot water, and stir it from time to time. Holding each bun by its base, dip the top into the fondant, allowing the excess to drip off (*above*). Put the dipped buns—base-down—on a wire rack.

Garlands of Raspberries, Almonds and Cream

1 **Piping the dough.** Prepare choux dough (*page 58, Steps 1 to 5*). Spoon it into a piping bag fitted with a 1 cm (½ inch) plain nozzle. On a baking tray lined with silicon paper, pipe out rings of dough—each one about 5 cm (2 inches) in diameter (*above*). Glaze the dough by brushing it with beaten egg, mixed with a little milk.

2 **Topping with almonds.** Arrange flaked blanched almonds (*page 12*) on top of each ring (*above*). Transfer the baking tray to a preheated 220°C (425°F or Mark 7) oven. After 20 minutes, remove the tray from the oven. Insert the tip of a sharp knife into the side of each ring to release steam. Bake the rings for a further 5 minutes, then cool them on a wire rack.

3 **Slicing the rings.** With a long, sharp knife, slice each ring in half horizontally (*above*). If necessary, create more space for the filling by removing some dough from inside the ring with your fingers. Arrange the split rings in pairs—a base and an almond-coated top—on a rack.

4 **Finishing the buns.** Leave the buns until the fondant has set—about 15 minutes. Make a paper piping bag and cut a tiny opening (*page 18*). Fill the bag with coffee-flavoured fondant (*recipe, page 165*) and pipe it in a pattern on the tops of the buns (*above*). Arrange the buns on a serving plate in a single layer (*right*).□

4 **Finishing the assemblies.** Fit a medium-sized star nozzle to a piping bag and fill it with whipped cream, flavoured with vanilla extract and sweetened with icing sugar. Pipe out the cream into each hollowed-out base (*above*), and lightly press a few fresh raspberries into the cream. Replace the top ring and dust it with icing sugar before serving (*right*).□

Ingenious Alliances of Choux and Shortcrust

Pastry shells made from shortcrust are firm and crisp; those made from choux are light and fragile. Assemblies that use choux and shortcrust together benefit from the virtues of both kinds of dough. Because of its rigidity, shortcrust usually provides the base for such composite pastries. In the demonstration on the right (*recipe, page 131*), rings of choux are piped on to rounds of shortcrust; after baking, the tartlets are filled with pastry cream and dusted with icing sugar. As a finishing touch, you can use a red-hot skewer to brand some caramelized stripes across the sugary surface.

For the tartlets demonstrated below (*recipe, page 131*), shortcrust again forms the base. The choux, though, is not part of a container—mixed with pastry cream, it becomes a filling for the shells. When the tartlets go back into the oven, the cream-and-choux combination remains moist inside beneath a delicate crust. To decorate the pastries, quadrants of sugar and redcurrant jelly alternate between the arms of a cross made from shortcrust strips.

Composite Effects from Contrasting Doughs

1 Piping rings. Prepare shortcrust dough enriched with eggs (*page 50*). Roll out 3 mm (⅛ inch) thick, prick it and stamp out 5 cm (2 inch) rounds. Place them on a baking sheet and brush their edges with beaten egg. Prepare choux dough (*page 58, Steps 1 to 5*). Using a piping bag with a 5 mm (¼ inch) nozzle, pipe a ring on to each round and brush with egg.

2 Filling the cases. Bake the pastries in a 220°C (425°F or Mark 7) oven for 12 to minutes or until crisp and golden. Cool on a rack. Prepare pastry cream (*page 16*)—here it is flavoured with orange liqueur. Use a piping bag with a 1 cm (½ inch) nozzle to pipe the cream into the centre of each pastry (*above*). Sift icing sugar thickly over the pastries.

Choux in an Unexpected Role

1 Stirring in pastry cream. Prepare egg-enriched shortcrust dough and roll it out 3 mm (⅛ inch) thick. Line 5 cm (2 inch) tartlet moulds with the dough. Prick the base and sides of each shortcrust case with a fork. For the filling, prepare pastry cream and choux paste, and then mix the two together (*above*).

2 Filling the pastries. Spoon about two teaspoons of the choux paste and pastry cream mixture into each case, mounding the filling slightly in the centre (*above*). Place the moulds on a baking sheet.

3 Decorating with dough strips. Roll out the dough trimmings and cut strips about 5 mm (¼ inch) wide and just under 5 cm (2 inches) long. Arrange the dough strips in a cross on the top of each tartlet. Make sure the strips do not touch the edge of the case or the crosses might break as the filling expands during baking. Glaze the dough strips with beaten egg.

3 **Decorating the pastries.** Protecting your hand with a cloth, hold the end of a steel skewer in a flame until the skewer is red hot. Touch the surface of each pastry for a few seconds with the hot skewer, to form a pattern of caramelized sugar (*above*). Serve the decorated pastries immediately (*right*).□

4 **Sifting sugar over the pastries.** Preheat the oven to 190°C (375°F or Mark 5) and bake the pastries until the filling is puffy and golden-brown—about 30 minutes. Unmould the pastries on to a wire rack to cool. Sift icing sugar over them (*above*).

5 **Piping on redcurrant jelly.** In a pan, warm redcurrant jelly over a gentle heat. Make a paper piping bag (*page 18*) and cut a small hole in the bag. Fill the bag with jelly. Pipe the jelly into two opposite sections of each cross (*above*); the icing sugar in these sections will dissolve under the redcurrant jelly. Serve the finished pastries immediately (*inset*).□

4
Yeast-Leavened Cakes
Fine Textures from Butter and Eggs

Yeast, the oldest of all leavens and the mainstay of the breadmaker, has an honoured place in patisserie. Festive babas and savarins, spicy buns and miniature brioches all owe their charm and character to the alchemy worked by the same single-celled organisms that raise our daily bread.

In fact, the alchemy is twofold: both yeast and flour have a role to play. In the presence of liquid and such nourishments as flour, the yeast cells multiply, releasing carbon dioxide as a by-product. Flour also contains proteins that combine with moisture to produce an elastic substance known as gluten; when the dough is kneaded, the gluten forms a web that retains the gas the yeast has produced. The chemical reactions are complex, but the practice is simple; in fact, the process was known and used by cooks thousands of years before scientists understood it. Given certain conditions, well-kneaded yeast dough will rise slowly and steadily. Then, during baking, the carbon dioxide will expand and provide an aerated texture, while the gluten will set to give the cake its final contours.

In patisserie, sweetening the dough with sugar and enriching it with eggs and butter are almost obligatory to enhance the flavour and develop a cake-like texture. However, the inclusion of butter—or any fat—in quantity poses a special problem. Mixed in with the other ingredients, the fat coats the flour, inhibiting the action of the yeast cells. As a general rule, therefore, the yeast in most patisserie dough is allowed to begin its fermentation before the butter is added.

The more butter a dough contains, the richer its flavour and the silkier its texture. The brioche dough made on page 74 has a higher proportion of enriching ingredients than it does flour. Combined with several lengthy risings, such proportions result in an exceptionally fine texture ideally suited to the delicate, cream-filled "peaches" fashioned on page 76.

The consistency of the dough also largely affects the way it is shaped. Stiff doughs are firm enough to make free-standing shapes (*page 66*) or to serve as bases or wrappings for fillings (*pages 68 and 70*). Loose doughs—those rich in eggs and milk—must be cooked in moulds; their open texture is typified by the babas and savarins on page 72, which are porous enough to absorb delectable quantities of flavoured syrup.

lled yeast cake, garnished with lemon glacé
g and chopped walnuts, is lifted from a
te for serving. After being rolled out, the
ugh was stamped into ovals, folded round a
g of ground poppy seeds and sultanas,
d shaped into neat crescents (*page 70*).

A Supple Dough that Rises into Flowers

A sweet, springy yeast dough (*recipe, page 162*) is easy to fashion into any shape you fancy, such as a flower (*right*), a knot, a crescent or a loop. Such a dough is not difficult to form, but certain steps must be taken to ensure that it rises properly.

The dough is composed of flour, milk, yeast, eggs and butter—which gives a luxurious, cake-like texture—as well as sugar and flavourings. Because of the butter—which could retard the action of the yeast if added too soon—the mixing of the ingredients takes place in two stages.

First, the yeast, milk, a little sugar and about one-third of the flour are mixed into a frothy batter and left to rise in a warm place. After the yeast has fermented, softened butter is added to the mixture. The butter should first be mashed until it is pliable enough to work into the batter with your fingertips. Fingers are also the best tools to use when mixing in the eggs, which should be introduced one at a time to achieve a smooth consistency. Finally, the remaining flour and sugar are added to the mixture, along with flavourings such as dried fruit and spices.

Before it can be shaped, the dough must be kneaded to make it smooth and elastic, then left in a warm place until it doubles in size. This rising, known as proving, permits the yeast to work and gently stretches the network of gluten in the dough. Once risen, the dough is ready to shape: here, the dough is gathered into small balls, flattened, and snipped with scissors to imitate flower petals.

Just before the cakes go into the oven, you can apply a wash of beaten egg to their surfaces. This not only helps a garnish, such as grated orange rind, to adhere to the uncooked dough, but will give the crust of the finished cakes a golden sheen. Once baked, yeast buns can, if you like, be decorated with chopped or slivered nuts, with a thin icing or with a sprinkling of coarse sugar crystals.

1 **Adding yeast.** Stir yeast into a little tepid milk or water. Put about one-third of the flour, sifted with salt, into a large bowl. Add one teaspoon of sugar, then make a well in the flour. When the yeast has completely dissolved, pour it into the well (*above*). Stir to a smooth paste. Leave, covered with plastic film, for about 20 minutes at room temperature.

2 **Incorporating butter.** Mash softened butter with the heel of your hand. When the yeast mixture has risen, divide the butter into small pieces and add each piece of butter separately (*above*). Rub in by hand, swirling the yeasty dough around to incorporate it. Mix in the rest the butter, piece by piece. If you wish, the bowl on a damp cloth to steady it.

6 **Shaping the dough.** Once the dough has risen, set it on a cool marble surface. Knead the dough again, for about 5 minutes. Cut off a portion of dough weighing roughly 30 g (1 oz). Clench your fist and thump the piece of dough to flatten it slightly. Roll the dough beneath your hand, cupping your palm as the dough gathers into a ball (*above*).

7 **Cutting flowers.** Dip scissor blades in flour to prevent sticking. Snip the dough, cutting to within about 1 cm (½ inch) of the centre, at five equal intervals to form the radial petals of a flower (*above*). Put the flower on a buttered baking sheet.

3 **Working in eggs.** Add the eggs one at a time. Break each egg into the dough. Pull your fingers through the dough (*above*) to mix it thoroughly. Add the remaining flour, sugar and any flavouring—here, grated orange rind, ground cinnamon, mace and cardamom. When all the ingredients are thoroughly blended, gather up the dough into a ball.

4 **Kneading the dough.** Transfer the dough to a floured surface. Press the heel of your hand into the dough's centre and push forward firmly—in one motion (*above*). Fold the extended section of dough back into the centre and repeat the pushing and folding actions for 15 to 20 minutes, until the dough is smooth and elastic.

5 **Proving the dough.** Place the kneaded dough in a large mixing bowl. Cover the bowl with plastic film. Leave the bowl in a warm place for about 2 hours or until the dough has doubled its original bulk.

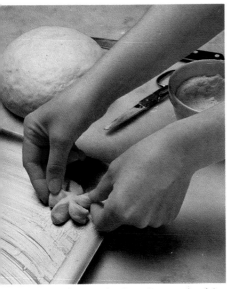

8 **Twisting the petals.** Grip the petals of the flower between your thumb and index finger. Twist the dough to make the petals more pronounced (*above*). Roll the rest of the dough into buns and shape them in the same way. Allow the dough to rise again until the flower buns have almost doubled in volume—about 40 minutes.

9 **Glazing the buns.** Beat an egg in a small bowl. Use a pastry brush to glaze each flower with the egg (*above*). Mix grated orange rind with castor sugar and sprinkle the mixture on to the centre of each bun.

10 **Baking the flowers.** Place the buns in a preheated 180°C (350°F or Mark 4) oven. Bake the flowers for about 20 minutes until they are golden-brown. Tap the base of one flower; if it sounds hollow, the bun is ready. Remove the buns from the oven and cool them on a wire rack. Serve the flowers heaped on a plate (*above*). □

A Creamy Cheesecake on a Firm Foundation

A sweet yeast dough can provide a firm and crisp foundation compatible with many different fillings. These can range from moist and creamy cheese mixtures to dry crumble toppings.

The dough used here contains little sugar, but extra butter is incorporated for fullness of flavour. When the dough is made, the yeast is not set aside to ferment first with flour and milk, but dissolved and then mixed together with the other ingredients. This method produces dough with a coarse open texture that contrasts pleasingly with a smooth filling.

Here, a rich mixture of curd cheese, soured cream, butter and dried fruit is used for the filling. After baking, the assembly is cut into individual cheesecakes (*right; recipe, page 139*). Other suitable fillings include firm-fleshed fresh fruit, such as apricots, plums or cherries, stoned and then sweetened with sugar. A spicy crumble of sugar, butter, flour and cinnamon sprinkled on to the dough yields *streusel* slices (*recipe, page 139*), or you can combine a layer of fruit, jam or curd cheese with a *streusel* topping.

1 Preparing dough. Make yeast dough (*recipe, page 162*) and allow it to rest for about 15 minutes. On a lightly floured marble surface, roll out the dough 3 mm (⅛ inch) thick. Press the dough into a buttered baking tin with your fingertips. To help prevent the filling from soaking into the uncooked dough, sprinkle a little fine semolina over it (*above*).

2 Mixing the filling. Cream sugar and butter together in a large mixing bowl (*page 36, Step 1*); stir in egg yolks. If you like, add chopped glacé cherries and crystallized orange and citron peel. Add semolina, soured cream and sultanas (*above*). Using a wooden spoon, mix all the ingredients thoroughly.

6 Adding the curd filling. Pour the filling on to the surface of the dough using the spoon to guide the mixture (*above*). Spread the filling evenly with the back of the spoon and level the surface.

7 Glazing the surface. In a small bowl, beat an egg. Using a pastry brush, glaze the surface of the filling with egg (*above*) until it is evenly covered. Use light, deft strokes so that the filling is not disturbed. Place the baking tin in the oven.

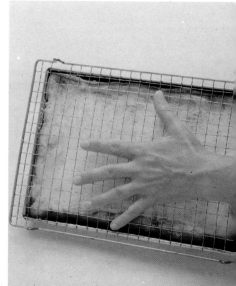

8 Unmoulding the cake. Bake the cake for about 40 minutes or until the surface is golden-brown. If the edges brown too quickly, cover the cake with aluminium foil. Insert a knife into the filling; if it comes out clean, the cake is done. Allow to cool in the tin. Run a knife round the edges and invert on to a wire rack (*above*), then place right side up on a cutting board.

3 **Sieving cheese.** Put curd cheese into a sturdy metal sieve and, using a pestle or a wooden spoon, force the curd cheese through the sieve into a large bowl. From time to time scrape cheese from the underside of the sieve into the bowl.

4 **Adding the curd cheese.** Add the sieved cheese to the bowl containing the rest of the filling ingredients (*above*). Stir the cheese into the filling mixture until it is thoroughly incorporated.

5 **Folding in egg whites.** Whisk egg whites until they form soft peaks. Use a metal spoon to fold a little egg white into the filling (*above*), then gently fold in the remainder of the egg whites. Preheat the oven to 180°C (350°F or Mark 4).

6 **Serving the slices.** With a sharp knife, trim away any dark brown edges from the cake. Cut the trimmed cake into slices about 2.5 by 6 cm (1 by 2½ inches); each slice will show colourful specks of fruit when presented on a plate (*right*).□

Classic Shapes with Exotic Fillings

Rolled out pastry-thin, a yeast dough makes a soft-textured wrapping that is flexible enough to envelop almost any filling. In the demonstration on the right, for instance, a rum-flavoured chestnut purée is piped on to strips of dough, which are rolled into thin cylinders and fashioned into rings (*recipe, page 140*). In the box below, the dough is moulded by hand into crescent shapes round a filling based on poppy seeds (*recipe, page 140*).

Provided it is firm enough to shape, almost any rich yeast dough can be used. The dough used for the rings is enriched with cream as well as with butter: if it becomes too soft to work, refrigerate the dough until it becomes firm again.

Uncooked fillings—chopped nuts, for example, or a mixture of curd cheese and dried fruit may be spooned or piped on to the dough. Allow cooked fillings, such as puréed fruit or the chestnuts used here, to cool first. Glaze the pastries with beaten egg before baking, and, if you like, coat them afterwards with an icing.

1 **Making the dough.** Mix yeast, a little flour and tepid milk in a large bowl. Stand the covered bowl in a warm place for about 30 minutes to allow the yeast to start working; bubbles will appear on the surface. Stir in more flour, melted butter, sugar and an egg yolk. Mix in cream (*above*) until the dough is smooth and cohesive. Let it rest for about 30 minutes.

2 **Mixing the filling.** Cut crosses in the flat ends of fresh chestnuts. Parboil the nuts for 10 minutes and then peel off the cut hulls and the skins beneath. Simmer the chestnuts in milk for about 45 minutes, until they are tender. Purée them in a food mill, or use a wooden pestle to press them through a metal sieve. Add butter, sugar, rum and cream to the purée.

Poppy Seeds Sealed in Glossy Envelopes

1 **Shaping crescents.** Make a yeast dough, rest it for 2 hours, and roll it out 3 mm (⅛ inch) thick. Flour an oval pastry cutter and stamp out the dough. In a food processor or mortar, grind poppy seeds to a fine powder. Bring milk to the boil; stir in the poppy seeds, semolina, sultanas, sugar and lemon rind and cook for a few minutes over gentle heat. Cool. Spread the filling on to each oval, leaving a margin of 2.5 cm (1 inch). Roll each oval lengthwise round its filling (*above, left*) keeping the ends pointed. Shape into crescents with seams underneath and place on a buttered baking sheet (*above, right*). Glaze with beaten egg and let rise in a warm place for 1 hour

2 **Decorating the crescents.** To prevent the crescents splitting, pierce their sides with a fork. Bake them in a 220°C (425°F or Mark 7) oven for 10 minutes, then at 190°C (375°F or Mark 5) for 15 to 20 minutes, until golden. Make icing—here, lemon glacé (*page 15*)—and spoon it over the crescents (*above*); sprinkle them with chopped nuts—here, walnuts are used—before the icing sets.

3 **Cutting pastry into strips.** Flour a cool work surface. Roll out the dough to a thickness of about 2 mm (1/10 inch). Trim the dough square and cut it into strips about 4 cm (1½ inches) wide. Slice the dough crosswise so that the strips are about 10 cm (4 inches) long (*above*).

4 **Enclosing the filling.** Fit a piping bag with a plain 5 mm (¼ inch) nozzle. Spoon the chestnut filling into the bag and twist the top of the bag to secure it. Pipe the filling down one side of each pastry strip about 5 mm (¼ inch) from the edge (*above, left*). Roll each strip of dough round the filling to form a tight cylinder (*above, centre*). With the seam underneath, bring the ends together to make a ring (*above, right*); pinch the ends firmly together to join them. Place the rings on a buttered and floured baking sheet; brush the tops with a little beaten egg and sugar. Allow the rings to rise slightly.

5 **Icing the rings.** Bake the rings in a 200°C (400°F or Mark 6) oven until golden-brown—15 minutes. Cool them on a rack over a tray. Brush them with apricot glaze (*page 14*). Prepare a thin glacé icing (*page 15*). Using a paper piping bag (*page 18*), pipe thin lines back and forth across the rings (*above*). Let the icing dry before serving (*right*). □

Spirited Finishes for Honeycombed Cakes

Some yeast doughs contain such a lot of liquid—mainly in the form of eggs—that they are best described as batters. Such mixtures have distinct advantages: in a copious amount of liquid the yeast becomes easily dispersed throughout the flour and can develop prolifically. As the yeast multiplies, carbon dioxide is produced which expands the dough. The result is porous, open-textured cakes that readily absorb flavouring syrups. Babas (*right; recipe, page 134*) and savarins (*box, below*) are two celebrated examples.

Yeast batters require as much kneading as stiffer doughs, but the technique must be adapted to suit the mixture's consistency. A combination of pulling and slapping (*Step 2, right*) is most effective. Once risen, the batter is stable enough for softened butter and, in the case of babas, rum-soaked raisins to be folded in.

The batter is baked in moulds: dariole moulds for babas and ring—or savarin—moulds for savarins. After cooking, the warm cakes are dipped in syrup, then served either warm or cold. Savarins also receive a topping of fruit or cream.

1 Adding yeast. Mix yeast with tepid water and allow the mixture to stand for about 10 minutes. Sift flour and salt into a large bowl. Make a well in the centre of the flour and break eggs into it. Add sugar. Pour the yeast mixture into the well in the flour (*above*). Use your hands to mix all of the ingredients into a smooth dough.

2 Kneading the dough. Mash butter by pressing it with the heel of your hand, and set it aside. To knead the dough, pull it upwards with the tips of your fingers (*above*) then vigorously slap it down into the bowl. Continue for about 5 minutes, until any lumps disappear and the dough becomes smooth and elastic.

Dimpled Rounds Brimming with Fruit

1 Filling moulds. Make a baba dough (*Steps 1 to 4, above*), omitting the raisins. Butter ring moulds; fill them two-thirds full with dough. Cover them and allow the dough to rise until the moulds are almost full—about 20 minutes. Set them on a baking sheet and bake in a 200°C (400°F or Mark 6) oven for about 15 minutes, until the cakes are golden-brown.

2 Garnishing with fruit. Make a light sugar syrup (*page 6*) flavoured with kirsch or rum. Turn the baked savarins out of their moulds and soak them in the syrup. Allow them to drain on a wire rack, then garnish the centre of each savarin with fresh fruit—here, a slice each of pineapple and kiwi fruit, an orange segment, a green grape and half a strawberry.

3 Serving the savarins. Prepare apricot glaze (*page 14*) and brush it over each savarin using a pastry brush (*above*). Transfer the savarins to a platter or to individual plates for serving.

3 **Covering the dough.** Place the softened butter, in small pieces, on the surface of the dough. Cover the bowl with a damp cloth. Stand the bowl in a warm place for about 1 hour, until the dough doubles in bulk and almost encloses the butter. Meanwhile, soak raisins in rum diluted with a little water until they are plump and swollen—about 1 hour.

4 **Folding in butter.** Drain the rum from the raisins through a sieve into a small bowl. Use your hands to fold the softened butter into the dough (*above*) until the mixture is smooth. Fold in the raisins.

5 **Filling moulds.** Using a pastry brush, butter dariole moulds and chill them until the butter just hardens. Apply a second coat of butter. Fill each mould one-third full with dough. Tap each mould against the work surface to settle the dough. Put the moulds on a baking sheet, cover with a cloth and leave for 1 hour, until the dough almost fills them.

6 **Dipping in syrup.** Bake the babas in a 200°C (400°F or Mark 6) oven for about 20 minutes until they are golden-brown and shrink from the sides of the moulds. Prepare a sugar syrup (*recipe, page 134*) and add rum to it. Unmould the babas and immerse them in the syrup. Turn them over several times and transfer them to a wire rack over a tray (*above*).

7 **Glazing the babas.** Make an apricot glaze (*page 14*). While the glaze is still warm, use a pastry brush to coat the babas with it (*above*). Leave the babas on the wire rack until excess syrup and glaze have drained away; transfer them to a serving plate.

8 **Serving the babas.** Cut angelica into diamond-shaped leaves; allow two for every baba. Cut glacé cherries into quarters. Press one cherry quarter on to the sticky surface of each baba, then place an angelica leaf on either side of the cherry (*above*). Serve the babas immediately or when completely cool.□

Spectacular Results from the Richest of Doughs

Silk-smooth, golden and supremely rich, brioche is the queen of yeast doughs—a title merited by the royal proportions of eggs and butter that go into its making. For every 500 g (1 lb) of flour, brioche doughs include up to an equal weight of butter and six or more eggs. Such a dough takes time and careful preparation, but the finished results, exemplified by the brioche "peaches" demonstrated on the following pages (*recipe, page 134*), more than justify the effort.

The dough itself is prepared in two stages. First, flour, yeast and eggs are mixed together. Then, after fermentation has begun, the butter is folded into the mixture. The high proportion of eggs makes the dough very loose, and you will need a scraper to handle it. A cool working surface—ideally, a marble slab—is also useful: it keeps the butter from turning oily as the dough is kneaded.

To promote its fine texture, brioche dough requires three risings. First, after kneading, it is set aside at room temperature until it has trebled in volume. Then the dough is punched down, eliminating large gas bubbles, before the second, more lengthy rising which takes place in the refrigerator. The low temperature slows the yeast, and the dough expands gently and evenly. The cold dough is also easier to mould into its final form. The third and last rising takes place just before the dough goes into the oven.

To make the peaches demonstrated overleaf, the dough is rolled out into a cylinder and cut into small slices, each of which is then shaped into a flattened hemisphere. After being baked, the hemispheres are joined in pairs by pastry cream, to imitate the form of the real fruit. Careful finishing ensures the decorative verisimilitude of the peaches, as well as contributing an interplay of different flavours. Apricot glaze, brushed over an undercoat of rum syrup, provides the basic colour of the fruit. Redcurrant jelly adds the characteristic peach bloom, and leaves fashioned from green-tinted marzipan complete the effect.

1 Starting the dough. Measure flour and sugar and put them in a large bowl. Add salt. Mix yeast in a little tepid water or milk. Make a well in the centre of the flour and pour in the dissolved yeast. Break eggs into the well, and then stir all the ingredients together with your fingers (*above*) to make a loose dough.

2 Kneading the dough. Turn the dough out on a cool work surface, such as marble. Gather as much of the dough as you can between your fingers and then pull it up quickly (*above*). With a flick of your wrist slap the dough back on to the work surface. Continue to knead the dough in this way for about 10 minutes, until it becomes smooth and elastic.

5 Kneading the dough. Knead vigorously with one hand, using the scraper to gather the dough together as it spreads. Continue kneading for about 5 minutes, until the butter is thoroughly blended. Place the kneaded dough in a bowl and cover it with plastic film. Allow the bowl to stand at room temperature for 3 to 4 hours, until it has trebled in bulk.

6 Gathering the dough. When the dough has risen, remove the plastic film. Punch down into the centre of the dough several times to expel gas. Cover the dough with plastic film again and set the bowl in the refrigerator for 6 to 8 hours or overnight, until the dough has doubled in volume. Pull the dough from the bowl (*above*) and transfer it to a floured work surface.

3 **Using a dough scraper.** As the dough spreads, pull it together again with a dough scraper to work it evenly (*above*). If the dough becomes too loose to hold together, fold a little sifted flour into it. If necessary, place the dough in a bowl in the refrigerator to firm it.

4 **Folding in butter.** Mash butter by working it with the heel of your hand. Pull the dough apart with your fingers and place a small piece of butter in its centre (*above, left*). Use the dough scraper to fold the butter into the dough (*above, right*). Add the rest of the butter in the same way, slapping the dough up and down. Make sure each piece of butter is well blended before you add the next.

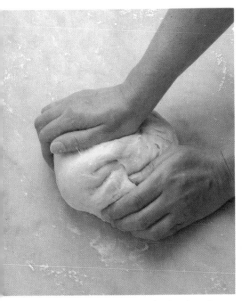

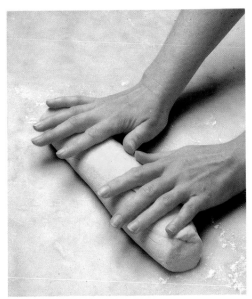

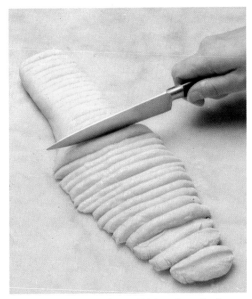

7 **Kneading the risen dough.** Gather the dough into a ball. Exerting a light, even pressure with the heel of your hand, push the dough away from you. At the same time, turn it slightly, then fold it back towards you. Knead in this manner for about 1 minute, until smooth.

8 **Forming a cylinder.** Lightly flour the work surface again. Mould the dough into a cylinder. With outstretched hands, roll the cylinder until it is smooth and even, and approximately 30 cm (12 inches) long (*above*). With a knife, mark it into equal portions about 1 cm (½ inch) wide.

9 **Cutting into slices.** With a sharp knife, slice the dough along the marks to obtain small, equal-sized pieces. Dust the blade of the knife with flour so that it cuts cleanly, without breaking the dough. ▶

10 **Making balls.** Use your cupped hand to shape each dough piece into a ball (*above*). Lightly butter a baking sheet and place the balls on the sheet at 7.5 cm (3 inch) intervals, to allow room for expansion while proving.

11 **Flattening the balls.** Flour the fingers of one hand and flatten the top of each ball (*above*). Cover the dough balls with a dampened towel to prevent a skin from forming, and leave the baking sheet at room temperature until the dough has doubled in size.

12 **Hollowing the baked brioche.** Place the baking sheet in a 230°C (450°F or Mark 8) oven for about 15 minutes until the shapes are golden. Transfer the shapes to a wire rack to cool. Using a sharp pointed knife, hollow out the base of each shape (*above*).

14 **Applying the first glaze.** Over a low heat, warm more rum syrup. Using a pastry brush, glaze the outsides of the brioche peaches with the rum syrup (*above*). Allow the glaze to dry—about 10 minutes.

15 **Applying apricot glaze.** Prepare an apricot glaze (*page 14*). With a pastry brush, apply the warm glaze so that the peaches are completely coated. Leave the peaches for a few minutes to allow the glaze to set.

16 **Brushing with redcurrant jelly.** Warm redcurrant jelly in a small pan. Using a pastry brush, apply the jelly to the centre of each half of the brioche peaches and at the top, creating the illusion of the red "blushes" of the real fruit. Dust each peach with castor sugar sprinkled from a small sieve. Put each peach in a paper case.

3 **Filling with cream.** Using a pastry brush, coat the inside of each hollow with rum syrup. Make pastry cream (*page 16*) and flavour it with rum. Fill each hollow with the pastry cream and smooth it flat with a knife (*above*). Join pairs of the filled shapes to form "peaches" and put them on the rack.

Colouring and Shaping Marzipan Leaves

1 **Colouring marzipan.** Make marzipan (*page 13*). Flatten the marzipan into a rough circle with the heel of your hand, and spoon spinach extract into the centre (*above*). Draw the marzipan together and knead it slightly until the green colour is well blended throughout.

2 **Cutting leaves.** Roll out the coloured marzipan to a thickness of about 3 mm ($\frac{1}{8}$ inch). Use a confectionery cutter or a knife to make small leaf shapes. Cut each shape in half lengthwise. Place the halves over an upturned dish to dry (*above*); leave them for 30 minutes or until they are firm enough to handle.

7 **Completing the peaches.** Make leaf shapes from marzipan that has been coloured with spinach extract (*box, above*); alternatively, cut leaf shapes from crystallized angelica. Place a leaf, pointing upwards, in the centre of the two halves of each peach (*above*) and then serve the peaches (*right*). □

5
Poached and Fried Cakes
Unusual Methods for Special Effects

Not all patisserie comes from the oven. The poaching kettle, the waffle iron, the frying pan and the vessel bubbling with hot oil—from these and other utensils come delicacies as diverse as the methods used to cook them. Variety is this chapter's theme, and its subjects range from fruit-laden dumplings to syrup-coated waffles and buttery *pain perdu*, from plump doughnuts to crisply fried pastries.

Dumplings (*page 80*) are simply portions of pliable dough—often enclosing a fruit stuffing—that have been dropped into gently simmering water and poached until cooked through. Provided the basic dumpling dough is firm enough to hold together in hot water, these little parcels may be made not only with a flour-based mixture but with curd cheese, rice flour, semolina or even mashed potatoes (*recipes, pages 143-145*).

Waffles, on the other hand, require a light, loose batter. Too liquid to hold any shape of its own, the batter will cook into a crisp honeycomb on the hot metal grid of a waffle iron (*page 82*). Flavourings such as rum or cinnamon add character to the batter; once cooked, the waffles need only a sprinkling of icing sugar to complete them. Like much patisserie, though, waffles invite more generous accompaniments—finely chopped nuts, a pool of syrup or honey, or a topping of ice cream, whipped cream, or jam.

Doughs for deep frying are often similar to those used in baking, but because the intense, enveloping heat of deep frying causes extremely rapid cooking, the end product is very different. The sweet yeast dough that yields crusty buns on page 66, for example, puffs out in a bath of hot oil to form light and tender doughnuts (*page 84*). The effect is even more pronounced in the case of noodle doughs, which are pliant enough to form into knots, bows and other shapes that are sharply accentuated by deep frying (*page 86*). Wrapped round cylindrical moulds, a wine-flavoured noodle dough yields crisp, golden tubes that will hold a creamy filling (*opposite and page 88*). And some fillings themselves can be deep fried, without a wrapping of dough to contain them. A firm pastry cream, for example, cut into shapes and coated only with egg and breadcrumbs, emerges from its bath of hot oil encased in a light golden shell (*page 90*).

Sugar-dusted *cannoli*—crisp, deep-fried shells of wine-flavoured pastry filled with a mixture of sweetened *ricotta*, chocolate and crystallized orange peel (*page 88*)—await serving. The cases were formed from ovals of noodle dough wrapped round small tubular moulds and secured with egg white. After deep frying, the delicate shells were unmoulded and filled.

Fruit-Stuffed Dumplings Gently Simmered

Sweet dumplings—parcels of dough with a fruit filling—are particularly popular in Germany and Eastern Europe where they are usually sprinkled with nuts or sugar and served hot with soured cream. The dumplings may be made from flour, semolina or more unusual ingredients such as potato or curd cheese, but all are cooked in the same way—dropped into simmering water and poached until done.

For successful dumplings, the dough should be soft, yet firm enough to hold together during cooking. Here, it is made from flour, egg and milk; to enrich it, a little butter is beaten with the eggs before the other ingredients are added (*recipe, page 142*). The high proportion of egg to fat can give the mixture a curdled appearance, which disappears when flour and milk are added and the dough is kneaded until silky and elastic.

For the dumpling filling, firm-fleshed fruits such as apricots, cherries, berries or the plums shown here are all suitable. The centres of larger, stoned fruits can be filled with chopped nuts, a whole almond or a mixture of sugar and ground spices.

1 Mixing eggs and butter. Remove eggs and butter from the refrigerator well in advance, to allow them to reach room temperature. Sift flour and salt together into a bowl. Measure milk into a jug. Put the butter in a second bowl. Add the eggs, one at a time, and beat them into the butter with a wooden spoon (*above*).

2 Combining the mixtures. Continue to beat until all the eggs have been added to the bowl and incorporated into the butter. Pour the egg mixture into the flour (*above*) and stir the ingredients together.

6 Filling the rounds. Place one plum half, cut side up, on each round of dough. Fill the centre of the plum with some of the sugar and cinnamon mixture and place another plum half on top. Cover the plum with a second circle of dough. Hold the dumpling firmly in one hand and press the edges between your thumb and forefinger to make a decorative seal.

7 Poaching the dumplings. Bring salted water to the boil in a large pan. Drop in the dumplings in batches of eight to 10, to avoid overcrowding the pan. Reduce the heat to a simmer and cook, uncovered, until the dumplings float to the surface— 10 to 12 minutes. Using a slotted spoon, remove the dumplings and drain them on a cloth-lined tray.

8 Garnishing the dumplings. Finely chop walnuts and fry them lightly in butter for a minute or two. Sprinkle the walnuts and the rest of the sugar and cinnamon mixture over the cooked dumplings.

3 **Adding milk.** Add milk, a little at a time, to the other ingredients in the bowl. Stir all the ingredients together, blending them well and incorporating all the flour from the sides of the bowl. Continue to add milk to the mixture and blend it in until the dough is pliable but still stiff.

4 **Kneading the dough.** Gather together the dough in the bowl (*above*) and transfer it to a marble slab. To knead the dough, push it away from you with the heel of your hand, then fold it back towards you, twisting it slightly. Continue kneading until the dough is smooth and silky in texture—5 to 10 minutes. Cover and leave to rest for 30 minutes.

5 **Stamping rounds.** Cut plums in half, remove the stones and dip the cut edges in lemon juice to prevent them turning brown. Put the halves on a tray, cut side down. In a small bowl, mix sugar and ground cinnamon. Roll out the dough on a floured surface to a thickness of about 3 mm ($\frac{1}{8}$ inch). Use a 7.5 cm (3 inch) cutter to stamp out rounds of dough (*above*).

9 **Serving the fruit dumplings.** Transfer the dumplings to a serving dish and serve them immediately while they are still hot (*above*). You can eat them just as they are (*right*) or you can accompany them with a little soured cream or whipped fresh cream. □

Crisp Confections from Griddle and Pan

Sealed between the hot grids of a waffle iron, a simple batter of flour, milk and eggs will cook rapidly to produce tender, delicately crisped cakes. The batter can be left plain, or it can be flavoured, as here, with a little oil and rum (*recipe, page 160*). The oil also helps to prevent the batter from sticking. To achieve an especially light texture, the egg whites are beaten before being folded into the batter.

Two types of waffle iron are available. The cast-iron type shown here is used over direct heat and must be turned to cook the batter on both sides. Electric waffle irons will cook both sides of the waffle simultaneously. The waffles can be served hot or cold, sprinkled with sugar or maple syrup, or sandwiched with jam, puréed fruit or whipped double cream.

Small cakes can also be created from slices of leftover bread or brioche (*page 74*). The slices are dipped in a mixture of eggs, sugar, rum or brandy, and milk or cream (*below; recipe, page 157*). Since dry bread is porous, it readily absorbs liquid. Fried in butter, drained and dusted with sugar, the slices are served hot with jam.

A Batter Enclosed in a Patterned Mould

1 Mixing the batter. Separate eggs. Sift flour into a bowl. Make a well in the flour and add olive oil, the yolks and, if you like, flavouring—here, a tablespoon of rum. Gradually add milk (*above*); pour it in a thin stream, whisking at the same time to incorporate it thoroughly.

2 Folding in egg whites. Continue to add milk until the consistency of the mixture resembles thick cream. Beat the egg whites until they form soft peaks. Tip the beaten whites into the bowl; using a metal spoon or a spatula, gently fold them into the batter.

A Sweet Transformation for Leftover Bread

1 Dividing brioche into sections. Using a sharp knife, cut two-day-old brioche, or other bread, into slices about 1 cm (½ inch) thick. Divide each slice into sections (*above*). To make the coating mixture, whisk whole eggs and sugar together in a bowl. Add some rum or brandy. Warm cream in a pan and add it to the mixture.

2 Dipping and frying. Over a low heat, melt butter in a frying pan. Using a fork, dip each section of brioche briefly in the coating mixture. Do not let the brioche soak or it will disintegrate. Drain the section on the fork (*above*), then place it in the pan. Fry the sections on both sides for about 2 minutes each, or until they are golden. Drain them on a napkin.

3 Serving the sections. Transfer the fried slices to a plate and sprinkle them with castor sugar. Serve them hot, garnished with a spoonful of jam—strawberry jam shown here—or with whipped double cream, honey or syrup. □

3 Filling the iron. Preheat a waffle iron over a medium heat for 5 minutes on each side or until water sprinkled on the grids steams immediately. Brush both grids with melted butter. Ladle batter on to the bottom grid to barely fill it. Close the iron; if batter oozes out, scrape it off. Cook over a medium heat for about 2 minutes; turn the iron over to cook the other side.

4 Removing the waffles. Open the iron. If the surface of the cake is not brown enough for your taste, close the iron and cook for a minute longer on each side. To remove the cake, free its edges with a metal spatula and lift it out (*above*). Slip the waffles on to a wire rack. Butter the grids again and cook the rest of the batter in the same way.

5 Filling the waffles. Cut the waffles into sections using a sharp knife; trim any rough edges. Sift icing sugar into a bowl. Prepare a filling—here, double cream whipped with icing sugar and one or two tablespoons of rum. Sandwich the cold waffles with the cream (*above*); place them on a rack set over a tray.

6 Serving the waffles. To finish the waffles, dust their tops with icing sugar shaken from the sieve. Transfer the filled waffles to a plate and serve them immediately; otherwise the cream will soak into the waffles and soften them.□

Doughnuts: Fashioning and Filling Perennial Favourites

Deep-fried patisserie has a character all its own, the result of the rapid cooking caused by the oil's all-enveloping heat. The method suits pastry doughs—pages 86-88—as well as the yeast dough used for the doughnuts demonstrated here.

In the case of yeast dough, the sudden exposure to heat causes the gas trapped inside the dough to expand, producing a light, airy texture. The surface of the dough turns an appetizing golden-brown, but remains soft and tender, giving the doughnuts a finish quite unlike the crust that forms on oven-baked doughs.

Traditionally, doughnuts are shaped into balls and rings before frying, as in this demonstration. Balls are the most straightforward: just pinch off a piece of dough and roll it under your cupped hand. For variety, you can roll the piece of dough into a sausage shape, which can also be twisted into a corkscrew. To make ring doughnuts, pierce a ball of dough with your forefinger (*Step 1, right*).

Doughnuts made from a more liquid mixture will produce crisper though less substantial results. To shape these drop doughnuts from a loose dough, simply squeeze them out from your clenched hand (*Step 1, box, opposite page*).

Doughnuts are ready to cook as soon as the dough has risen. Most vegetable oils, including corn oil, groundnut oil and olive oil, are suitable for deep frying. Heat the oil to a temperature of about 190°C (375°F). You can check the temperature with a deep-frying thermometer, or drop a small piece of bread or dough into the oil; if the bread sizzles immediately, the oil is ready. To maintain the oil at the optimum temperature, fry the doughnuts in small batches—the exact number will depend on the size of your pan. Overfilling the pan will lower the temperature of the oil, hinder the sealing of the dough and cause the doughnuts to absorb oil.

Doughnuts are delicious just as they are, but if you like, you can use a piping bag to fill them with jam, cream or pastry cream before serving (*box, right*). Decorative finishes range from a sprinkling of sugar to coatings of icing or chocolate; a dip in warmed honey is a luxurious alternative (*box, opposite page*).

1 **Forming a ring.** Prepare a sweet yeast dough (*recipe, page 162*). Flour a tray. Divide the dough into 30 g (1 oz) pieces, roll each piece into a ball and poke a floured forefinger through the centre. Circle your finger to widen the hole to about 2 cm (¾ inch) in diameter. Set the rings on the tray, cover with a towel and allow to rise until doubled in volume.

2 **Deep frying the rings.** Fill a deep pan two-thirds full with oil; heat the oil to 190°C (375°F). Gently stretch each risen dough ring back into shape. Slide each ring into the hot oil. Cook the rings for about a minute on either side, turning them with a skimmer or a slotted spoon until they are evenly brown. Remove them and drain on kitchen paper.

An Efficient Technique for Adding Jam

1 **Filling with jam.** Deep fry doughnut balls; drain and cool them. Fill a large piping bag fitted with a 5 mm (¼ inch) nozzle with jam—here, raspberry. Cover a tray with castor sugar. With a small, sharp knife, cut into the centre of each doughnut. Push the nozzle into the cut; squeeze jam into the doughnut (*above*). Place the doughnut on the tray of sugar.

2 **Serving the doughnuts.** Fill the rest of the doughnuts with jam in the same way, then roll them in the castor sugar to coat them completely. Serve the doughnuts piled on a cake stand (*above*) or plate.

3 **Coating with sugar.** In a wide, shallow dish, mix castor sugar and a little ground cinnamon. Allow the dough rings to cool slightly, then place them, a few at a time, in the dish. Sprinkle the sugar over the rings (*above*). Serve the sugared rings in a napkin-lined container (*right*).□

Golden Globes Dipped in Honey

1 **Deep frying the dough.** Prepare a loose, sweet yeast dough (*recipe, page 162*). Wet your hand in a bowl of water, then scoop up a handful of the dough. Clench your fist and gently squeeze out a piece of dough the size of a walnut. Use a metal spatula to cut it off so that it slides into the oil (*above*). Fry the doughnuts a few at a time and drain them on kitchen paper.

2 **Dipping in honey.** Set a wire rack over a tray. In a wide, shallow pan, warm honey and a little lemon juice over low heat until the mixture is well combined; take the pan off the heat. Using a slotted spoon, dip the doughnuts in the honey to coat them completely; lift them out (*above*) and set them on the rack to drain.

3 **Finishing and serving.** To complete the doughnuts, lightly dust them with ground cinnamon shaken from a fine-meshed sieve, then sprinkle them with chopped pistachio nuts. Place the doughnuts in paper cases and serve immediately.

Fanciful Shapes from a Pliable Dough

By varying the method of cutting, folding and twisting a simple noodle dough, you can produce a wide assortment of pastry shapes that can be cooked and served together. Made from flour, egg, sugar, water and melted butter, sweet noodle dough is particularly pliable and can be worked into intricate forms without tearing or disintegrating (*recipe, page 162*).

Pin-wheels, for instance, can be made from squares of dough merely by cutting the corners and folding them over (*Step 1*). Oval and rectangular shapes yield elaborate twists (*Steps 2 and 3*). Knots are simply strips of dough, looped round and tied in the middle (*Step 4*).

These shaped pastries are deep fried, which accentuates their shape and gives them a crisp, light texture. Dropped in hot oil, the pastries puff slightly and turn golden-brown in a couple of minutes.

A stiff, creamed batter (*box below; recipe, page 164*) can be shaped and deep fried in the same way as noodle dough. In this case, rounds of dough are cut and stacked to resemble flowers or rosettes.

1 Making pin-wheels. Prepare a sweet noodle dough. To relax the dough, cover and leave it at room temperature for about 1 hour, then roll it into a sheet 3 mm (⅛ inch) thick. Cut the dough into 7.5 cm (3 inch) squares, then make a diagonal cut from each corner, stopping about 1 cm (½ inch) from the centre of each square. To make the surface of the dough adhesive, brush the centre of each square with a little egg white (*above, left*). Fold alternate points of dough into the centre so that the points touch but do not overlap (*above, right*); press the points gently into place.

Three-Tiered Rosettes Gilded in Oil

1 Forming rosettes. Roll out stiff, creamed batter 5 mm (¼ inch) thick; stamp out circles, using a 6 cm (2½ inch) fluted cutter. Make cuts at regular intervals round the edge of each circle, stopping 5 mm (¼ inch) from the centre. Brush the centres of two circles with egg white and stack them with a third circle on top. Press a spoon handle into the middle to make a hollow.

2 Completing the rosettes. Deep fry the rosettes for about 5 minutes or until golden-brown, turning them once. Drain them and then cool them on a wire rack. To decorate the rosettes, dust them with icing sugar, then place a spoonful of jelly—here, redcurrant jelly—or sieved jam in the centre of each one.

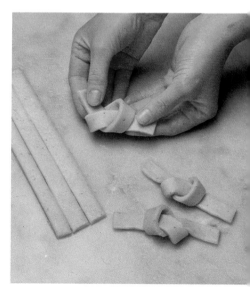

4 Forming knots. Roll the dough into a rectangle 3 mm (⅛ inch) thick and about 20 cm (8 inches) long. Cut the dough into strips 2 cm (¾ inch) wide. Loop each strip round and tie it into a loose knot (*above*); gently pull the ends straight.

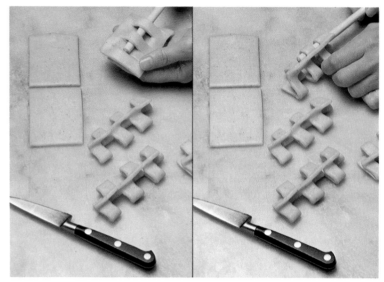

Making twisted ovals. Roll out the dough 3 mm (⅛ inch) thick and stamp it into ovals using a pastry cutter. Cutting to within 1 cm (½ inch) of the edge, make two lengthwise slits so that the three bands of dough are of roughly equal width (*above, left*). Lift the two outer bands towards the centre, then push one of them through the opposite slit. Pull the other side band in the opposite direction (*above, right*); press the bands slightly to flatten them.

3 **Making ladders.** Roll out the dough 3 mm (⅛ inch) thick. Cut the dough into 9 by 6 cm (3½ by 2½ inch) rectangles. Make five equally spaced incisions across the rectangles, cutting to within 1 cm (½ inch) of the edge each time. Thread the handle of a wooden spoon over and under alternate strips of dough (*above, left*). Raise the spoon handle to pull up three loops of dough. Move the handle to one side to fold the loops on to themselves and create three loops on the other side. Carefully withdraw the handle (*above, right*) and press the loops slightly to flatten them.

5 **Deep frying and serving.** Fill a deep pan two-thirds full of oil; heat the oil to 190°C (375°F). It is ready when a scrap of dough dropped into it sizzles immediately and floats to the top. Fry the pastry shapes in batches, turning them with a skimmer after about 1 minute (*above*). Drain and cool the pastries on kitchen paper, toss them in vanilla sugar and serve (*right*). □

Diverse Treatments for Distinctive Doughs

Deep-fried pastries are perfect containers for a filling. Whether the dough is shaped and fried first, then filled afterwards, or filled before being cooked, the results are crisp and appetizing.

In the demonstration on the right (*recipe, page 148*), a wine-flavoured noodle dough is wrapped round small cylindrical moulds and plunged into hot oil. After being cooled, the moulds are removed and the pastry tubes—known as *cannoli*—are then ready for stuffing. Here, sweetened *ricotta* studded with pieces of crystallized fruit and chocolate is used, but almost any creamy mixture could be substituted.

A filling that is to be cooked along with its dough must be firm enough to hold together during deep frying. Below, semolina dough is wrapped round a filling of minced dates, then cut into slices for deep frying (*recipe, page 149*). Once cooked, the slices can be eaten just as they are; here, dipping in honey provides a luxurious finishing touch.

Cannoli: Wine-Flavoured Shells with a Creamy Filling

1 Shaping dough. Make a wine-flavoured noodle dough, roll it out 3 mm ($\frac{1}{8}$ inch) thick and stamp into ovals. Lightly oil metal *cannoli* moulds, or, as here, 15 cm (6 inch) lengths of 2.5 cm (1 inch) dowel. Wrap each oval of dough lengthwise round a mould, dab the overlapping edges with egg white (*above*) and press one over the other to seal the join.

2 Deep frying the pastries. Fill a deep pa[n] not more than two-thirds full with oil. Heat the oil to 190°C (375°F) or until a scrap of dough dropped into the oil sizzles immediately. Fry in small batches to avoid cooling the oil. As soon as the pastries are puffed and golden—about [ ] minutes—remove them with a skimmer (*above*) and drain on kitchen paper.

Mass-Producing Filled Sweetmeats

1 Preparing dates. Stem and halve fresh dates and remove the stones. Peel the dates with a small, sharp knife (*above*). Mince the dates using a grinder fitted with a medium disc, or finely chop them with a heavy knife. Finely chop orange rind. Mix the dates and rind together.

2 Filling pastry. Prepare semolina dough and roll it into a 1 cm ($\frac{1}{2}$ inch) thick rectangle. You need not flour the work surface; the dough contains enough oil to prevent sticking. Cut the rectangle in two. Spoon the filling on to the dough, covering half of each piece (*above*). Spread the filling to within about 2 cm ($\frac{3}{4}$ inch) of the outside edge.

3 Sealing and slicing. To seal the dough, fold the unfilled half over the filled half so that the edges meet; firmly press the edges together with your fingertips. Sea[l] the other piece of dough in the same way. Using a large knife, cut each roll int[o] 1 cm ($\frac{1}{2}$ inch) slices (*above*).

3 **Removing the moulds.** As they cool, the pastries become more fragile; remove them from their moulds as soon as they are cool enough to handle. Grasping the end of a mould in one hand, hold the pastry with the other hand and pull it free with a gentle twisting action (*above*). Cool the pastries completely and fill them just before serving.

4 **Filling the pastries.** Sieve *ricotta* and icing sugar into a bowl. Stir in chopped crystallized fruit—here, orange peel— and chopped, hard chocolate (*page 10*). Using a small metal spatula or a spoon, fill each pastry from both ends (*above*). Smooth the filling level at the ends and place the pastry on a wire rack.

5 **Finishing and serving.** Put icing sugar in a small sieve; shake it gently over the filled pastries to cover them with sugar. Serve the *cannoli* immediately, otherwise the filling will soak into the pastry and make it less crisp.□

4 **Cooking and serving.** Heat oil to 190°C (375°F) and fry the slices until they are golden-brown—2 to 3 minutes. Drain the slices. Warm honey in a wide, shallow pan. Set a wire rack over a tray. Using a fork, dip the fried slices in the honey to coat them (*above*), then place them on the rack so that excess honey can drip off. Serve the slices warm or cold (*right*).□

Pastry Cream Diamonds in a Protective Coating

Delicate pastry cream, used extensively as a filling in patisserie, can be enjoyed on its own. By making the cream firmer than for a filling, you can cut it into pieces that can be deep fried to produce crisp, golden shells with soft, almost liquid, centres (*right; recipe, page 158*).

To make the cream stiff enough for cutting into neat shapes, more flour is used in proportion to egg, and the mixture is cooked for a little longer than ordinary pastry cream. You can, if you like, add flavourings; here, a vanilla pod and finely grated lemon rind. A generous dash of Marsala or a few chopped bitter almonds are other possibilities. More unusual are the roasted, crushed sesame seeds incorporated into a Chinese version of the cream (*recipe, page 159*).

After it has thickened, the cream must be spread out flat and then chilled thoroughly before it can be cut or stamped into shapes—diamonds, as here, or triangles, squares or rounds. The pieces are dipped in egg and breadcrumbs and deep fried for a few minutes. They can be dusted with sugar and served hot or warm.

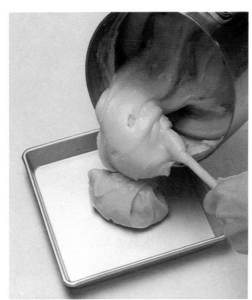

1 Making the cream. In a pan, beat whole eggs, yolks, flour, sugar and salt until smooth. Bring milk to the boil. Remove from the heat, add a vanilla pod and infuse for 15 minutes. Remove the pod. Add the milk to the egg mixture and whisk over a medium heat until smooth—about 15 minutes. Whisk in butter. Pour into an oiled tin to a depth of 1 cm ($\frac{1}{2}$ inch).

2 Cutting the cream. Spread the cream out, then pour melted butter over its surface to prevent a skin forming. Let the cream cool, then refrigerate it for 2 hour or until it is firm enough to cut. Cut the cream into 4 cm ($1\frac{1}{2}$ inch) strips. Remove loose flakes of butter. Using a spatula, transfer the strips to a work surface and cut at a slant to make diamonds.

3 Coating the shapes. Using a fork, dip each shape into beaten egg (*above*) and then in breadcrumbs. Pat the crumbs into place to cover the cream evenly. In a deep pan, heat oil to 190°C (375°F). Fry the shapes—a few at a time—for 3 minutes, or until a light, golden-brown. Using a slotted spoon, transfer them to kitchen paper to drain.

4 Serving. When you have fried all the shapes, sprinkle icing sugar over them, using a fine-meshed sieve. Arrange the pastry cream shapes on a napkin-lined plate for serving (*above*). Use a cake slice or a metal spatula to transfer them to individual plates. □

Anthology
of Recipes

selecting the recipes for the Anthology that follows, the Editors and consultants have drawn upon the cookery literature and traditions of 27 countries. The recipes range from the luscious pastries of Austria and Hungary to traditional brownies and cup cakes from America; from regional British specialities such as Bakewell tarts and Chelsea buns to the nut-filled, syrup-soaked pastries of Greece and the fritters and doughnuts characteristic of cuisines as diverse as those of France, Germany, Spain, Mexico and the Middle East.

The Anthology spans four centuries and includes the works of 92 authors. Some recipes have been selected from rare and out-of-print books in private collections; a large number have never before been published in English.

Throughout the Anthology, as in the first half of the book, the emphasis is on techniques fully accessible to the home cook which do justice to fresh, high-quality ingredients. Since many early cookery writers did not specify quantities, oven temperatures or cooking times, this information has been judiciously included and, where appropriate, introductory notes in italics have been added by the Editors.

Modern terms have been substituted for archaic language, but to preserve the character of the original and to create a true anthology, the authors' texts have been changed as little as possible. Some instructions have necessarily been expanded, but in cases where the cooking directions seem somewhat abrupt, the reader need only refer to the appropriate demonstration in the front of the book to find the technique in question explained in words and pictures. Cooking terms and ingredients that may be unfamiliar to the reader are explained in the combined General Index and Glossary at the end of the book.

For ease of use, the Anthology is organized into categories which correspond to the chapters of the techniques section of the book; within the categories, recipes are grouped according to their main ingredient. Standard preparations—pastry doughs, cake batters, fillings and icings—appear at the end.

All recipe ingredients are listed in order of use, with the title ingredient first. Metric and imperial measurements for each ingredient are listed in separate columns. The two sets of figures are not exact equivalents, but are consistent for each recipe. Working from either metric or imperial weights and measures will produce equally good results, but the two systems should not be mixed for the same recipe. All spoon measures are level.

Meringues

Chef Wennberg's Orange Meringues

The technique of making meringue "oranges" is demonstrated on page 30. In order to make the meringue halves completely dry for hollowing out, you can bake the meringues for 3 to 4 hours at 115°C (240°F or Mark ¼). Fondant icing (recipe, page 165), coloured and flavoured with orange syrup and grated orange rind, may be used instead of the icing given here. Instead of brushing on a chocolate dot for the stem of the orange, you can use a clove with its centre removed.

The meringue shells and the filling can be prepared in advance, but they must be assembled just before serving.

To make about 12 meringues

5	egg whites, at room temperature	5
350 g	castor sugar	12 oz
2 tsp	grated orange rind	2 tsp
	icing sugar, sifted	

Orange mousse

150 g	castor sugar	5 oz
12.5 cl	orange juice	4 fl oz
4	egg yolks	4
2 tsp	grated orange rind	2 tsp
½ litre	double cream	16 fl oz

Icing

300 g	castor sugar	10 oz
17.5 cl	water	6 fl oz
1 tbsp	golden syrup	1 tbsp
1 kg	icing sugar, sifted	2 lb
2 tsp	grated orange rind	2 tsp
	yellow food colouring	
60 g	sweet chocolate, melted	2 oz

For the meringues, beat the egg whites until stiff. Beat in the sugar, 1 tablespoon at a time, until the mixture is very stiff. Fold in the grated orange rind. Line baking sheets with silicon paper. With a spoon or a piping bag, shape the meringues into mounds resembling half an orange. Sprinkle with icing sugar. Bake in a preheated 140°C (275°F or Mark 1) oven for about 40 minutes or until crusty. Remove the meringues from the paper. Turn them upside-down and hollow them out with a teaspoon. Take care not to break the shell. Store in an airtight container until you are ready to use them.

For the orange mousse, boil the sugar and orange juice for 5 minutes over a medium heat. Beat the egg yolks in the top of a double boiler until very thick. Gradually beat in the orange syrup. Beat over hot (not boiling) water until smooth and thick. Fold in the grated orange rind. Remove from hot water and beat until cool. Whip the cream and fold it into the cooled orange custard. Pour the mixture into a freezing tray and freeze until firm. Stir several times during the freezing process to prevent ice crystals from forming.

For the icing, combine the castor sugar, water and golden syrup over a low heat. When the sugar has dissolved, bring the mixture to the boil and cook until clear. Remove from the heat and cool for 5 minutes. Gradually beat in the icing sugar and grated orange rind. Beat until smooth and lukewarm. Keep over hot (not boiling) water. Stir enough food colouring into the icing to make it a bright orange colour.

To assemble the meringues, fill the meringue shells with orange mousse and press two shells together to form one orange. Place the filled meringues on a wire rack over greaseproof paper, and spoon icing over the entire surface. Let the icing harden. With a thin brush, dot the top of the orange meringue with a little melted chocolate to resemble the stem of an orange. Serve immediately.

NIKA STANDEN HAZELTON
THE ART OF DANISH COOKING

Nut Meringues

Japonais

Ground almonds may be substituted for the ground hazelnuts used here. Ways of assembling these meringues with fillings and icings are shown on page 32.

To make about 50 meringues

200 g	hazelnuts, blanched and finely ground	7 oz
10	egg whites	10
300 g	castor sugar	10 oz

Beat the egg whites to stiff peaks with 100 g (3½ oz) of the sugar. Sift the remaining sugar and the ground hazelnuts together and fold them delicately into the egg whites. Using a piping bag with a plain 5 mm (¼ inch) nozzle, pipe the mixture in spirals 2.5 cm (1 inch) in diameter on to silicon paper. Cook the meringues in a preheated 170°C (325°F or Mark 3) oven, with the door slightly open, for about 1 hour or until the meringues are dried out and very slightly golden in colour.

AUGUSTE J. ROULET
LE LIVRE DES FRIANDISES

Heavenly Tarts

You can make these a day ahead.

To make 6 to 8 meringues

350 g	sugar	12 oz
1/4 tsp	cream of tartar	1/4 tsp
4	eggs, yolks separated from whites	4
3 tbsp	lemon juice	3 tbsp
1 tbsp	grated lemon rind	1 tbsp
1/2 litre	double cream	16 fl oz

Sift together 250 g (8 oz) of the sugar and the cream of tartar. Beat the egg whites until soft peaks form; add the sugar mixture gradually and continue beating until very stiff. Spoon the meringue mixture in mounds on a baking sheet covered with greaseproof paper; shape hollows in the mounds with a spoon. Bake in a preheated 140°C (275°F or Mark 1) oven for 1 hour. Remove the meringues from the paper and leave them to cool.

Beat the egg yolks slightly, and stir in the remaining sugar and the lemon juice and rind. Cook this mixture in the top of a double boiler until it is very thick—8 to 10 minutes. Leave the mixture to cool.

Whip the cream, combine half of it with the lemon and egg mixture and use this to fill the meringue shells. Cover them with the remaining whipped cream. Place in the refrigerator for 24 hours before serving.

NELL B. NICHOLS (EDITOR)
FARM JOURNAL'S COMPLETE PIE COOKBOOK

Persian Cookies

Nan-e Shirini

To make about 20 meringues

6	egg whites	6
250 g	sugar	8 oz
2 tbsp	lemon juice	2 tbsp
1 tbsp	grated orange rind or 1/2 tsp vanilla extract	1 tbsp
125 g	walnuts, chopped	4 oz

Beat the egg whites in a bowl until stiff. Add the sugar gradually and beat for a few minutes longer. Add the lemon juice and orange rind or vanilla extract. Add the chopped walnuts. Drop spoonfuls of the mixture on to a greased baking sheet. Bake in a preheated 180°C (350°F or Mark 4) oven for 15 minutes or until the meringue is firm and dry.

NESTA RAMAZANI
PERSIAN COOKING

Butterscotch Meringues

To make about 15 meringues

2	egg whites	2
1/3 tsp	cream of tartar	1/3 tsp
	salt	
125 g	soft brown sugar	4 oz
60 g	walnuts, chopped	2 oz
30 cl	double cream, whipped	1/2 pint

First, prepare the baking sheet on which the meringues are to be baked. Rub a few drops of oil over the sheet, then dust it with flour. Tip the sheet and give it a sharp knock, so that only a light dusting of flour is left on the surface.

Beat the egg whites with the cream of tartar and a pinch of salt until they are stiff. Stir in the brown sugar, 1 tablespoon at a time, beating the mixture after each addition until it is stiff. Fold in the walnuts. Spoon the mixture in rounds, 1 tablespoonful at a time, on the prepared baking sheet and bake them in a preheated 50° to 100°C (150° to 200°F or Mark 1/4) oven for 1 to 1 1/2 hours or until they are dry. Remove the meringues immediately from the sheet. When they are cold, put them together in twos with the whipped cream.

MARGARET FAIRLIE
TRADITIONAL SCOTTISH COOKERY

Vienna Almond Kisses

Wiener Mandelbusserln

If edible rice paper is unavailable, the baking sheet can be lined with greaseproof paper instead. In that case, the paper will have to be peeled off the meringues after they have cooled.

To make about 15 meringues

160 g	ground almonds	5½ oz
3	egg whites, stiffly beaten	3
200 g	sugar	7 oz
½	vanilla pod, seeds scraped out and reserved	½
	salt	
	rice paper	
250 g	chocolate, broken into pieces	8 oz
30 g	butter	1 oz

Mix the egg whites lightly with half the sugar. Mix the rest of the sugar with the vanilla seeds, a pinch of salt and the almonds. Place the bowl containing the almond mixture over a pan of simmering water and stir until the mixture is very warm; then fold in the egg whites.

Line a baking sheet with rice paper and place on it small heaps of the dough. Bake in a preheated 170°C (325°F or Mark 3) oven for about 20 minutes. The kisses should be crisp on the outside and soft inside. Allow them to cool.

Trim off the edges of the rice paper with scissors. Melt the chocolate over gentle heat with the butter and a little water. Dip the kisses half way into the chocolate and let them dry.

ARNE KRÜGER AND ANNETTE WOLTER
KOCHEN HEUTE

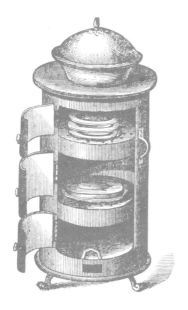

Chocolate Kisses

Schokoladenbaiser auf Oblaten

If rice paper wafers are unobtainable, use 4 cm (1½ inch) circles of rice paper or greaseproof paper. The greaseproof paper will have to be peeled off the meringues after they have cooled.

To make about 60 meringues

140 g	chocolate, grated	4½ oz
150 g	icing sugar	5 oz
4	egg whites, stiffly beaten	4
100 g	almonds, slivered	3½ oz
About 60	rice paper wafers	About 60
About 60	almonds, blanched (optional)	About 60

Mix the sugar into the egg whites and beat over hot water until very stiff. Meanwhile, melt the grated chocolate in a bowl over hot water. Fold the chocolate into the egg white mixture with the slivered almonds.

Grease a shallow baking tin and arrange the rice paper wafers on it. Place a spoonful of the mixture on each wafer. Garnish each with a blanched almond, if desired. Dry the meringues rather than bake them, in a preheated 150°C (300°F or Mark 2) oven for 30 minutes.

MÁRIA HAJKOVÁ
MÚČNIKY

Poppy Seed Kisses

Mohnbusserln

To make about 50 meringues

100 g	poppy seeds, ground	3½ oz
150 g	icing sugar	5 oz
2 tbsp	vanilla sugar	2 tbsp
3	egg whites, stiffly beaten	3
2	cloves, ground	2

Add the icing sugar and vanilla sugar to the egg whites, and beat over hot water until the mass is very stiff. Cool slightly, then beat in the poppy seeds and cloves. Make small mounds of the mixture on greased baking sheets, and bake in a preheated 180°C (350°F or Mark 4) oven for 15 minutes, or until lightly browned.

MÁRIA HAJKOVÁ
MÚČNIKY

Creamed, Melted and Whisked Cakes

Cup Cakes

To make about 15 cakes

125 g	butter	4 oz
125 g	castor sugar	4 oz
2	eggs, lightly whisked	2
125 g	flour	4 oz
$\frac{1}{4}$ tsp	baking powder	$\frac{1}{4}$ tsp

Cream the butter and sugar thoroughly and beat in the whisked eggs. With the last of the egg, add the flour and baking powder. Divide the mixture among paper baking cases, filling them two-thirds full, and bake them in a pre-heated 200°C (400°F or Mark 6) oven for 15 minutes. When the cakes are cool, they may be finished by one or more of the following methods:

Butterfly cakes are probably the best known variety. Choose cakes which are quite flat on top and, with a sharp knife, cut a thin slice from the top of each cake. Cut this piece in two. Spread the cake with jam and pipe a generous star of whipped cream in the centre. Replace the two half-slices of cake, butterfly fashion, and dust with icing sugar.

Crown cakes: Again, cut a thin slice from the top of each cake, but this time cut it into four or six even-sized pieces. Spread each cake with jam and pipe a high star of whipped cream in the centre. Then replace the pieces showing the cream in the middle. Decorate with a tiny piece of glacé cherry and dust with icing sugar.

Basket cakes are made by once more removing a slice from the top of each cake. Spread the cake with jam and pipe with whipped cream—rather more generously to one side. Replace the slice at a pretty angle to show off the cream. Finish with a piece of angelica or a glacé cherry and dust with icing sugar.

Cork cakes: Using a small cutter, 1 cm ($\frac{1}{2}$ inch) across, cut a cork-shaped piece from the top of each cake. An éclair pipe is ideal for this purpose, while even an apple corer will suffice. Fill the bottom of the cavity with jam, pipe a star of whipped cream on the jam and replace the cork at a rather jaunty angle. Dust with icing sugar.

Iced cup cakes: If there is a little rim of the paper case above the level of the cake then it is a simple matter to ice it with water icing. Make up 60 to 90 g (2 to 3 oz) of icing sugar into water icing by blending it with about 2 teaspoons of water,

and, using a teaspoon, run a little over the top of each cake. The paper case will prevent the icing running down the sides and looking messy. Decorate with a silver ball, a glacé cherry and angelica or a piece of walnut.

MARGARET BATES
TALKING ABOUT CAKES WITH AN IRISH AND SCOTTISH ACCENT

Filled Cakes from Vergara

Bizcochos Rellenos de Vergara

The technique of boiling sugar syrup to the soft-ball stage is shown on page 6.

To make about 40 cakes

6	eggs	6
250 g	sugar	8 oz
250 g	flour	8 oz
45 cl	fondant icing (*page 165*)	$\frac{3}{4}$ pint
	ground cinnamon	
	Egg yolk filling	
250 g	sugar	8 oz
12	hard-boiled egg yolks	12

Put the eggs in a saucepan and beat them over hot water or over a very low heat until they are thick. Add the sugar and continue to beat the mixture until it falls from the whisk in a thick ribbon. Gradually stir in the flour.

Line a baking sheet with greaseproof paper and pour the dough on to it in strips about 4 cm (1½ inches) wide, spacing them well apart. Bake the dough in a preheated 180°C (350°F or Mark 4) oven for 15 minutes or until lightly coloured.

When the cakes are cool, turn the paper over and brush the underside with cold water so that the cake strips can be detached easily. Cut the strips into 5 cm (2 inch) pieces.

For the filling, boil the sugar with 1 tablespoon of water until the syrup reaches the soft-ball stage. Put the egg yolks in a saucepan and beat the syrup into them gradually. Cook the mixture over hot water, stirring constantly, until it comes away from the sides of the pan. Pour it into a bowl.

Hollow out the base of each cake slightly and fill them with the egg yolk filling. Sandwich them together in pairs to enclose the filling.

Melt the fondant icing and spoon it over the cakes. Put them back on the baking sheet. Sprinkle them with cinnamon and put them back in the oven for 2 minutes to dry them.

MARIA MESTAYER DE ECHAGÜE (MARQUESA DE PARABERE)
CONFITERÍA Y REPOSTERÍA

Dimple Cakes or Ladies' Navels

Kadin Göbeği

Kaymak, *a type of Turkish clotted cream, can be bought in Middle Eastern delicatessens. If it is unobtainable, use clotted cream or lightly whipped double cream.*

To make about 16 cakes

125 g	butter, softened	4 oz
125 g	sugar	4 oz
4	eggs	4
500 g	flour	1 lb
	milk	
	kaymak	
	Syrup	
175 g	sugar	6 oz
15 cl	water	$\frac{1}{4}$ pint

Cream the butter and beat in the sugar until the mixture is light and fluffy. Continue beating and gradually add the eggs and flour. Moisten with a little milk if necessary, but keep the dough fairly stiff. Form the dough into balls about the size of an orange, and make a depression in the top of each one with your finger. Arrange the cakes on a greased baking sheet and bake them in a preheated 180°C (350°F or Mark 4) oven until they are lightly browned, about 20 minutes.

Meanwhile, dissolve the sugar in the water over a low heat. Raise the heat and boil the syrup for about 1 minute. Pour the syrup over the cakes, so that they become spongy but not sodden, then remove them from the syrup and put a blob of cream in each dimple.

VENICE LAMB
THE HOME BOOK OF TURKISH COOKERY

Mint Prianiki

Peppermint oil can be bought from most chemists.

Other flavourings for *prianiki* instead of peppermint oil are 1 tablespoon of raspberry syrup or 2 tablespoons of rose-water.

To make 24 prianiki

30 drops	peppermint oil	30 drops
3	eggs	3
250 g	sugar	8 oz
175 g	flour	6 oz
$\frac{1}{2}$ tsp	baking powder	$\frac{1}{2}$ tsp

Beat the eggs and sugar together until they are white and fluffy. Gradually mix in the flour sifted with the baking powder, and stir in the peppermint oil, making sure that it is well distributed. Grease a baking sheet with butter and dust it with flour, shaking off the excess. With a teaspoon, place rounds of the mixture on to the sheet and bake them for 20 minutes in a preheated 190°C (375°F or Mark 5) oven.

SOFKA SKIPWITH
EAT RUSSIAN

Mendaro Cakes

Bizcochos de Mendaro

The technique of boiling sugar syrup to the small-thread stage is shown on page 6.

These cakes may also be shaped like elongated éclairs. They must be eaten very fresh.

To make about 80 cakes

8	eggs, yolks of 6 separated from whites	8
250 g	castor sugar	8 oz
$\frac{1}{2}$	lemon, rind grated	$\frac{1}{2}$
250 g	flour, sifted	8 oz
	White icing	
500 g	sugar cubes	1 lb
10 cl	water	$3\frac{1}{2}$ fl oz
1 or 2	egg whites	1 or 2
	vinegar	

Place the whole eggs and the six yolks in a bowl; reserve 1 tablespoonful of sugar and add the rest to the eggs. Stir without beating until the sugar has dissolved. Add the lemon rind and flour; mix well. Beat the egg whites to soft peaks with the reserved sugar. Fold them into the dough carefully. Put the dough in a piping bag with a plain nozzle and squeeze small mounds of it on to baking trays lined with greaseproof paper. Bake the cakes in a preheated 180°C (350°F or Mark 4) oven for about 15 minutes or until they are lightly coloured.

For the icing, boil the sugar and water together until the syrup reaches the small-thread stage. Whisk one egg white to soft peaks and gradually beat in the syrup and two drops of vinegar. Whisk vigorously until the mixture is thick and glossy. If the mixture is too runny, thicken it by beating it vigorously over a gentle heat. If it is too thick, thin it with a few drops of water or a little of a second egg white.

Remove the cakes from the oven and glaze them with the icing. Return to the oven for a minute or two to dry the icing.

MARIA MESTAYER DE ECHAGÜE (MARQUESA DE PARABERE)
CONFITERÍA Y REPOSTERÍA

Devonshire Creams

If wished, the sponges may be baked in shallow tartlet tins.

To make about 20 cakes		
125 g	castor sugar	4 oz
2	eggs, yolks separated from whites, whites stiffly beaten with a pinch of salt	2
90 g	flour	3 oz
¼ tsp	baking powder	¼ tsp
	raspberry jam	
	whipped cream	
	icing sugar	

Gradually and alternately, whisk 90 g (3 oz) of the castor sugar and the egg yolks into the beaten egg whites. Continue beating until the mixture is a creamy colour, and thickens, so that it leaves a heavy trail. When this stage is reached, remove the beater and gently sift in the flour and baking powder. Then, using a metal spoon, fold in these dry ingredients. Meanwhile, have two or three baking sheets prepared. These should be greased and dusted with flour. Drop the sponge mixture out in teaspoonfuls, allowing room for them to spread. Dust with the rest of the castor sugar, and bake in a preheated 220°C (425°F or Mark 7) oven for 5 to 7 minutes, or until the cakes are browned.

When the cakes are cold, sandwich them in pairs with a little raspberry jam and whipped cream. Serve them dusted with icing sugar.

MARGARET BATES
TALKING ABOUT CAKES WITH AN IRISH AND SCOTTISH ACCENT

Wine Cubes

Weinwürfel

To make about 40 cubes		
20 cl	sweet white wine	7 fl oz
8	egg yolks	8
140 g	icing sugar	4½ oz
6	egg whites, stiffly beaten	6
½	lemon, rind grated	½
70 g	flour, sifted	2½ oz
250 g	apricot jam	8 oz

Beat six of the egg yolks and the sugar well together until light coloured and fluffy. Mix the egg whites with the lemon rind and fold into the yolk mixture with the flour. Turn the mixture into a greased shallow baking tin, and bake in a preheated 180°C (350°F or Mark 4) oven for about 15 minutes or until firm. Allow the cake to cool.

Cut the cake in half horizontally and spread the bottom half with some of the apricot jam. Replace the top layer. Cut the filled cake into squares and place the squares on an oven-proof dish. Beat the wine with the remaining egg yolks and spoon the mixture over the cake squares. Sieve the remaining jam and spread it over the tops of the squares. Return the cakes to the oven for 5 minutes to set the jam.

MÁRIA HAJKOVÁ
MÚČNIKY

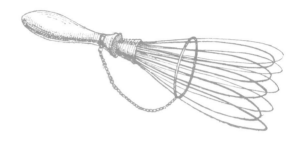

Dainty Catalan Cakes

Bizcochos Melindros

To make 80 to 100 cakes		
4	egg yolks	4
150 g	castor sugar	5 oz
1 tsp	vanilla extract	1 tsp
1	lemon, rind grated	1
200 g	flour	7 oz
5	egg whites, stiffly beaten	5
	icing sugar	

Beat the egg yolks with the castor sugar, vanilla extract and lemon rind to a creamy, spongy consistency. Sift the flour and incorporate it into the egg yolk and sugar mixture. Fold in the egg whites carefully. Take a piping bag with a medium-sized ribbon nozzle and fill it with the mixture. Squeeze out oblong shapes, about 7 cm (2¾ inches) long, on to a baking sheet lined with silicon paper. Leave a space of about 5 cm (2 inches) between each cake.

Bake in a preheated 180°C (350°F or Mark 4) oven for 10 to 15 minutes, until the surfaces of the cakes are light golden. Do not open the oven door during the first 10 minutes of baking or the cakes will shrink.

When the cakes are cooked, leave them to cool, then separate them from the paper and dust them with icing sugar. They keep fresh for several days in a tin.

MARÍA DOLORES CAMPS CARDONA
COCINA CATALANA

Lemon Cup Cakes

If possible, make the icing the night before making the cakes.

To make 12 cup cakes

$\frac{1}{2}$	lemon, rind grated, juice strained	$\frac{1}{2}$
6	eggs, yolks separated from whites, whites stiffly beaten	6
500 g	granulated sugar	1 lb
12.5 cl	boiling water	4 fl oz
250 g	flour, sifted	8 oz
	Icing	
2	oranges, rind grated, juice strained	2
$1\frac{1}{2}$	lemons, rind grated, juice strained	$1\frac{1}{2}$
450 g	icing sugar	15 oz

Make the icing by stirring the orange and lemon juice into the icing sugar. Mix to a smooth consistency and then add the orange and lemon rind. Set the icing aside until it is needed, stirring it occasionally.

Beat the egg yolks well; add the granulated sugar and beat together thoroughly. Add the lemon juice and rind, the boiling water and the flour. Fold in the egg whites. Half-fill buttered and floured muffin tins with the batter. Bake in a preheated 230°C (450°F or Mark 8) oven for 5 to 6 minutes.

Remove the cakes from the tins and, while they are still hot, dip them in the icing. Place the cakes on a rack set over greaseproof paper to allow any excess icing to drain off.

ST. STEPHEN'S EPISCOPAL CHURCH
BAYOU CUISINE

Orange Slices

Tranches à l'Orange

To make about 30 slices

3	oranges, rind grated, juice strained	3
14	eggs	14
500 g	sugar	1 lb
500 g	flour, sifted	1 lb
350 g	butter, melted	12 oz
1	lemon, rind grated	1
	apricot jam	
45 cl	orange-flavoured fondant icing (*page 165*)	$\frac{3}{4}$ pint

Break the eggs into a basin, add the sugar and whisk over a pan of hot water on a gentle heat until the mixture is luke-warm; then remove the bowl from the heat and whisk the mixture to a light colour, like a cream. Stir in the flour, butter, orange juice and grated orange and lemon rind and mix it gently together. Fill two buttered and floured square cake tins with the batter and bake in a preheated 180°C (350°F or Mark 4) oven for about 25 minutes or until the cakes have shrunk slightly from the sides of the tins. Turn the cakes out of the tins and leave to cool.

When cold, trim each piece smooth and place one on the other, putting apricot jam between and on the top; then ice over with the orange fondant icing and cut the cake into strips about 12.5 cm (5 inches) long and 4 cm ($1\frac{1}{2}$ inches) wide.

ÉMILE HÉRISSÉ
THE ART OF PASTRY MAKING

Aladdin Cakes

To make 8 cakes

8 g	flour	$\frac{1}{4}$ oz
30 g	ground almonds	1 oz
60 g	castor sugar	2 oz
2	eggs, yolks separated from whites, whites stiffly beaten	2
250 g	chocolate buttercream (*page 166*)	8 oz
75 g	powdered chocolate, or sifted grated chocolate	$2\frac{1}{2}$ oz
8	crystallized violets	8
15 g	angelica	$\frac{1}{2}$ oz

Sift the flour, ground almonds and sugar on to a sheet of paper. Add the yolks of the eggs to the whites and lightly stir in the flour, almonds and sugar. Put the mixture out in 24 rounds about 2.5 cm (1 inch) in diameter (by means of a piping bag and a plain nozzle), not too near together, on a buttered and floured baking sheet. Bake for about 10 minutes in a preheated 180°C (350°F or Mark 4) oven so that they are lightly coloured and firm. Remove the cakes from the baking sheet with a knife whilst they are hot.

When the cakes are cold, trim them to an even shape with a cutter. Spread a little of the buttercream on each, and put three together, one on top of the other. Cover each little pile neatly with buttercream and dust thickly with powdered or grated and sifted chocolate. Decorate the top with a crystallized violet and some fancifully cut pieces of angelica. Serve in paper cake cases.

MABEL I. RIVERS
TIPS FOR TEA

Little Almond Cakes

This simple mixture plays tricks in the oven. It is put from a teaspoon into little paper cases and baked. At first it rises but, since there is no flour, it falls again to give a little case of almond mixture suitable for filling. For variety, ground Brazil nuts might be used instead of the ground almonds.

To make 30 to 36 cakes

125 g	ground almonds	4 oz
90 g	butter	3 oz
90 g	castor sugar	3 oz
	apricot jam	
	double cream, whipped, and sweetened or flavoured to taste	

Cream the butter and sugar together and gradually work in the ground almonds. Place teaspoonfuls of the mixture into little paper sweet cases. Bake in a preheated 180°C (350°F or Mark 4) oven for 10 to 15 minutes, or until lightly coloured.

When the cakes are cold, peel off the paper cases. Before serving, fill them with a little good-quality apricot jam and pipe with a star of whipped cream.

MARGARET BATES
TALKING ABOUT CAKES WITH AN IRISH AND SCOTTISH ACCENT

Savoy Sponges

Biscottini alla Savoiarda

To make about 48 sponges

7	eggs, yolks of 3 separated from whites, whites stiffly beaten	7
325 g	sugar	11 oz
1 tsp	ground cinnamon	1 tsp
300 g	flour, dried in a 150°C (300°F or Mark 2) oven for 15 minutes	10 oz

Beat the four whole eggs and the egg yolks with 300 g (10 oz) of the sugar in a bowl. Add the cinnamon and flour. Combine these ingredients and add the egg whites. Pour the mixture into small buttered tins or paper cases. Sprinkle with the remaining sugar and bake in a preheated 170°C (325°F or Mark 3) oven for about 30 minutes or until the cakes are golden, soft in the middle and dry. When they are cooked, remove them from the tins and serve them plain.

GINO BRUNETTI (EDITOR)
CUCINA MANTOVANA DI PRINCIPI E DI POPOLO

Almond Cheesecakes

In the 18th and 19th centuries it was quite common for tartlets or little cakes such as these to be called cheesecakes even though they contained no cheese or curd.

To make 10 cakes

125 g	almonds, blanched	4 oz
3	bitter almonds, blanched	3
1 tbsp	water	1 tbsp
125 g	icing sugar	4 oz
1 tbsp	double cream	1 tbsp
2	egg whites, stiffly beaten	2

Pound the almonds and the bitter almonds with the water, add the sugar, cream and egg whites; mix them quickly, put into small individual cake moulds and bake for 20 minutes in a preheated 180°C (350°F or Mark 4) oven.

FREDERICK BISHOP
THE WIFE'S OWN BOOK OF COOKERY

Spice Muffins

To make 12 muffins

½ tbsp	ground ginger	½ tbsp
½ tsp	ground cloves	½ tsp
½ tsp	ground cinnamon	½ tsp
250 g	flour	8 oz
½ tsp	bicarbonate of soda	½ tsp
1 tsp	baking powder	1 tsp
½ tsp	salt	½ tsp
½ tsp	ground white pepper	½ tsp
30 g	lard	1 oz
175 g	sugar	6 oz
2	eggs, well beaten	2
125 g	molasses or black treacle	4 oz
4 tbsp	buttermilk	4 tbsp

Sift together the flour, bicarbonate of soda, baking powder, ginger, cloves, cinnamon, salt and pepper. Set aside. Work the lard and sugar together in a bowl, beat in the eggs vigorously, then stir in the molasses. Stir in the flour mixture and buttermilk alternately. Pour the batter into greased muffin tins and bake in a preheated 180°C (350°F or Mark 4) oven for 25 to 30 minutes, or until a cake tester or toothpick inserted in the centre of one muffin comes out dry. Serve the muffins warm with butter.

THE EDITORS OF AMERICAN HERITAGE
THE AMERICAN HERITAGE COOKBOOK

Spanish Cinnamon Cakes

Mostachones

To make about 24 cakes

	ground cinnamon	
200 g	sugar	7 oz
4	eggs, yolks separated from whites, whites stiffly beaten	4
220 g	flour	7½ oz

Add the sugar, the egg yolks and finally the flour to the beaten egg whites. Pour the mixture into paper cake cases, sprinkle the tops with cinnamon and bake in a preheated 180°C (350°F or Mark 4) oven for about 15 minutes, or until the cakes are firm and browned.

JUAN MUJAL ROIG
GRAN LIBRO DE COCINA ESPAÑOLA

Cinnamon Cup Cakes

To make 18 cup cakes

1 tbsp	ground cinnamon	1 tbsp
175 g	flour, sifted	6 oz
2 tsp	baking powder	2 tsp
	salt	
250 g	sugar	8 oz
125 g	butter, softened	4 oz
2	eggs	2
12.5 cl	milk	4 fl oz

	Whipped cream frosting	
¼ litre	double cream	8 fl oz
60 g	sugar	2 oz
½ tsp	ground cinnamon	½ tsp

Sift together the flour, the baking powder, a pinch of salt and the cinnamon. Set aside. Gradually work the sugar into the butter as thoroughly as possible. Beat in the eggs, one at a time, beating hard after each addition. Stir in the flour mixture and the milk alternately. Spoon the batter into greased muffin tins and bake in a preheated 180°C (350°F or Mark 4) oven for 25 minutes or until a toothpick inserted in the centre of a cake comes out clean.

For the frosting, combine the cream with the sugar. Chill in the refrigerator for at least 2 hours, then beat with a rotary or electric beater until stiff. Flavour with the cinnamon. Spread the frosting over the cakes just before serving.

THE EDITORS OF AMERICAN HERITAGE
THE AMERICAN HERITAGE COOKBOOK

Parham Cheese Loaves

From an unpublished manuscript book of recipes from Parham, the Sussex house which was for long owned by the Curzon family, descendants of Robert Curzon, famous traveller and author of *Monasteries in the Levant*, comes this variation of the cheesecake, which is original and delicious. It has a warm flavour, and requires no pastry. It is important to have very dry cheese; or moisture will come out during cooking and spoil the texture of the finished dish.

To make 18 to 24 small loaves

500 g	curd cheese, sieved	1 lb
60 g	white breadcrumbs	2 oz
60 g	sugar	2 oz
5 or 6	egg yolks, very well beaten	5 or 6
½ tsp each	grated nutmeg and ground mace	½ tsp each
¼ tsp	ground cloves	¼ tsp
1 tsp	salt	1 tsp

Beat together all the ingredients. Butter small soufflé or pie dishes, dariole moulds, ramekins or even one large charlotte tin. Fill the buttered tin or tins by only four-fifths.

Bake in a preheated 180°C (350°F or Mark 4) oven. For small sizes allow approximately 20 minutes' baking; for one large one, 35 to 40 minutes.

ELIZABETH DAVID
SPICES, SALT AND AROMATICS IN THE ENGLISH KITCHEN

Easter Cookies

Koulourakia

To make about 60 rings

250 g	butter	8 oz
500 g	sugar	1 lb
6	eggs, beaten	6
12.5 cl	milk	4 fl oz
1 kg	flour, sifted	2 to 2½ lb
4 tsp	baking powder	4 tsp
½ tsp	ground cinnamon	½ tsp
1 tsp	vanilla extract	1 tsp
½ tsp	ground allspice	½ tsp
2 tbsp	anisette or 2 tsp anise extract	2 tbsp
2	egg yolks, beaten	2
60 g	sesame seeds	2 oz

Cream the butter until soft, add the sugar and mix thoroughly; add the whole eggs, then the milk. Combine the flour with the baking powder, and gradually sift it into the batter; add the cinnamon, vanilla, allspice and anisette. Knead the dough, adding more flour as needed to form a smooth and firm dough. (Test the dough by rolling it in your hand; if it is firm and does not stick, it is the right consistency.)

Roll pieces of dough in the palms of your hands into cylinders about 7.5 cm (3 inches) long and 1 cm (½ inch) thick; then shape the cylinders into small rings by pressing the ends together with your fingers to form circles. Brush the rings with egg yolk, and dip them in sesame seeds. Place them on baking sheets, and bake them in a preheated 180°C (350°F or Mark 4) oven for 15 minutes until they are lightly brown.

EVA ZANE
GREEK COOKING FOR THE GODS

Winster Wakes Cakes

These traditional cakes are made each year in the old market town of Winster, Derbyshire, in celebration of Midsummer or St. John the Baptist's Day. The festival is always observed on "Wakes Sunday", the Sunday following 24 June. The following recipe has been handed down from generation to generation for the last century and a half. The cakes are accompanied by home-made wine or ale and many visitors on Wakes Sunday are presented with this recipe for the famous cakes.

To make about 48 cakes

250 g	butter	8 oz
200 g	sugar	7 oz
400 g	flour	14 oz
½ tsp	baking powder	½ tsp
	salt	
1	egg	1
3 tbsp	currants	3 tbsp

Cream the butter and 175 g (6 oz) of the sugar. Sift together the flour, baking powder and a pinch of salt. Beat the egg until thick and yellow and add it to the butter and sugar mixture. Gradually stir in the flour, mixing the dough thoroughly.

Roll out the dough very thin. Press in the currants. Cut the dough into 8 cm (3¼ inch) circles, sprinkle them with the remaining sugar and bake in a preheated 180°C (350°F or Mark 4) oven for 15 minutes or until golden.

DOROTHY GLADYS SPICER
FROM AN ENGLISH OVEN

Majorcan Dried Fruit Cakes

Bizcochos de Frutas Secas

To make about 50 cakes

125 g	currants, finely chopped	4 oz
125 g	raisins, finely chopped	4 oz
30 g	butter	1 oz
400 g	sugar	14 oz
20 cl	milk	7 fl oz
400 g	flour	14 oz
2 tsp	baking powder	2 tsp

Cream the butter and sugar together. Pour in the milk, stir well and add the flour and baking powder. Lastly mix in the chopped currants and raisins. Put the mixture into lined and buttered individual cake moulds and bake in a preheated 180°C (350°F or Mark 4) oven for 20 minutes or until the cakes are risen and brown.

LUIS RIPOLL
NUESTRA COCINA

Bishop's Buns

To make about 35 buns

200 g	butter	7 oz
175 g	soft brown sugar	6 oz
¼ tsp each	ground ginger and ground cinnamon	¼ tsp each
350 g	flour	12 oz
2	eggs, well beaten	2
125 g	sultanas	4 oz
60 g	currants	2 oz
2 tsp	baking powder	2 tsp
1	lemon, rind grated	1
60 g	almonds, blanched and slivered	2 oz

Cream the butter and sugar for 10 minutes. Add the spices to the flour, then gradually add the flour, the beaten eggs and the dried fruit alternately to the butter and sugar mixture; finally add the baking powder and the grated lemon rind, mixing well to incorporate all the ingredients. This mixture will be fairly stiff as no milk is added. Put small portions (about 1 tablespoonful) on to a well-greased baking sheet, and spike each one with the slivered almonds. Bake in a preheated 180°C (350°F or Mark 4) oven for 15 to 20 minutes.

RIA SYSONBY
LADY SYSONBY'S COOK BOOK

Creole Porcupines

The technique of grating fresh coconut is shown on page 12.

To make 60 porcupines

30 g	butter, melted	1 oz
250 g	brown sugar	8 oz
2	eggs, well beaten	2
175 g	pecan nuts, chopped	6 oz
175 g	stoned dates, chopped	6 oz
350 g	grated coconut	12 oz

Add the butter to the sugar and eggs. Add the pecan nuts, dates and a third of the coconut. Mix well and form into small balls. Roll each ball in the remaining coconut. Bake the balls in a preheated 150°C (300°F or Mark 2) oven until they are just beginning to brown, 25 to 30 minutes. Remove them from the oven and let them cool.

FRANCES D. AND PETER J. ROBOTTI
FRENCH COOKING IN THE NEW WORLD

Date Nut Tea Cakes

To make 24 cakes

90 g	stoned dates, chopped	3 oz
60 g	walnuts, chopped	2 oz
175 g	light brown sugar	6 oz
2	eggs, beaten	2
60 g	flour	2 oz
$\frac{1}{3}$ tsp	baking powder	$\frac{1}{3}$ tsp
$\frac{1}{2}$ tsp	salt	$\frac{1}{2}$ tsp

Beat the sugar into the eggs. Stir in the flour mixed with the baking powder and salt, then stir in the dates and walnuts.

Grease very small tartlet tins and put a generous teaspoonful of the mixture into each tin. Bake in a preheated 230°C (450°F or Mark 8) oven for 10 minutes or until firm. Turn the cakes out of the tins while hot, and cool them on a wire rack.

CHARLOTTE TURGEON AND FREDERIC A. BIRMINGHAM
THE SATURDAY EVENING POST ALL-AMERICAN COOKBOOK

Ginger Crowns

To make 8 crowns

1 tbsp	finely chopped preserved ginger	1 tbsp
1 tsp	syrup from jar of preserved ginger	1 tsp
60 g	ground almonds	2 oz
60 g	castor sugar	2 oz
1 or 2	egg yolks	1 or 2
8	small pieces preserved ginger	8

Icing		
2 tbsp	icing sugar	2 tbsp
1 tsp	syrup from jar of preserved ginger	1 tsp

Put the almonds, sugar and chopped ginger in a bowl. Stir in the ginger syrup and mix all to a stiff paste with the egg yolks.

Divide the mixture roughly in half and, from one piece, shape eight small balls like marbles. Roll the other piece out fairly thinly and cut it into strips, the width of each strip being a little greater than the diameter of the ball of mixture. If possible, one side of each strip should be cut with a fluted edge. Wrap the strips around the little balls in such a way as to make miniature crowns.

These are best left overnight before baking. Brown them quickly by placing them in a preheated 220°C (425°F or Mark 7) oven for a few minutes.

Blend the icing sugar and ginger syrup with a little boiling water to make a smooth icing. Fill the centre of each crown with a little icing and decorate with a small piece of ginger.

MARGARET BATES
TALKING ABOUT CAKES WITH AN IRISH AND SCOTTISH ACCENT

Chestnut Finger Cakes

To make 16 cakes

175 g	flour	6 oz
1 tsp	baking powder	1 tsp
1 tsp	vanilla extract	1 tsp
2 tbsp	milk	2 tbsp
90 g	butter	3 oz
150 g	castor sugar	5 oz
2	eggs	2
2 tsp	grated chocolate	2 tsp
4 tbsp	water	4 tbsp
125 g	sugar cubes	4 oz

Chestnut filling		
6	*marrons glacés*	6
1 tbsp	icing sugar	1 tbsp
1 tbsp	cream	1 tbsp
1 tsp	vanilla extract	1 tsp
1 tsp	maraschino	1 tsp

To make the filling, pass the *marrons glacés* and icing sugar through a fine-meshed sieve; mix to a stiff paste with the cream, vanilla extract and maraschino.

Sift the flour and baking powder on to a sheet of paper. Add the vanilla extract to the milk. Cream the butter and castor sugar until white, beat in the eggs one at a time, and stir in the flour and milk alternately. Grease a rectangular baking tin and line it with greaseproof paper; spread the mixture in the tin and bake it in a preheated 180°C (350°F or Mark 4) oven for about 40 minutes, or until a skewer inserted in the middle comes out clean. When cold, cut the cake up into pieces about 2.5 by 7.5 cm (1 by 3 inches). Split each one open, put in a little chestnut filling, and close up again.

Melt the grated chocolate in 1 tablespoon of the water, boil it up and keep it warm. Put the sugar cubes and the remaining water in a small pan, let the sugar dissolve, then boil quickly until it turns a golden-brown colour. Pour in the prepared chocolate, boil up the mixture, and by means of a hot teaspoon, coat the top of each little cake. Put the remainder of the chestnut filling in a piping bag with a small plain nozzle and decorate the edges of the cakes.

MABEL I. RIVERS
TIPS FOR TEA

Blueberry Buckle

If blueberries are unavailable, bilberries can be substituted.

	To make 16 squares	
300 g	blueberries	10 oz
60 g	butter, softened	2 oz
175 g	sugar	6 oz
1	egg	1
175 g	flour	6 oz
2 tsp	baking powder	2 tsp
½ tsp	salt	½ tsp
12.5 cl	milk	4 fl oz
	Crumb topping	
125 g	sugar	4 oz
45 g	flour	1½ oz
½ tsp	ground cinnamon	½ tsp
60 g	butter, cubed	2 oz

To prepare the topping, mix together the sugar, flour and cinnamon in a small bowl. With two knives or a pastry blender, cut the butter into the sugar and flour mixture until it resembles coarse meal.

In a large bowl, cream together the butter and sugar until fluffy. Blend in the egg. In another bowl, sift together the flour, baking powder and salt. Add the flour mixture to the creamed mixture alternately with the milk, beating after each addition. Gently fold the blueberries into the batter. Pour the batter into a greased and floured 20 cm (8 inch) square baking tin. Sprinkle it evenly with crumb topping.

Bake in a preheated 190°C (375°F or Mark 5) oven for 40 to 45 minutes or until a toothpick inserted in the centre comes out clean. Place the baking tin on a rack and cool slightly. Cut the cake into squares and serve them warm, or cold and topped with whipped cream.

THE JUNIOR LEAGUE OF PASADENA
THE CALIFORNIA HERITAGE COOKBOOK

Corsican Caramel Cakes

Pastizzi

Bay leaves may be used instead of orange leaves.

These nourishing little cakes are baked for the principal religious holidays, and in particular for the pilgrimage of Lavasina, in the Cap Corse region of Corsica.

	To make 20 cakes	
1 litre	milk	1¾ pints
1 or 2	orange leaves	1 or 2
5 tbsp	semolina	5 tbsp
	salt	
3 tbsp	sugar	3 tbsp
4	eggs	4
	Caramel	
125 g	sugar	4 oz
1 tbsp	water	1 tbsp

Make the caramel first. Dissolve the sugar in the water over a gentle heat, then raise the heat and boil the syrup until it turns a rich amber colour. Pour a little caramel into the bottom of 20 small bucket-shaped moulds, turning each mould so that caramel coats the bottom and sides.

Boil the milk with the orange leaves. Then remove the leaves and stir in the semolina and a pinch of salt. Cook the mixture, stirring, over a low heat, then remove from the heat and add the sugar and the eggs. Stir them in well. Fill the caramelized moulds with the mixture and bake in a preheated 220°C (425°F or Mark 7) oven for 10 minutes, or until the cakes are firm and light brown. Turn the cakes out of their moulds and leave them to cool.

NICOLE VIELFAURE AND A. CHRISTINE BEAUVIALA
FÊTES, COUTUMES ET GÂTEAUX

Rice Buns

These buns are not only very light and delicious, but they also look most attractive.

To make 12 buns

175 g	ground rice	6 oz
175 g	flour	6 oz
125 g	butter	4 oz
125 g	sugar	4 oz
1 tsp	baking powder	1 tsp
2	egg yolks	2
12.5 cl	milk	4 fl oz
2 tbsp	raspberry jam	2 tbsp

Mix together the flour and ground rice, rub in the butter, add the sugar and baking powder and mix with the egg yolks and the milk. The mixture must be stiff. Work it into a roll and cut the roll into 12 pieces. Roll each piece into a ball. Work a hole in the centre of each ball and spoon in half a teaspoonful of raspberry jam. Close up the holes, put the buns on a baking sheet and bake them in a preheated 180°C (350°F or Mark 4) oven for 20 minutes or until they are a nice brown colour.

RIA SYSONBY
LADY SYSONBY'S COOK BOOK

Rice Cakes

Pasticcini di Riso

To make 20 cakes

150 g	round-grain rice	5 oz
$\frac{3}{4}$ litre	milk	$1\frac{1}{4}$ pints
70 g	sugar	$2\frac{1}{2}$ oz
30 g	butter	1 oz
30 g	crystallized fruit, chopped	1 oz
	salt	
2 tbsp	rum	2 tbsp
3	eggs, yolks separated from whites, whites stiffly beaten	3
	breadcrumbs	

Cook the rice in the milk over a low heat, stirring continuously. After about 15 minutes, add the sugar, butter, crystallized fruit and a pinch of salt. Cook until the mixture is like a pudding, about 1 hour, stirring frequently. Cool, then add the

rum, the egg yolks, and finally the egg whites. Grease 20 individual cake moulds and dust them lightly with the breadcrumbs. Fill them with the rice mixture and bake in a preheated 180°C (350°F or Mark 4) oven for 20 minutes or until lightly browned. Serve when cool.

LEONE BOSI (EDITOR)
DOLCI PER UN ANNO

Crisp Brownies

Other nuts such as pecan nuts, hazelnuts or almonds can be substituted for the walnuts. The brownies can be iced with chocolate frosting (recipe, page 165) when they are cool.

To make about 20 brownies

125 g	flour	4 oz
$\frac{1}{2}$ tsp	baking powder	$\frac{1}{2}$ tsp
60 g	semi-sweet chocolate	2 oz
75 g	butter	$2\frac{1}{2}$ oz
2	eggs, well beaten	2
250 g	sugar	8 oz
$\frac{1}{2}$ tsp	vanilla extract	$\frac{1}{2}$ tsp
60 g	walnuts, chopped	2 oz

Sift the flour and baking powder together. Melt the chocolate and the butter over a gentle heat, remove from the heat and stir in the eggs and the sugar. Fold in the flour and baking powder. Stir in the vanilla extract and the nuts. Pour the batter into a greased, square cake tin and bake in a preheated 180°C (350°F or Mark 4) oven for 30 minutes or until a skewer inserted in the centre comes out clean. Mark the cake into squares or rectangles while it is still warm.

LOIS LINTNER SUMPTION AND MARGUERITE LINTNER ASHBROOK
AROUND-THE-WORLD COOKY BOOK

Chocolate Cream Cheese Brownies

To make about 30 brownies

125 g	semi-sweet chocolate or chocolate chips	4 oz
45 g	butter	$1\frac{1}{2}$ oz
2	eggs	2
175 g	granulated sugar	6 oz
60 g	flour	2 oz
$\frac{1}{2}$ tsp	baking powder	$\frac{1}{2}$ tsp
$\frac{1}{2}$ tsp	salt	$\frac{1}{2}$ tsp
60 g	walnuts, chopped	2 oz
1 tsp	vanilla extract	1 tsp
$\frac{1}{4}$ tsp	almond extract	$\frac{1}{4}$ tsp

	Cream cheese mixture	
30 g	butter, softened	1 oz
90 g	cream cheese, softened	3 oz
60 g	sugar	2 oz
1	egg	1
1 tbsp	flour	1 tbsp
1 tsp	vanilla extract	1 tsp

Melt the chocolate and butter in the top of a double boiler over simmering water. Remove the pan from the heat and set it aside. To prepare the cream cheese mixture, cream the softened butter and cream cheese in a medium-sized bowl until fluffy. Blend the sugar, egg, flour and vanilla extract into the creamed mixture and set it aside.

In another mixing bowl, beat the eggs and add the sugar, continuing to beat until blended. Into the sugar and egg mixture, sift the flour, baking powder and salt, then stir in the melted chocolate mixture, walnuts, vanilla and almond extract. Spread half of this mixture evenly in a greased 23 cm (9 inch) square tin and spread the cream cheese mixture on the top. Drop the remaining chocolate mixture over the cream cheese with a spoon. Swirl the top just slightly with a fork to give a marbled effect. Bake in a preheated 180°C (350°F or Mark 4) oven for 40 to 50 minutes or until a cocktail stick inserted in the centre comes out clean. Cool slightly. Cut the cake into squares to serve.

THE JUNIOR LEAGUE OF PASADENA
THE CALIFORNIA HERITAGE COOKBOOK

Moors' Heads

Indiáner

Some cooks cover both halves of each cake with chocolate.

To make 12 cakes

4	eggs, yolks separated from whites	4
	salt	
150 g	granulated sugar	5 oz
75 g	flour	2½ oz
125 g	sweet chocolate	4 oz
15 g	butter	½ oz
¼ litre	double cream	8 fl oz
3 tbsp	vanilla sugar	3 tbsp

Whip the egg whites with a pinch of salt until they are foamy and stand in peaks. Add the egg yolks, one by one, beating after each addition for about 2 minutes. Add the sugar and whip for another 2 minutes. Add the flour, little by little, and stir until the batter is very smooth.

Butter 12 muffin tins. Fill them to three-quarters capacity with the batter. Bake them in a preheated 180°C (350°F or Mark 4) oven for 10 to 12 minutes. Let them cool slightly in the moulds, then turn them out on to a wire rack.

When the cakes are completely cool, cut them across into halves and scrape out the centre of each half.

To make the glaze, place the chocolate in a bowl over a pan of water or the top part of a double boiler and soften it, while stirring. When the chocolate is completely melted, remove from the heat. When cool, whip in the butter. Dip the top halves of the cakes into the chocolate glaze and place them in the refrigerator to harden.

Whip the double cream till it becomes stiff, then mix in the vanilla sugar. Fill the hollowed-out, unglazed halves of the cakes with the sweetened whipped cream. Place the chocolate-glazed halves on top. Whipped cream should show through around the middle.

GEORGE LANG
THE CUISINE OF HUNGARY

Chocolate Sponges

Spumette di Cioccolata

To make about 20 cakes

45 g	cocoa powder	1½ oz
6	eggs, yolks separated from whites, whites stiffly beaten	6
175 g	icing sugar	6 oz
175 g	potato flour	6 oz
	castor sugar	

Beat the egg yolks, gradually beating in the cocoa powder and the icing sugar. Beat for 20 minutes. Fold in the stiffly beaten egg whites and, when the ingredients are well combined, add the potato flour. Place spoonfuls of the mixture on a baking sheet lined with greaseproof paper, or in small paper cases greased with butter. Do not fill the cases to the top. Sprinkle with castor sugar. Bake in a preheated 170°C (325°F or Mark 3) oven for 15 minutes or until firm.

IPPOLITO CAVALCANTI, DUCA DI BUONVICINO
CUCINA TEORICO-PRATICA

Black Bottom Cup Cakes

To make 18 cup cakes

175 g	cream cheese	6 oz
1	egg	1
300 g	sugar	10 oz
	salt	
175 g	plain chocolate, broken into small pieces	6 oz
175 g	flour	6 oz
30 g	cocoa powder	1 oz
1 tsp	bicarbonate of soda	1 tsp
$\frac{1}{4}$ litre	water	8 fl oz
8 cl	vegetable oil	3 fl oz
1 tbsp	vinegar	1 tbsp
1 tsp	vanilla extract	1 tsp
	Walnut topping	
60 g	walnuts, chopped	2 oz
2 tbsp	sugar	2 tbsp

Beat the cream cheese until it is smooth. Add the egg, 75 g ($2\frac{1}{2}$ oz) of the sugar and a pinch of salt. Beat until well blended, then stir in the chocolate pieces.

Sift together the flour, the remaining sugar, the cocoa powder, bicarbonate of soda, and half a teaspoon of salt.

Combine the water, oil, vinegar and vanilla extract; mix well. Add the oil mixture to the cocoa powder mixture. Beat until well blended. Spoon the batter into 6 cm ($2\frac{1}{2}$ inch) paper cases set in tartlet or bun tins, filling the cases about one-third full. Place a large teaspoonful of the cream cheese mixture on top of the batter in each paper case.

To make the topping, combine the sugar and the walnuts; mix well. Sprinkle each cup cake with this mixture.

Bake in a preheated 180°C (350°F or Mark 4) oven for 35 minutes, or until a skewer inserted in the centre comes out clean. Remove the cup cakes from their tins and cool on racks.

ELISE W. MANNING
FARM JOURNAL'S COMPLETE HOME BAKING BOOK

Honey Pogácsas

Mézespogácsa

In the demonstration on page 38, the cakes were cut slightly larger than here, so that they could be decorated more elaborately with glacé cherry pieces and triangles of candied citron peel in addition to blanched almonds.

To make about 30 cakes

250 g	honey	8 oz
90 g	butter	3 oz
1	egg	1
3	egg yolks	3
90 g	sugar	3 oz
500 g	flour	1 lb
1 tsp	bicarbonate of soda	1 tsp
$\frac{1}{2}$ tsp	grated lemon rind, ground cinnamon or ground cloves	$\frac{1}{2}$ tsp
1 tbsp	soured cream	1 tbsp
	almonds, blanched and halved	

Warm the honey just enough to melt the butter in it, remove the pan from the heat and add the egg and two of the yolks, the sugar and finally the flour sifted with the bicarbonate of soda. Work the ingredients into a smooth dough and flavour to taste with a little grated lemon rind, ground cinnamon or cloves.

Roll out the dough to a thickness of about 9 mm ($\frac{3}{8}$ inch) and cut out very small rounds. Set these out on a greased baking sheet, brush the tops carefully with the remaining egg yolk mixed with the soured cream, and decorate each cake with half an almond. Bake in a preheated 190°C (375°F or Mark 5) oven for 6 to 8 minutes.

FRED MACNICOL
HUNGARIAN COOKERY

Prianiki with Honey and Spices

To make 24 cakes

2 tbsp	honey	2 tbsp
$\frac{1}{4}$ tsp each	grated nutmeg, ground cinnamon, ginger, cloves and cardamom	$\frac{1}{4}$ tsp each
1 tbsp	olive oil	1 tbsp
2	eggs	2
125 g	sugar	4 oz
175 g	flour	6 oz
$\frac{1}{2}$ tsp	baking powder	$\frac{1}{2}$ tsp

Syrup (optional)		
100 g	sugar	3½ oz
2 tbsp	water	2 tbsp
1	egg white, stiffly beaten	1

Mix together the honey and oil. Beat the eggs and sugar until white and fluffy. Sift the flour with the baking powder and stir in the spices. Gradually mix the spiced flour into the beaten eggs and sugar and then add the honey and oil mixture. The dough should be stiff but not dry. Cool the dough for 1 hour in the refrigerator.

Roll the dough into small balls in the palms of your hands and place, well separated, on a greased baking sheet. Bake in a preheated 190°C (375°F or Mark 5) oven for 20 minutes.

Spiced *prianiki* are usually glazed while still hot by being dipped into a syrup made by boiling together the sugar and water for 5 minutes, and then folding in the egg white. Cool the glazed cakes on a wire rack.

SOFKA SKIPWITH
EAT RUSSIAN

Calabrian Honey Cakes
Mustazzuoli

The authentic honey to use in this recipe is fig honey, but any clear, well-flavoured honey can be substituted.

In Calabria these cakes are made in various shapes: hearts, fishes, birds, horses and baskets.

To make about 120 cakes

600 g	honey	1¼ lb
About 850 g	flour	About 1¾ lb
4	eggs, lightly beaten	4
100 g	almonds, blanched, toasted and chopped	3½ oz
2 tsp	ground cloves	2 tsp
1 tbsp	pounded dried orange rind, or grated fresh rind	1 tbsp
200 g	sugar	7 oz

Combine the honey with enough flour for it all to be absorbed. Add the lightly beaten eggs, chopped almonds, ground cloves, orange rind and the sugar. Mix well, then form the dough into fairly small rectangular pieces, about 5 mm (¼ inch) thick, 2.5 cm (1 inch) wide and 5 cm (2 inches) long. Bake them in a preheated 220°C (425°F or Mark 7) oven until they are golden, about 15 minutes.

OTTAVIO CAVALCANTI
IL LIBRO D'ORO DELLA CUCINA E DEI VINI DI CALABRIA E BASILICATA

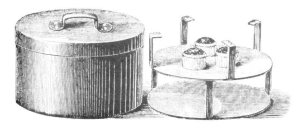

Phoenician Honey Cakes
Melomacarona

Finikia is another name for these small honey cakes offered to callers at a Greek home at Christmas and New Year. The recipe for these cakes is said to have been brought to Greece by the Phoenicians.

To make about 30 cakes

About 1 kg	flour, sifted	About 2 lb
½ litre	olive oil	16 fl oz
125 g	sugar	4 oz
12.5 cl	retsina or white wine	4 fl oz
12.5 cl	orange juice	4 fl oz
4 tbsp	brandy	4 tbsp
½ tsp	ground cloves	½ tsp
½ tsp	grated nutmeg	½ tsp
1 tbsp	ground cinnamon	1 tbsp
	salt	
	chopped almonds	
Syrup		
600 g	honey	1¼ lb
250 g	sugar	8 oz
¼ litre	cold water	8 fl oz
1	lemon, juice strained	1

Work the flour little by little into the oil, adding the sugar, the other liquids, the cloves, nutmeg, 1 teaspoonful of the cinnamon and a pinch of salt, until a fairly stiff dough is achieved; add more liquid if the dough is too stiff and more flour if it is too soft to handle. Knead the dough well for about 15 minutes. Pinch off a piece at a time and form each piece into a ball the size and shape of an egg; flatten the balls lightly on an oiled baking sheet. Bake them in a preheated 200°C (400°F or Mark 6) oven for 15 minutes until they are brown.

Meanwhile, dissolve the honey and sugar in the water and lemon juice, then boil until the syrup is frothy. When the cakes are cooked, take them from the oven and while they are still warm, lower each one into the hot syrup for 2 to 3 minutes. Place them on greaseproof paper to cool. Sprinkle them with chopped almonds and the remaining cinnamon.

JOYCE M. STUBBS
THE HOME BOOK OF GREEK COOKERY

Honey Cake from Warsaw

Piernik Warszawski

This cake is better the day after it is made. Keep it covered.

To make 32 slices

350 g	honey	12 oz
250 g	sugar	8 oz
3 tbsp	water	3 tbsp
30 g	butter	1 oz
¼ litre	soured cream	8 fl oz
3	egg yolks	3
1 tsp	ground allspice	1 tsp
1 tsp	ground cinnamon	1 tsp
1 tsp	ground cloves	1 tsp
1 tsp	grated orange rind	1 tsp
1 tsp	bicarbonate of soda	1 tsp
500 g	flour	1 lb
3 tbsp	dry breadcrumbs	3 tbsp
150 g	jam	5 oz

Icing

175 g	plain chocolate	6 oz
30 g	butter	1 oz
4 tbsp	single cream, hot	4 tbsp

To make the batter, brown 1 tablespoon of the sugar in a saucepan. Add the water and stir until the sugar has dissolved. Add the rest of the sugar, the butter and the honey. Bring to the boil, then remove from the heat and add the soured cream, egg yolks, spices and orange rind. Mix well. Add the bicarbonate of soda and flour. Beat at low speed for 5 minutes or until smooth. Butter a 30 by 23 cm (12 by 9 inch) baking tin; sprinkle with the breadcrumbs and pour the mixture into it. Bake the cake in a preheated 180°C (350°F or Mark 4) oven for 1 hour.

Cool the cake. Remove it from the tin and cut it with a long sharp knife into two layers. Spread the jam over the bottom layer and cover with the top layer.

To make the icing, melt the chocolate and the butter in the cream over a low heat. Do not boil. Spread the icing over the cake. Cut the cake into long narrow pieces before serving.

ALINA ŻERAŃSKA
THE ART OF POLISH COOKING

Peanut Butter Brownies

To make 16 brownies

175 g	peanut butter	6 oz
4 tbsp	oil or melted butter	4 tbsp
250 g	honey	8 oz
2	eggs	2
¼ tsp	salt	¼ tsp
90 g	prunes, stoned and chopped	3 oz
90 g	dried figs, chopped (optional)	3 oz
45 g	peanuts, chopped	1½ oz
45 g	whole wheat flour	1½ oz

In a medium-sized bowl, combine all the ingredients in the order given. Mix well. Spread the batter evenly in an oiled 22 cm (9 inch) square baking tin. Bake in a preheated 180°C (350°F or Mark 4) oven for 20 to 25 minutes, or just until the surface is firm to the touch. Remove the tin from the oven, cool the cake slightly, and cut it into 16 squares.

FAYE MARTIN
RODALE'S NATURALLY DELICIOUS DESSERTS AND SNACKS

Lemon-Nut Squares

To make 15 squares

2 tbsp	lemon juice, strained	2 tbsp
3½ tbsp	grated lemon rind	3½ tbsp
60 g	nuts, chopped	2 oz
2	eggs	2
5 tbsp	oil or melted butter, cooled	5 tbsp
200 g	honey, warmed	7 oz
4 tbsp	buttermilk	4 tbsp
175 g	whole wheat flour	6 oz
1 tsp	salt	1 tsp
¾ tsp	bicarbonate of soda	¾ tsp

Beat the eggs in a large bowl. Add the oil or butter, 175 g (6 oz) of the honey, the buttermilk and 1½ tablespoons of the lemon rind. Mix until thoroughly combined.

Stir together the flour, salt and bicarbonate of soda, making sure there are no lumps in the soda. Add this to the egg mixture and beat well. Stir in the nuts.

Bake in a greased 30 by 20 cm (12 by 8 inch) baking tin in a preheated 180°C (350°F or Mark 4) oven for 20 to 25 minutes, or until the cake is browned. Cool the cake for 5 minutes, then pour over the top a mixture of the remaining honey, lemon rind and the lemon juice. Cut the cake into squares and serve it warm or at room temperature.

FAYE MARTIN
RODALE'S NATURALLY DELICIOUS DESSERTS AND SNACKS

Georgia Pecan Brownies

To make 20 brownies

125 g	pecan nuts, chopped	4 oz
125 g	honey, warmed	4 oz
2	egg whites, stiffly beaten	2
1 tbsp	maple syrup (optional)	1 tbsp
100 g	fine dry wholemeal breadcrumbs	3½ oz
	salt	

Add the honey to the egg whites gradually, beating until stiff and smooth. Carefully beat in the maple syrup, if used.

Mix the nuts, breadcrumbs and a pinch of salt. Fold them gently into the egg whites. Spread the mixture in a buttered 28 by 18 cm (11 by 7 inch) shallow baking tin. Bake in a preheated 170°C (325°F or Mark 3) oven for about 25 minutes. Cool the cake in the tin and cut it into rectangles.

FAYE MARTIN
RODALE'S NATURALLY DELICIOUS DESSERTS AND SNACKS

Passion Fruit Slices

Gâteau aux Fruits de la Passion

You will need about 2.5 kg (5 lb) of passion fruit altogether.

To make 24 slices

	sponge cake batter (*page 164*)	
	Passion fruit jelly	
15 g	gelatine	½ oz
2 to 3 tbsp	cold water	2 to 3 tbsp
¼ litre	passion fruit juice	8 fl oz
250 g	sugar	8 oz
	Passion fruit mousse	
15 g	gelatine	½ oz
½ litre	passion fruit juice	16 fl oz
200 g	sugar	7 oz
10 cl	water	3½ fl oz
3	egg whites, stiffly beaten	3
¾ litre	double cream, whipped to soft peaks	1¼ pints
	Glaze	
6 tbsp	sugar syrup (*page 6*) cooked to 102°C (214°F)	6 tbsp
6 tbsp	passion fruit juice	6 tbsp

First prepare the sponge cake. Brush the base and sides of a Swiss roll tin with melted butter and line it with greaseproof paper. Pour the batter into the tin and bake in a preheated 220°C (425°F or Mark 7) oven for 7 minutes or until the cake is golden-brown and springs back when pressed with a fingertip. Turn the cake out on to a wire rack and allow it to cool.

Meanwhile, prepare the passion fruit jelly. Lightly oil a rectangular tin measuring about 30 by 20 by 5 cm (12 by 8 by 2 inches). Sprinkle the gelatine on to the cold water in a small pan and allow the gelatine to soften until all the liquid has been absorbed. Place the passion fruit juice and sugar in another pan and stir over a low heat until the sugar has dissolved. Raise the heat and bring to the boil, then simmer the liquid. As scum floats to the surface, remove it with a spoon. Continue simmering until no more scum appears.

Melt the softened gelatine in the pan over a low heat until the liquid is clear. Add this liquid to the passion fruit and sugar mixture. Strain and pour the jelly into the oiled tin to form a layer no deeper than 3 mm (⅛ inch). Refrigerate the tin, making sure that it is level.

While the jelly is setting, prepare the mousse. First, soften the gelatine with a little passion fruit juice. Dissolve the sugar in the water over a low heat, stirring gently so as not to brush sugar crystals against the sides of the pan. Increase the heat and boil the syrup to the hard-ball stage, 121° to 130°C (250° to 266°F). Dip the base of the pan in cold water to arrest the cooking. Pour the hot syrup on to the beaten egg whites in a thin stream, whisking continuously, and continue beating until all the syrup has been incorporated and the meringue is cool. It should be white, very shiny and form a stiff peak on the end of the whisk. Melt the softened gelatine over a low heat. Add the remainder of the passion fruit juice. Fold the gelatine and juice into the meringue, then fold in the whipped cream.

Pour the mousse into the tin on top of the set jelly; it should form a layer about 2.5 cm (1 inch) thick. Keep it refrigerated.

Make the glaze by mixing together the sugar syrup and the passion fruit juice.

Trim the sponge to fit the top of the tin of jelly and mousse. Brush the underside of the sponge with the glaze; this will moisten and flavour the sponge and also help it to stick to the mousse. Place the sponge, glaze side down, on top of the mousse, and press gently. Refrigerate the cake for at least 2 hours to firm it, or cover it and leave overnight.

To unmould the cake, cut a piece of card slightly bigger than the tin. Run a hot knife round the sides of the tin and dip the base of the tin in hot water for a few seconds to melt the jelly very slightly. Hold the card tightly against the tin and invert. If the cake does not come out, dip the base again in hot water. Trim the sides of the cake with a long-bladed knife made of stainless steel so that it does not impart a metallic taste. Cut the cake into slices about 2.5 cm (1 inch) wide.

PETITS PROPOS CULINAIRES 10

Gipsy Slices

Zigeunerschnitten

Pariser Creme *is another name for chocolate ganache.*

To make about 16 slices

30 g	chocolate	1 oz
15 g	butter	½ oz
2	eggs	2
60 g	sugar	2 oz
60 g	flour	2 oz
	Pariser Creme	
60 g	chocolate, grated	2 oz
15 cl	double cream	¼ pint

Make the *Pariser Creme* in advance. Put the grated chocolate in a thick saucepan, add the cream and bring to the boil, stirring constantly. Allow the mixture to rise once, then remove the saucepan from the heat and stir the mixture until it is cool. Chill it well. Whisk it lightly, until it will just hold its shape. Chill again before using.

To make the cake, break the chocolate into small pieces, place in a bowl together with the butter and set them to soften in a warm place. Put the eggs and sugar in a bowl and whisk over steam until thick. Remove from the heat and whisk until cool. Lightly fold in the flour and finally the softened butter and chocolate. Spread the mixture about 1 cm (½ inch) thick on a baking sheet covered with buttered greaseproof paper. Bake in a preheated 200°F (400°C or Mark 6) oven for 10 minutes or until firm and just beginning to colour. Remove the paper while the cake is still hot. Cut the cake into slices, then cut through each slice once and fill with *Pariser Creme.*

GRETEL BEER
AUSTRIAN COOKING

Zola Cake

To make 16 slices

1	egg	1
1	egg yolk	1
1½ tbsp	sugar	1½ tbsp
1½ tbsp	flour	1½ tbsp
1 tsp	butter, melted	1 tsp
	Marzipan	
200 g	ground almonds	7 oz
200 g	castor sugar	7 oz
	water or egg white (optional)	

	Zola cream	
30 cl	milk	½ pint
2	egg yolks	2
3 tbsp	sugar	3 tbsp
15 g	gelatine, dissolved in a little boiling water	½ oz
35 cl	double cream, stiffly whipped	12 fl oz
	rum or vanilla extract	

Beat the egg, the egg yolk and the sugar until light and creamy. Stir in the flour and the melted butter. Line a rectangular baking tin with greaseproof paper, pour in the sponge cake batter and bake in á preheated 180°C (350°F or Mark 4) oven for about 20 minutes, or until the cake is firm and shrinks away slightly from the edges of the tin. Turn the cake out of the tin and leave it to cool on a wire rack.

Work the ground almonds and castor sugar well together; should the mixture not stick together, add a little water or egg white. When the mixture is nice and pliable, roll it out very thinly. Line a rectangular baking tin, the same size as the tin the sponge cake was made in, with the marzipan.

To make the Zola cream, whisk the milk, egg yolks and sugar together over a gentle heat until the mixture thickens, *but do not let it boil.* Remove the pan from the heat and stir in the dissolved gelatine. Allow the mixture to cool. When it is cold, stir in 20 cl (7 fl oz) of stiffly whipped cream, and a few drops of rum or vanilla extract to taste.

Pour the Zola cream into the marzipan-lined tin. Place the sponge cake on top and leave until the cream has set. Turn the cake out on to a serving dish, so that the sponge forms the base, and garnish it with the remaining whipped cream, squeezed over the marzipan in a nice pattern with a piping bag. Cut the cake into slices and serve.

INGA NORBERG (EDITOR)
GOOD FOOD FROM SWEDEN

Small Apricot Cakes

Aprikosentörtchen

If you use fresh apricots, poach them gently in a sugar syrup made from 15 cl (¼ pint) of water and 125 g (4 oz) of sugar for 8 to 10 minutes, or until they are soft but not disintegrating.

To make 12 cakes

250 g	poached fresh apricots or preserved apricots, drained, halved and stoned	8 oz
3	eggs, yolks separated from whites, whites stiffly beaten	3
3 tbsp	hot water	3 tbsp
120 g	sugar	4 oz
½	lemon, rind grated	½
60 g	flour	2 oz
60 g	cornflour	2 oz
1 tsp	baking powder	1 tsp
	Lemon buttercream	
40 g	cornflour	1½ oz
½ litre	milk	16 fl oz
1	lemon, juice strained, rind of ½ grated	1
	salt	
100 g	sugar	3½ oz
1	egg yolk	1
150 g	butter, creamed	5 oz

Beat the egg yolks, water, sugar and lemon rind together with a whisk until they are thick and foamy. Sift the flour with the cornflour and baking powder, and add to the mixture. Finally fold in the egg whites. Spread the dough in a Swiss roll tin lined with buttered greaseproof paper. Bake in a preheated 190°C (375°F or Mark 5) oven for about 20 minutes or until golden. Turn the cake out on to a rack and peel off the paper.

For the cream, beat the cornflour with a little of the milk. Bring the remaining milk to the boil with the lemon rind and a pinch of salt. Add the cornflour mixture and the sugar and stir well. Add the egg yolk and cook, without boiling, stirring constantly, until the mixture thickens. Stir in the lemon juice and allow to cool. Then beat the cooled cream, spoonful by spoonful, into the creamed butter.

Cut out rounds of the cooled cake with a wine glass. Spread with the cream, and garnish each with an apricot half.

ROTRAUD DEGNER
DAS SCHNELLKOCHBUCH FÜR FEINSCHMECKER

Pastries

Apple Custard Tarts

Pear custard tarts may be made in the same way. Halve, peel and core the pears and poach them for about 10 minutes in a light sugar syrup [*page 6*] before arranging them, cut side down, in the baked tartlet shells and pouring the cream over.

To make 12 tartlets

4	apples, peeled, cored and sliced	4
250 g	shortcrust dough (*page 163*)	8 oz
60 g	butter	2 oz
2	eggs	2
15 cl	double cream	¼ pint
60 g	sugar	2 oz
½ tsp	vanilla extract	½ tsp
	grated nutmeg	
	ground cinnamon	

Roll out the dough, line 12 individual tartlet moulds and bake them blind in a preheated 190°C (375°F or Mark 5) oven for 10 to 15 minutes or until the edges are just beginning to colour. Sauté the apples rapidly in the butter, tossing rather than stirring them, over a high heat, for 4 to 5 minutes or until they are lightly coloured and beginning to soften.

Beat together the eggs, cream, sugar, vanilla extract and a suspicion of nutmeg. Arrange the apples in the pastry shells, sprinkle with a bit of cinnamon and pour over the cream mixture. Bake in a preheated 190°C (375°F or Mark 5) oven until the cream is just set, about 12 minutes.

PETITS PROPOS CULINAIRES 2

Apple Ginger Tarts

To make the apple purée, put 250 g (8 oz) of peeled, cored and chopped apples into a saucepan with 4 tablespoons of water. Cover the pan and set it on a low heat for about 15 minutes, until the apple is soft enough to be beaten to a purée.

To make 12 tarts

250 g	thick apple purée	8 oz
15 g	crystallized ginger, finely chopped	½ oz
4 tbsp	double cream or pastry cream (*page 166*)	4 tbsp
250 g	shortcrust dough (*page 163*)	8 oz
1 tbsp	apricot jam	1 tbsp

Garnish

	icing sugar	
12	glacé cherries	12
12	small pieces crystallized ginger	12

To prepare the filling, mix the apple purée with the ginger and the cream or pastry cream.

Line 12 small tartlet tins with the dough and bake them slowly near the top of a preheated 150°C (300°F or Mark 2) oven for 20 to 25 minutes, or until they are crisp and golden-brown. Cool. Remove the pastry shells from the tins and fill each one first with a little apricot jam and then with the apple and ginger filling. Dust the tops with icing sugar and put a cherry and a piece of ginger in the centre of each.

MONA MELWANI
DELICIOUS WAYS WITH GINGER

Breton Apple Turnovers

Chocarts

To make 6 turnovers

1 kg	apples, peeled, cored and chopped into small pieces	2 to 2½ lb
250 g	sugar	8 oz
1 tsp	ground cinnamon	1 tsp
1 tsp	grated lemon rind	1 tsp
1	egg yolk	1

Puff dough

500 g	flour	1 lb
	salt	
½ litre	water	16 fl oz
500 g	butter, softened	1 lb

Place the apple pieces in an earthenware dish with the sugar, ground cinnamon and lemon rind. Mix them well together and leave them for 3 hours.

To make the dough, mix the flour with a pinch of salt. Add the water, a little at a time, and work the flour and water together with your hands into a smooth ball of dough.

Roll out the dough as thinly as possible. Cover it with the softened butter. Lift up the edges of the dough and fold them over so that the butter is completely covered. Turn the dough through 90 degrees, roll it out and fold it again. Leave it to rest in the refrigerator for 10 minutes.

During the next hour, roll out and fold the dough in the same way five times, about every 10 minutes. Finally, roll the dough out 5 mm (¼ inch) thick and cut it into rounds 20 cm (8 inches) in diameter.

Drain the apples and reserve their juice. Place some pieces of fruit on one half of each circle of dough. Dampen the edges of the dough slightly, fold over the other half to cover the filling, and press the edges firmly together.

Beat the egg yolk lightly with the reserved apple juice and brush this glaze over the pastries. Place them on a floured baking sheet and bake them in a preheated 220°C (425°F or Mark 7) oven for 30 minutes.

These pastries should preferably be served hot.

LA CUISINE BRETONNE

Apple Pockets

Rombosses

To make 6 apple pockets

6	apples, peeled, cored and thickly sliced	6
350 g	shortcrust dough (*page 163*)	12 oz
1	egg, beaten	1
60 g	coffee sugar crystals	2 oz

Divide the dough into six small portions. Roll out each piece of dough on a well-floured pastry board to a square 5 mm (¼ inch) thick. Put one of the sliced apples in the middle of each square. Fold one corner to the middle; brush its end with egg. Fold over a second corner and stick it to the first. Continue the operation until all four corners are stuck together on top. Stud the tops with coffee sugar crystals. Bake the pastries in a preheated 180°C (350°F or Mark 4) oven for 30 minutes.

JULIETTE ELKON
A BELGIAN COOKBOOK

Redcurrant Tart

Ribiselkuchen

The meringue can be piped in a latticework over the redcurrants for a decorative effect, as shown on page 57. Instead of drying out the meringue in a low oven, you can cook it very briefly in a hot oven—220°C (425°F or Mark 7) for 5 minutes. The surface of the meringue will become a delicate golden colour but it will remain soft inside.

To make about 30 slices

500 g	redcurrants, stalks removed	1 lb
250 g	flour	8 oz
160 g	butter	5½ oz
2	eggs, yolks separated from whites, whites stiffly beaten	2
250 g	sugar	8 oz
1 tsp	grated lemon rind	1 tsp
5 tbsp	water	5 tbsp

Work together the flour and butter until crumbly. Add the egg yolks, three tablespoons of sugar and the lemon rind and mix until the dough is firm and smooth. Leave to rest in a cool place for at least 30 minutes.

Boil 2 tablespoons of sugar in the water. Add the redcurrants and boil for a few moments only. Lift the redcurrants out with a perforated spoon. Keep to one side. Carry on boiling the syrup to reduce and thicken it.

Roll out the dough very thinly and place it on a baking sheet. Bake it blind in a preheated 190°C (375°F or Mark 5) oven for 15 to 20 minutes or until it is a very light golden colour. Leave it to cool. Brush the pastry with the thick syrup and arrange the redcurrants on top.

Fold the remaining sugar into the beaten egg whites. Spread the mixture over the redcurrants at once. Return the tart to the oven, with the heat reduced to 150°C (300°F or Mark 2), and leave for 20 minutes. The meringue top should dry out rather than bake.

Cut the tart into suitable slices and eat them hot or cold.

ROSL PHILPOT
VIENNESE COOKERY

Small Raspberry Tartlets

Pastry made with ground almonds instead of flour, and mixed to a dough with egg white and orange-flower water, was popular in the 18th century for tarts and pastry biscuits. This crackling crust is difficult to manage; by substituting ground almonds for part of the flour when making a sweet shortcrust you can get something of the well-flavoured crispness without the dough being too brittle to manipulate.

To make 30 to 36 tartlets

200 g	flour	7 oz
100 g	ground almonds	3 oz
30 g	vanilla sugar	1 oz
	salt	
150 g	butter	5 oz
1	egg	1
500 g	raspberries	1 lb
100 g	castor sugar	3 oz
	redcurrant jelly, melted to a syrup with 1 tbsp water, then cooled until tepid (optional)	
30 cl	double cream, whipped with 60 g (2 oz) castor sugar	½ pint

Mix the flour, ground almonds, vanilla sugar and a pinch of salt, rub in the butter and mix to a dough with the egg. No water is necessary if you use a large egg.

Chill for 1 hour, then roll out in batches and cut circles to fit into your tartlet tins.

Prick the base of the tarts with a fork—it is not necessary to put in foil and beans—and bake for 10 minutes in a preheated 200°C (400°F or Mark 6) oven. If the pastry is not as brown as you would like, lower the heat to 180°C (350°F or Mark 4) and give them another 5 minutes.

Cool the cases. Just before serving, toss the raspberries lightly with the castor sugar and distribute them among the cases. Glaze them if you like with the redcurrant glaze; brush it over the fruit while just tepid. Top each tart with a swirl of sweetened whipped cream.

JANE GRIGSON
FOOD WITH THE FAMOUS

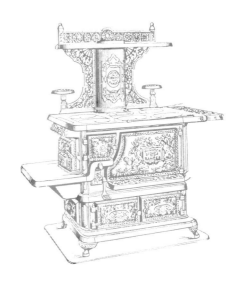

Raspberry Meringue Pastries

Delicieuses

To make the raspberry purée, rub 250 g (8 oz) of ripe raspberries through a nylon sieve.

To make about 30 pastries

250 g	shortcrust dough (*page 163*)	8 oz
15 cl	raspberry purée	¼ pint
2	egg whites	2
4 tbsp	castor sugar	4 tbsp
125 g	almonds, blanched and slivered	4 oz

Roll the dough out thinly and cut it into strips 8 cm (3 inches) wide. Cover the strips with a thin layer of raspberry purée. Beat the egg whites until they hold soft peaks. Add 2 tablespoons of the castor sugar, a little at a time, beating well between each addition. Using a piping bag with a plain, not too small nozzle, pipe five stripes of the meringue mixture side by side lengthwise on each strip of dough. Pipe another four stripes lengthwise on top to lie on the joins of the stripes underneath. Sprinkle the meringue first with almonds and then with the remaining sugar. Cut the pastries into 4 cm (1½ inch) pieces and put them into a preheated 200°C (400°F or Mark 6) oven for 10 minutes to brown lightly.

BANKETBAKKERSPRODUCTEN

Small Tea Cakes with Jam

Berlingos

To make about 36 cakes

250 g	butter	8 oz
375 g	flour	13 oz
200 g	granulated sugar	7 oz
2	sugar cubes, rubbed on the rind of a lemon, then crushed	2
	salt	
7	hard-boiled egg yolks, sieved	7
2	eggs, yolks separated from whites, whites stiffly beaten	2
	castor sugar	
	apricot, cherry, raspberry or redcurrant jam	

Work the butter and flour together until crumbly. Add the granulated sugar, lemon sugar, a pinch of salt and the hard-boiled and raw egg yolks. Work all the ingredients together to make a smooth dough. Roll the dough out 5 mm (¼ inch) thick

and cut it into 5 cm (2 inch) rounds. Place the rounds on a baking sheet, spread them with stiffly beaten egg whites, sprinkle them with castor sugar and form hollows in the centre of the egg white by pressing with the rounded end of a whole egg, dipped in sugar. Brush each hollow with water. Place the pastries in a preheated 180°C (350°F or Mark 4) oven and bake them for 15 minutes, or until golden.

Cut the cakes off the baking sheet while still warm and, when they are cool, fill the hollows with jam.

SOPHIE WILHELMINE SCHEIBLER
ALLGEMEINES DEUTSCHES KOCHBUCH FÜR ALLE STÄNDE

Little Fruit Baskets

Gyümöloskosárkák

Other fillings could be fresh raspberries or wild strawberries, or freshly grated chocolate mixed with whipped cream.

To make 12 baskets

125 g	butter	4 oz
150 g	flour	5 oz
4 tbsp	vanilla icing sugar	4 tbsp
	salt	
½	lemon, rind grated	½
2	egg yolks	2
½ tbsp	soured cream	½ tbsp
	Filling	
½ litre	double cream	16 fl oz
3 tbsp	vanilla icing sugar	3 tbsp
250 g	redcurrant jam, sieved	8 oz

Cut the butter into the flour with a pastry blender or with two knives until the mixture forms crumbs. Mix in the vanilla icing sugar, a pinch of salt, the lemon rind, egg yolks and cream. Knead until the mixture becomes a homogeneous dough. Cover with a cloth and leave to rest in the refrigerator.

Cut three-quarters of the dough into 12 even pieces. Roll the pieces out thinly and use them to line 6 cm (2½ inch) fluted tartlet moulds. Cut the remaining quarter of dough into 12 pieces. Roll out each piece to a length of 15 cm (6 inches), twist it into a corkscrew then bend it into a thin crescent. Make sure that the curve of the crescent is as wide as the widest part of the mould so that it will fit.

Place the lined moulds and the crescents on separate baking sheets and bake them in a preheated 190°C (375°F or Mark 5) oven for 12 to 15 minutes, or until they are well baked and coloured. Remove the pastry shells from the tins and allow them to cool completely before filling them.

To prepare the filling, whip the cream with the icing sugar and then gently mix with the jam. Fill each basket with some of the cream mixture, and place a twisted crescent as the handle of the basket. The whipped cream will hold it in place.

GEORGE LANG
THE CUISINE OF HUNGARY

Orange Tart Shells with Strawberries

These tarts may be prepared 6 to 8 hours before serving.

To make 10 tarts

175 g	lard	6 oz
250 g	flour, sifted	8 oz
1 tsp	salt	1 tsp
1 tbsp	grated orange rind	1 tbsp
4 to 5 tbsp	orange juice	4 to 5 tbsp

Pastry cream

4	egg yolks	4
175 g	granulated sugar	6 oz
1 tsp	vanilla extract	1 tsp
30 g	flour	1 oz
½ litre	milk	16 fl oz

Filling and glaze

150 g	redcurrant jelly	5 oz
2 tbsp	granulated sugar	2 tbsp
600 g	strawberries, hulled	1¼ lb
	icing sugar	

To prepare the dough, cut the lard into the flour in a large mixing bowl until the consistency is similar to coarse crumbs. (Rub the mixture with your fingers if necessary.) Add the salt and orange rind and mix well. Stir in the orange juice and mix until the dough holds together. Work the dough into a smooth ball. Wrap it in wax paper and chill for at least 2 hours.

On a lightly floured board, roll out the dough 3 mm (⅛ inch) thick and cut it into ten 9 cm (3½ inch) circles. Press the circles over the outsides of upside-down muffin tins. Prick the bottom of each tart shell *twice* with a fork. Bake in a preheated 220°C (425°F or Mark 7) oven for 10 minutes, until just brown. Watch carefully, as they burn easily. Cool the shells and remove them from the tins.

Meanwhile, to make the pastry cream, place the milk in a heavy, medium-sized saucepan and bring it almost to the boil over a medium heat. Set it aside. Combine the egg yolks, sugar and vanilla extract in a medium-sized mixing bowl. Beat with an electric beater on medium-high speed until the mixture makes ribbons, 3 to 4 minutes. Beat the flour into the mixture. Slowly add the milk, beating constantly. Pour the custard back into the saucepan and place over a moderate heat. Bring it to the boil, stirring constantly with a wooden spatula. Reduce the heat to low and continue to cook, still stirring, for 5 to 6 minutes, or until the cream is very thick. Take it off the heat and chill at once by placing the pan in a bowl of crushed ice. Stir until the pastry cream is cool.

To make the glaze, put the redcurrant jelly and the sugar in a small saucepan. Place over a medium-high heat for 2 to 3 minutes, stirring constantly, until the mixture is thick enough to coat the spoon and the last drops are sticky as they fall from the spoon (107° to 109°C or 225° to 228°F on a sugar thermometer). Do not boil beyond this point. Pour the glaze while it is still warm.

Fill each tart shell with about 1 tablespoon of the pastry cream. Place the strawberries on top, dividing them evenly among the shells. Pour about 1 tablespoon of the warm glaze over the strawberries in each tart. Chill the tarts until you are ready to serve them. Just before serving, sprinkle the top of each tart with icing sugar.

THE JUNIOR LEAGUE OF PASADENA
THE CALIFORNIA HERITAGE COOKBOOK

Polish Pastries

Polonais

To make 16 pastries

250 g	rough-puff dough (*page 163*), folded and rolled six times	8 oz
8	plums, stoned	8
8	apricots, stoned	8
50 g	apricot jam, warmed	2 oz

Roll the dough out thinly to a rectangle 30 cm (12 inches) long by 20 cm (8 inches) wide. Cut it into 16 small rectangles 5 cm (2 inches) wide, and place these on a dampened baking sheet. Place a plum or an apricot in the centre of each rectangle. Brush the points of the rectangle lightly with water and fold the corners of dough over the fruit, pressing the points together in the middle. Cook the pastries in a preheated 190°C (375°F or Mark 5) oven for about 20 minutes. Take the pastries from the oven and brush them immediately with warmed apricot jam.

ACADÉMIE DES GASTRONOMES, ACADÉMIE CULINAIRE DE FRANCE
LA HAUTE CUISINE FRANÇAISE

Plum Slices

Zwetschkenschnitten

To make about 40 slices

1 kg	blue plums, halved and stoned	2 to 2½ lb
400 g	flour	14 oz
200 g	butter	7 oz
2	eggs	2
150 g	castor sugar	5 oz
1 tsp	grated lemon rind	1 tsp

Sponge mixture

4	eggs	4
60 g	granulated sugar	2 oz
30 g	vanilla sugar	1 oz
60 g	flour	2 oz

Rub together the flour and butter. Add the eggs, 90 g (3 oz) of sugar and the lemon rind, and work to form a smooth pastry dough. Leave it to rest for 30 minutes in the refrigerator.

For the sponge mixture, beat together the eggs, granulated sugar and vanilla sugar until the mixture is pale and fluffy. Fold in the flour.

Roll out the pastry dough about 5 mm (¼ inch) thick. Put it on a baking sheet. Bake blind in a preheated 190°C (375°F or Mark 5) oven until it is slightly coloured and only half baked, about 10 minutes. Cover the pastry with the plums, cut side up. Spread the sponge mixture evenly over the plums. Return to the oven, reducing the heat slightly. Bake until a testing skewer comes out clean, about 20 to 25 minutes. Serve sliced, dusted with the remaining castor sugar.

ROSL PHILPOT
VIENNESE COOKERY

Plum Tarts

Ciastka ze Śliwkami

These tarts are best eaten on the day they are made.

To make 40 tarts

40	blue plums, halved and stoned	40
150 g	butter	5 oz
325 g	flour	11 oz
90 g	icing sugar	3 oz
2 tsp	baking powder	2 tsp
1	egg	1
1	egg yolk	1
3 tbsp	soured cream	3 tbsp

Icing

1	lemon, juice strained	1
About 60 g	icing sugar	About 2 oz
	whipped cream	

Cut the butter into the flour and rub it in with your fingertips. Add the icing sugar and baking powder and mix. Combine with the egg, egg yolk and soured cream. Knead the dough, then cover it and refrigerate it for 30 minutes.

Roll the dough out thinly and place it on a buttered 38 by 30 cm (15 by 12 inch) baking sheet. Spread the dough with your fingers until the sheet is almost covered. Arrange the plums in rows, skin down. Bake in a preheated 180°C (350°F or Mark 4) oven for 30 to 45 minutes, or until the pastry is browned and the plums are soft. Cool.

To make the icing, mix the lemon juice with enough icing sugar to have the thickness of soured cream. Spread this over the cake. Cut into 40 slices and serve with whipped cream.

ALINA ŻERAŃSKA
THE ART OF POLISH COOKING

Small Cherry Pies

Pasticcini alla Marenata

This 19th-century recipe used alkermes—a sweet red liqueur spiced with nutmeg, cinnamon and cloves. Cherry brandy or kirsch has been used here instead.

To make about 12 pies

250 g	shortcrust dough enriched with eggs (*page 163*)	8 oz
2 tbsp	castor sugar, flavoured with 2 tsp ground cinnamon	2 tbsp

Cherry filling

500 g	red cherries, stoned	1 lb
100 g	sugar	3½ oz
1	lemon, rind grated	1
4 tbsp	water	4 tbsp
2 tbsp	cherry brandy or kirsch	2 tbsp

To prepare the cherry filling, cook the cherries on a low heat, covered with the sugar, lemon rind and water, for about 20 minutes, until you obtain a jam. Allow the jam to cool and then add a little cherry brandy or kirsch.

Roll out the dough and use half of it to line tartlet tins. Fill them with the cherry jam and cover them with another layer of dough. Bake the tarts in a preheated 200°C (400°F or Mark 6) oven for 15 minutes, or until the pastry is browned.

Serve cold, sprinkled with the cinnamon-flavoured sugar.

GIUSEPPE RIVA
TRATTATO DI CUCINA SEMPLICE PER CONSERVARE LO STOMACO

Meringue Tarts

Frivolités Meringue

To make apricot purée, poach 250 g (8 oz) of fresh apricots in 45 cl (¾ pint) of light sugar syrup (page 6) for about 8 minutes or until they are tender. Drain and stone the apricots, then press them through a sieve. Alternatively, soak 175 g (6 oz) of dried apricots in enough water to cover them for about 8 hours. Drain the apricots and sieve them.

To make 16 tarts

170 g	flour	6 oz
62 g	castor sugar	2 oz
1	egg	1
1	egg yolk	1
62 g	butter, softened	2 oz
	Apricot cream	
4	egg yolks	4
100 g	granulated sugar	3½ oz
25 g	flour	1 oz
20 cl	milk	7 fl oz
1	vanilla pod	1
	salt	
200 g	apricot purée	7 oz
	Meringue	
3	egg whites	3
250 g	castor sugar	8 oz

Sift the flour and make a well in the middle. Place the sugar, the egg and the egg yolk in the well and mix them together by hand to dissolve the sugar. Add the softened butter and incorporate it with your fingers into the egg and sugar mixture. Gradually knead in the flour. When the dough forms a loose mass, gather it into a ball, turn it out on to a floured surface and knead it by pushing small pieces of dough away from you along the surface with the heel of your hand. Gather together the pieces and repeat the pushing operation. Leave the dough to rest in the refrigerator.

To make the apricot cream, beat the egg yolks and sugar together until they are pale and thick. Add the flour. Bring the milk to the boil with the vanilla pod. Remove the vanilla pod and pour the hot milk over the beaten egg mixture. Add a pinch of salt and stir well. Pour the mixture into a saucepan and place it over a medium heat. Bring it to the boil, stirring constantly, then lower the heat and leave it to cook gently for about 2 minutes. Remove the cream from the heat and leave it to cool. When it is completely cold, stir in the apricot purée.

To make the meringue, beat the egg whites until they form stiff peaks. Gradually sprinkle in 175 g (6 oz) of castor sugar and continue to beat until the meringue is smooth and glossy.

Line 16 small fluted brioche moulds with the sweet pastry dough. Place a little apricot cream at the bottom of each and bake the tarts in a preheated 220°C (425°F or Mark 7) oven for 6 minutes, or until the pastry is firm but not coloured.

When the tarts are cooked, remove them from the oven. Place the meringue mixture in a piping bag with a plain nozzle. Pipe a large dab of meringue over the top of each tart; then pipe three successive dabs of meringue on top of the first one, each slightly smaller than the one before, so that each tart is topped with a pointed peak of meringue. Sprinkle the tarts with the remaining castor sugar and replace them in the oven for 2 minutes so that the surface of the meringue is just crisp but it remains soft inside.

ACADÉMIE DES GASTRONOMES, ACADÉMIE CULINAIRE DE FRANCE
LA HAUTE CUISINE FRANÇAISE

Russian Rhubarb Cakes

Crakinoskis à la Rhubarbe

To make about 36 cakes

300 g	rhubarb, diced	10 oz
4	eggs	4
350 g	butter, softened	12 oz
500 g	sugar	1 lb
350 g	flour	12 oz
1 tbsp	lemon juice	1 tbsp
½ tsp	ground cinnamon	½ tsp
¼ tsp	grated nutmeg	¼ tsp

Combine the eggs, butter, 350 g (12 oz) of the sugar, the flour, lemon juice and spices and beat vigorously until smooth. Roll out the dough on a floured board to a thickness of 3 mm (⅛ inch). Cut with a large, round biscuit cutter. Line individual moulds or large muffin tins with the dough. Fill with the diced rhubarb and sprinkle with the remaining sugar. Bake in a preheated 200°C (400°F or Mark 6) oven for 45 minutes, or until the pastry is golden-brown and the rhubarb is soft.

TANTE MARIE'S FRENCH KITCHEN

Pecan Gems

Use the tiniest muffin tins you can find for these pastries—
they should be less than 5 cm (2 inches) in diameter.

To make 24 pastries

125 g	butter	4 oz
90 g	cream cheese	3 oz
125 g	flour	4 oz

Pecan nut filling

1	egg	1
1 tsp	vanilla extract	1 tsp
250 g	dark brown sugar	8 oz
90 g	pecan nuts, chopped	3 oz
60 g	butter (optional)	2 oz

Let the butter and cream cheese soften at room temperature,
then cream them together. Mix in the flour, form the dough
into a ball and chill it in the refrigerator for at least 1 hour.

To line the muffin tins, pull off small portions of the dough
and press it against the bottom and sides of the tins, using
your fingers or thumb. Do not roll the dough.

For the filling, beat the egg and stir in the vanilla extract
and sugar. In each muffin tin place a few nut pieces and a
spoonful of the egg mixture. For extra richness, add a tiny
piece of butter to each. Bake in a preheated 170°C (325°F or
Mark 3) oven until the filling is set and the pastry is delicately
browned—about 20 minutes, but this will vary somewhat
with the size of the muffin tins and the depth of the egg filling.

CHARLOTTE TURGEON AND FREDERIC A. BIRMINGHAM
THE SATURDAY EVENING POST ALL-AMERICAN COOKBOOK

Spanish Nut Tartlets

Tartelettes aux Noisettes d'Espagne

To make about 40 tartlets

175 g	hazelnuts, ground	6 oz
5	eggs	5
250 g	granulated sugar	8 oz
15 g	vanilla sugar	$\frac{1}{2}$ oz
60 g	flour, sifted	2 oz
90 g	butter, melted	3 oz
	raspberry or apricot jam	
45 cl	fondant icing (*page 165*) flavoured with kirsch	$\frac{3}{4}$ pint
	glacé cherries	

Sugar pastry

500 g	flour	1 lb
250 g	granulated sugar	8 oz
3	eggs	3
150 g	butter	5 oz
1	lemon, rind grated	1

For the pastry, sift the flour on to a board, make a hole in the
middle, and put in the remaining pastry ingredients. Mix the
whole together into a stiff paste.

For the filling, break the eggs into a basin, add the granulated sugar and vanilla sugar, and whisk over a low heat until
lukewarm; remove from the heat, but continue whisking the
mixture until it becomes light. Then stir in the hazelnuts,
then the flour and butter.

Line some deep tartlet tins with the pastry dough, then put
a little jam in the bottom of each and fill them up with the
hazelnut mixture. Bake in a preheated 180°C (350°F or Mark
4) oven for about 15 minutes.

When cold, ice the tartlets over with kirsch-flavoured
fondant, and put a cherry in the centre of each.

ÉMILE HÉRISSÉ
THE ART OF PASTRY MAKING

Chestnut Tartlets

Tartelettes Marrons

To make about 40 tartlets

125 g	peeled, cooked chestnuts, mashed	4 oz
90 g	butter	3 oz
125 g	icing sugar	4 oz
30 g	vanilla sugar	1 oz
	Italian meringue (*page 165*)	
45 cl	fondant icing (*page 165*), half coloured pink, half flavoured with chocolate	$\frac{3}{4}$ pint

Sugar pastry

500 g	flour	1 lb
250 g	granulated sugar	8 oz
3	eggs	3
150 g	butter	5 oz
1	lemon, rind grated	1

Put the butter into an earthenware dish, beat it to a fine
cream with a wooden spoon, then add the icing sugar and
vanilla sugar and the mashed chestnuts.

For the pastry, sift the flour on to a board and make a hole
in the middle. Put in the remaining pastry ingredients. Mix
the whole together into a stiff dough.

Line some oval tartlet moulds with the dough, prick it all over and bake the tartlet shells in a preheated 190°C (375°F or Mark 5) oven for about 15 minutes.

When the tartlets are cold, fill them with the chestnut cream and pipe the meringue over it; then ice them with the pink and chocolate fondant icing.

ÉMILE HÉRISSÉ
THE ART OF PASTRY MAKING

Pensée Tartlets

Penséetaartjes

If you wish, you can bake these almond-filled tartlets in individual aluminium foil cases.

To make 10 tartlets

160 g	flour	5 oz
80 g	icing sugar	3 oz
	salt	
120 g	butter	4 oz
1	egg, beaten	1
50 g	apricot jam, sieved and warmed	2 oz
30 g	glacé icing (*page 166*)	1 oz
	Almond filling	
120 g	ground almonds	4 oz
120 g	sugar	4 oz
1	egg	1
$\frac{1}{4}$	lemon, rind grated, juice strained	$\frac{1}{4}$
15 g	butter, melted, or 1½ tbsp cream	½ oz

Prepare a soft almond paste by mixing together the ground almonds, sugar, egg, grated lemon rind and lemon juice. Finish by stirring in the melted butter or cream.

To make the dough, sift the flour into a bowl and add the sugar and a pinch of salt. Rub the butter into the flour until the mixture resembles coarse breadcrumbs. Add a quarter of the beaten egg and stir with a fork to bind the mixture together. Roll the pastry dough out on a floured board to a thickness of about 5 mm (¦ inch). Use a biscuit cutter to cut out 10 small circles. Use these to line the bottoms of buttered

tartlet tins and line the sides with strips of dough about 3 cm (1¦ inch) wide. Save all the dough scraps to make the lattice covers. Fill the tartlets with the almond paste. Roll the remaining dough out thinly and cut it into very narrow strips. Use these to make a lattice-work top to each tartlet. Where necessary, trim the top edge of the dough wall and fold it over the filling to obtain a closely fitting edge round the tart.

Brush the lattice-work and the dough edges with the remaining beaten egg and bake the tartlets in a preheated 170°C (325°F or Mark 3) oven for about 30 minutes or until they are golden-brown. While the pastry is still warm, spread the warmed apricot jam over the tartlets. Leave them to cool, then remove them from the tins and cover with glacé icing.

H. H. F. HENDERSON, H. TOORS AND H. M. CALLENBACH
HET NIEUWE KOOKBOEK

Andalusian Easter Cakes

Hornazos de Pascua

Hornazos are traditionally eaten at Easter, and made only at that time of the year.

To make 6 cakes

30 g	baking powder	1 oz
1½ tsp	salt	1½ tsp
¼ litre	hot water	8 fl oz
1 kg	flour	2 to 2½ lb
3 tbsp	olive oil	3 tbsp
500 g	almonds, blanched, roasted and ground	1 lb
25 g	ground cinnamon	¾ oz
2	lemons, rind grated	2
6	eggs, beaten	6
750 g	sugar	1½ lb

Dissolve the baking powder and salt in the water. Little by little add the flour to make a very firm dough.

Gradually pour in the oil and stir until a very smooth dough is obtained. Divide the dough into six pieces. Form these into rounds about the size of saucers, and about 1 cm (½ inch) thick.

Raise the sides of the rounds and form them into cup shapes. Mix the almonds with the cinnamon and lemon rind and place a layer of this mixture in each cup. Pour in a layer of beaten egg and place another layer of the almond mixture on top. Sprinkle sugar over the filling. Bake the cakes in a preheated 180°C (350°F or Mark 4) oven until the cakes are golden, 30 to 45 minutes.

ANA MARIA CALERA
COCINA ANDALUZA

Coppelia Squares

Coppelias

To make 20 squares

125 g	flour	4 oz
65 g	icing sugar	2¼ oz
90 g	butter	3 oz
2	egg yolks	2
125 g	apricot jam	4 oz
10	glacé cherries, halved	10
50 g	pistachio nuts, finely chopped	2 oz

Almond cream		
150 g	marzipan *(page 166)*	5 oz
4	egg yolks	4
75 g	butter, softened	2½ oz
1½ tbsp	kirsch	1½ tbsp

Sift the flour and icing sugar together into a bowl, make a well in the middle and put the butter and egg yolks into the well. Blend the eggs and butter together with your fingertips. With a knife, chop the flour into the butter and egg mixture gradually, until all the flour is incorporated and you have a crumbly dough. Gather the dough into a ball and refrigerate it for 30 minutes.

Roll out the dough and line a buttered and floured rectangular baking tin with it. Spread the dough with 40 g (1½ oz) of the apricot jam. To make the almond cream, mix together the marzipan, egg yolks, softened butter and kirsch; spread this cream over the dough. Bake in a preheated 180°C (350°F or Mark 4) oven for 20 minutes, or until lightly coloured.

When the cake is cooked, remove it from the oven and spread the remaining apricot jam over the surface, then leave it to cool. When it is cold, cut it into small squares. Place a half cherry on top of each square and make a frame round the edges with the finely chopped pistachio nuts.

ACADÉMIE DES GASTRONOMES, ACADÉMIE CULINAIRE DE FRANCE
LA HAUTE CUISINE FRANÇAISE

Almond Slices

Mandelschnitten

To make 16 slices

90 g	butter	3 oz
40 g	sugar	1½ oz
135 g	flour	4½ oz
2 tbsp	apricot or raspberry jam	2 tbsp
125 g	plain chocolate, melted over hot water	4 oz

Almond paste		
90 g	almonds, blanched and chopped	3 oz
125 g	granulated sugar	4 oz
3	egg whites, stiffly beaten	3
½ tsp	flour	½ tsp

Cream the butter and sugar, add the flour and work to a dough. Roll the dough out to about 3 mm (⅛ inch) thick and line a buttered baking sheet with it. Bake in a preheated 180°C (350°F or Mark 4) oven until the top is lightly set (about 5 minutes). Remove from the oven and raise the heat to 200°C (400°F or Mark 6).

To make the almond paste, add the almonds and the sugar to the beaten egg whites and stir over the lowest possible heat in a heavy saucepan until the mixture is light pink—about 5 minutes. Remove from the heat and stir in the flour.

Spread the half-baked pastry with the jam and then with the almond paste. Return the pastry to the oven until golden-brown, about 10 minutes. Cut into squares while still hot, then carefully dip one side of each square into melted chocolate and set on greaseproof paper to dry.

GRETEL BEER
AUSTRIAN COOKING

Small Almond Cakes

To make about 60 cakes

250 g	almonds, blanched	8 oz
3	egg whites	3
350 g	icing sugar	12 oz
125 g	caramelized orange flowers	4 oz
4 tbsp	cream	4 tbsp
500 g	rough-puff dough *(page 163)*	1 lb
8 cl	milk	3 fl oz
1	egg, beaten	1
	glacé icing *(page 166)*, made with 125 g (4 oz) icing sugar	

Beat the almonds to a paste with the egg whites, then add the icing sugar, the caramelized orange flowers and the cream. Roll out the puff dough very thin and cut it into small squares. Put a small portion of the above mixture on each of half of the squares; moisten the edges with milk, cover them with the remaining squares, glaze them with beaten egg, prick them and bake them in a preheated 200°C (400°F or Mark 6) oven for 20 minutes, or until the pastry is golden-brown and risen. When the pastries are cool, ice them with the glacé icing.

FREDERICK BISHOP
THE WIFE'S OWN BOOK OF COOKERY

Almond-Filled Pastries

Gevulde Koeken

To make 8 pastries

200 g	marzipan (*page 166*) made with 100 g (3½ oz) ground almonds	7 oz
240 g	flour	8 oz
	salt	
120 g	castor sugar	4 oz
180 g	butter	6 oz
1	egg, beaten	1
1 tbsp	milk	1 tbsp
4	almonds, blanched and halved	4

Sift the flour and a pinch of salt into a bowl. Add the sugar and rub in the butter until the mixture resembles coarse meal. Add half the egg and mix with a fork to make a soft dough. Roll the dough out on a floured board to a thickness of about 5 mm (¼ inch). Use a biscuit cutter about 10 cm (4 inches) in diameter to cut 16 rounds of dough. Place eight of these on a buttered baking sheet. Soften the marzipan with the milk and spread it over the dough circles, leaving the edge of each round uncovered. Cover with the remaining eight rounds and press the edges together. Place a halved almond in the centre of each and brush the tops with the remaining beaten egg. Bake the pastries in a preheated 170°C (325°F or Mark 3) oven for about 30 minutes or until golden-brown.

H. H. F. HENDERSON, H. TOORS AND H. M. CALLENBACH
HET NIEUWE KOOKBOEK

Marzipan Tartlets for Ladies

Pasticcini alla Dama

This 19th-century recipe used alkermes—a sweet red liqueur spiced with nutmeg, cinnamon and cloves. Cherry brandy or kirsch has been used here instead.

To make about 24 tartlets

500 g	rough-puff dough (*page 163*)	1 lb
2	eggs, beaten	2
90 g	almonds, chopped	3 oz
60 g	castor sugar	2 oz

Marzipan		
500 g	almonds, blanched	1 lb
350 g	castor sugar	12 oz
16	egg yolks	16
½ tsp	vanilla extract	½ tsp
3	egg whites, stiffly beaten	3
60 g	crystallized lime peel, chopped	2 oz
100 g	sultanas, chopped	3½ oz
	cherry brandy or kirsch	

To prepare the marzipan, pound the almonds in a mortar wi h half the sugar. When they are well pounded, pass them through a coarse sieve. Add the remaining sugar. Put the mixture in a large bowl and beat in the egg yolks until the paste increases in volume. Add the vanilla extract and then fold in the beaten egg whites. Finally add the crystallized lime, sultanas and a drop of cherry brandy or kirsch.

Roll out the rough-puff dough and use half of it to line some small copper or tin moulds. Fill each one with the marzipan and cover with a second layer of dough. Brush each one with beaten egg and sprinkle with chopped almonds and sugar. Bake in a preheated 180°C (350°F or Mark 4) oven until the tartlets are golden in colour, about 40 minutes.

GIUSEPPE RIVA
TRATTATO DI CUCINA SEMPLICE PER CONSERVARE LO STOMACO

Maids of Honour

To make about 30 tarts

500 g	rough-puff dough (*page 163*)	1 lb
150 g	icing sugar, sifted	5 oz
3	egg yolks	3
60 g	ground almonds	2 oz
1 tbsp	brandy	1 tbsp
250 g	cottage cheese	8 oz
1	lemon, rind grated, juice of ½ strained	1

Butter and flour deep patty tins. Roll out the dough and stamp into 9 cm (3½ inch) diameter rounds with a cutter. Press into the patty tins.

Mix together the remaining ingredients in a large bowl. Fill the tins to within a fraction of the rim with the cheese mixture, and bake in a preheated 180°C (350°F or Mark 4) oven for 35 to 40 minutes or until puffed and golden on top.

FREDA MURRAY
LACOCK TEA TIME RECIPES

Bakewell Puddings

Special oval tins are used in Bakewell for this pudding, having sloping sides as deep as one's thumb. They are about 15 cm (6 inches) across and look not unlike a tiny hip bath. In default of this, tartlet tins with deep sides might be used.

To make about 24 small puddings

350 g	rough-puff dough (*page 163*)	12 oz
350 g	raspberry jam	12 oz
	Filling	
8	eggs	8
250 g	sugar	8 oz
250 g	butter	8 oz
125 g	ground almonds	4 oz

Line greased tartlet tins with the rough-puff dough and leave them overnight in the refrigerator. Next day, cover the dough with raspberry jam. Prepare a rich filling by beating the eggs and sugar together until they are pale and runny. Then melt the butter and run it in, beating it all together before adding the ground almonds. Pour the mixture into the tins. Bake the puddings in a preheated 200°C (400°F or Mark 6) oven for 20 minutes or until the filling is set.

SHEILA HUTCHINS
ENGLISH RECIPES AND OTHERS FROM SCOTLAND, WALES AND IRELAND

Bakewell Tarts

This is an early 19th-century recipe from Derbyshire.

To make 24 tarts

250 g	shortcrust dough enriched with eggs and sugar (*page 163*)	8 oz
6 tbsp	strawberry jam	6 tbsp
3	eggs	3
1	egg yolk	1
125 g	castor sugar	4 oz
125 g	butter	4 oz

Roll the dough out thinly and line patty tins with it. Cover the bottom of each with a thin layer of strawberry jam. Now make the following mixture. Beat the eggs, the egg yolk and the sugar together. Put the butter into a brass or aluminium pan over a medium heat and let it boil up. Skim it carefully. As it continues to boil, stir into it the beaten egg and sugar mixture; again, beat all well together. Place a thick layer of this mixture over the strawberry jam in each tart and bake in a preheated 200°C (400°F or Mark 6) oven for 15 minutes, until the tarts are delicately brown.

FLORENCE WHITE (EDITOR)
GOOD THINGS IN ENGLAND

Macaroon and Apricot Jam Tarts

Mirlitons

Any other jam of your choice may be substituted for the apricot jam in these tarts.

To make 10 tarts

6	large dry macaroons, crushed to a powder	6
5 tsp	apricot jam	5 tsp
250 g	rough-puff dough (*page 163*)	8 oz
2	eggs	2
125 g	granulated sugar	4 oz
1 tsp	rum	1 tsp
3 tbsp	icing sugar	3 tbsp
60 g	almonds, slivered	2 oz

Line 10 individual deep tartlet moulds with the rough-puff dough, rolled to about 3 mm (⅛ inch) thick. Place half a teaspoon of apricot jam in the bottom of each mould. Beat the eggs with the granulated sugar and rum until light and fluffy. Stir the powdered macaroons into the egg mixture. Blend thoroughly and fill the tartlet moulds approximately two-thirds full with egg mixture. Dust with icing sugar and almonds. Bake in a preheated 200°C (400°F or Mark 6) oven for approximately 20 minutes, or until golden-brown.

DOMINIQUE D'ERMO
THE CHEF'S DESSERT COOKBOOK

Almond Stuffed Rolls

Floyeres

Floyeres will keep for several days.

To make 24 rolls

125 g	blanched almonds or peeled walnuts, ground or crushed	4 oz
1	egg, beaten	1
60 g	sugar	2 oz
6 sheets	ready-made phyllo dough	6 sheets
About 90 g	butter, slightly melted	About 3 oz

	Syrup	
250 g	sugar	8 oz
60 cl	water	1 pint
1 tsp	lemon juice	1 tsp
1	small stick cinnamon	1

Mix the nuts with the egg and sugar. This makes the filling. Cut each sheet of phyllo into four strips and brush with butter. Put a heaped teaspoonful of filling on to one end of each strip and roll up as for a Swiss roll. Place on a buttered baking sheet and bake in a preheated 180°C (350°F or Mark 4) oven until a golden-brown, about 25 minutes.

Put the syrup ingredients into a small shallow pan and bring to the boil, then simmer until the syrup is of a medium thickness. As soon as the rolls are cooked, take them from the oven, put two or three on a perforated spoon and dip them into the still-simmering syrup. Do this once or twice, then put the rolls on to a large platter. When all the rolls have been dipped in the syrup, leave them until they are cold.

ROBIN HOWE
GREEK COOKING

Sweet Ravioli

Tortelli Dolci

Fruit mustard pickles, which may be bought in jars, are a combination of fruits preserved in a sweet mustard sauce. Amaretti are dry, bitter-almond macaroons.

To make about 60 pastries

50 g	dried chestnuts, soaked overnight	2 oz
700 g	fruit mustard pickles	1½ lb
10	large *amaretti*, crumbled	10
17.5 cl	rum or brandy	6 fl oz
	mustard (optional)	
500 g	shortcrust dough enriched with eggs (page 163)	1 lb

Boil the chestnuts in water to cover until they are soft. Drain and sieve them. Mix the chestnut purée with the fruit mustard pickles, *amaretti* and rum or brandy; add a few drops of mustard if the taste of the pickles is not strong enough.

Roll out the dough into a thin sheet. Place teaspoonfuls of the filling on one half of the dough, spacing them evenly in rows. Fold over the other half of the dough, and cut into squares with a ravioli cutter, ensuring that the filling is in the centre of each square and the edges are well sealed. Place on a greased baking sheet and bake in a preheated 180°C (350°F or Mark 4) oven for 15 minutes, or until golden-brown.

FERRUCCIO BOTTI (MASTRO PRESCIUTTO)
GASTRONOMIA PARMENSE

Almond Ravioli

Tortelli

Fruit mustard pickles, which may be bought in jars, are a combination of fruit preserved in a sweet mustard sauce. To cook the chick peas, soak them in cold water for 7 to 8 hours. Discard the soaking water, replace it with fresh cold water, and bring to the boil. Simmer for 2 to 3 hours, until the peas are very soft, then drain.

To make 80 to 90 pastries

100 g	almonds, blanched	3½ oz
50 g	bitter almonds, blanched	2 oz
200 g	walnuts	7 oz
200 g	cooked chick peas, sieved	7 oz
200 g	fruit mustard pickles	7 oz
200 g	orange marmalade	7 oz
100 g	pine-nuts	3½ oz
	oil for deep frying (optional)	

Lemon dough

1	lemon, rind grated, juice strained	1
500 g	flour, sifted	1 lb
200 g	butter, cut into pieces	7 oz
200 g	sugar	7 oz
5	egg yolks	5
8 cl	brandy	3 fl oz
About 8 cl	white wine	About 3 fl oz

Chop the almonds, bitter almonds and walnuts together very finely. Mix with the remaining filling ingredients.

For the dough, rub together the flour, butter and sugar until crumbly. Add the egg yolks, lemon rind and juice, and the brandy and work well together, adding white wine as necessary to make a smooth dough.

Roll out the dough and place teaspoonfuls of the filling at equal intervals over half the dough. Fold over the other half of the dough and cut into squares with a ravioli cutter, making sure that a spoonful of filling is in the centre of each square. Place on greased baking sheets and bake in a preheated 180°C (350°F or Mark 4) oven for 15 minutes. Alternatively, deep fry the pastries in hot oil; if you intend to fry the pastries, the dough should be very firm.

FERRUCCIO BOTTI (MASTRO PRESCIUTTO)
GASTRONOMIA PARMENSE

Kataifi

Kataifi is bought by the kilo and is to be found in Greek delicatessens. To watch *kataifi* being made is a fascinating experience. A batter of flour and water is poured into a hopper which feeds a fine stream on to a very hot rotating turntable in ever-widening circles, from which the operator scoops up loops of the thread-like *kataifi* with his hand at just the right moment before it becomes overcooked and brittle. *Kataifi* looks very like shredded wheat, which can in fact be used when fresh *kataifi* is unobtainable. In that case, the rolls of shredded wheat should be dipped in milk before being used.

To make 20 squares

500 g	*kataifi*	1 lb
125 g	walnuts and almonds, chopped	4 oz
125 g	butter, melted	4 oz
90 g	sugar	3 oz
1 tsp	ground cinnamon	1 tsp
	Syrup	
250 g	sugar	8 oz
¼ litre	water	8 fl oz
150 g	honey	5 oz
1	lemon, juice strained	1

Line a greased baking tin with half the *kataifi*. Mix together the nuts, melted butter, sugar and cinnamon. Spread this mixture in the tin and cover it with the rest of the *kataifi*. Mark the top into squares and bake in a preheated 180°C (350°F or Mark 4) oven for about 20 minutes, or until golden.

Heat the syrup ingredients together to boiling point. Allow the syrup to cool a little and pour it over the *kataifi*. When it is well soaked in syrup, cut it into squares for serving.

JOYCE M. STUBBS
THE HOME BOOK OF GREEK COOKERY

Baklava

Baklava is rich and sticky, and very delicious when made a day or two before it is required.

To make 20 squares

250 g	butter	8 oz
250 g	sugar	8 oz
¼ litre	hot water	8 fl oz
250 g	walnuts, chopped	8 oz
500 g	ready-made phyllo dough	1 lb
1 tsp	ground cinnamon	1 tsp

	Syrup	
250 g	sugar	8 oz
350 g	honey	12 oz
¼ litre	water	8 fl oz
1	lemon, juice strained	1

Heat half of the butter with the sugar and hot water. Add the chopped nuts. Melt the remaining butter separately. Line a well-buttered baking tin with three or four sheets of phyllo, brushing each one with the melted butter. Spread a thin layer of nut filling on the dough, sprinkle with cinnamon and cover with two more sheets of buttered phyllo. Continue in this way, using alternate layers of nuts and phyllo. Tuck the ends and sides in to contain the filling.

Cover the last layer of nuts with three or four sheets of phyllo, each one brushed liberally with melted butter. Brush the top with melted butter and score it into squares or diamonds with a sharp knife. Bake in a preheated 180°C (350°F or Mark 4) oven until golden and crisp, about 30 minutes.

Boil all the syrup ingredients together for 10 minutes. Pour the hot syrup over the hot baklava. Leave it to cool before cutting into pieces for serving.

JOYCE M. STUBBS
THE HOME BOOK OF GREEK COOKERY

Wine and Walnut Filled Hamantaschen

The Jewish feast of Purim commemorates the downfall of Haman, the vizier of King Ahasuerus (Artaxerxes II) who formulated his own "Final Solution" by planning the massacre of the entire Jewish population of Persia. Haman ended up on the gallows he had prepared for his enemies, and his name is perpetuated in a variety of unusual cakes and sweetmeats. By tradition these are three-cornered—some say like Haman's ears, others like his purse which he planned to fill with Jewish gold.

To make 56 hamantaschen

500 g	flour	1 lb
2 tsp	baking powder	2 tsp
60 g	icing sugar	2 oz
300 g	butter	10 oz
2	egg yolks, lightly beaten with 4 tbsp water	2
1	egg white, beaten until foamy	1
	castor sugar	

125 g	walnuts	4 oz
125 g	stoned dates	4 oz
250 g	mixed sultanas, currants and raisins	8 oz
1 tbsp	sweet white wine or sherry	1 tbsp
1 tbsp	golden syrup, warmed	1 tbsp
$\frac{1}{2}$	lemon, rind grated, juice strained	$\frac{1}{2}$
1 tbsp	apricot jam	1 tbsp
$\frac{1}{2}$ tsp	ground cinnamon	$\frac{1}{2}$ tsp

Mix all the ingredients for the filling together. To make the dough, mix the flour, baking powder and icing sugar. Rub in the butter until the mixture resembles coarse breadcrumbs. Sprinkle with the egg yolks and water and gather the mixture into a ball. Chill the dough for 30 minutes. Roll out the dough 5 mm ($\frac{1}{4}$ inch) thick and cut it into 7.5 cm (3 inch) circles. Put a spoonful of filling on each dough circle, then draw up the edges to form a pyramid and pinch them firmly together. Brush the *Hamantaschen* with the beaten egg white and sprinkle with castor sugar. Bake in a preheated 220°C (425°F or Mark 7) oven for 15 minutes or until the *Hamantaschen* are a rich brown colour.

EVELYN ROSE
THE COMPLETE INTERNATIONAL JEWISH COOKBOOK

Kichel Hamantaschen

The quantities given for each fruit filling make enough for the whole quantity of dough. If you want to make a mixed batch of Hamantaschen, *using two or three fillings, you should reduce the filling quantities accordingly.*

To make about 24 Hamantaschen

2	eggs, well beaten	2
125 g	castor sugar	5 oz
10 cl	oil	4 fl oz
1 tsp	vanilla extract	1 tsp
$\frac{1}{2}$	orange, rind grated	$\frac{1}{2}$
About 300 g	flour, sifted with 1$\frac{1}{2}$ tsp baking powder	About 12 oz

Apple filling (optional)

500 g	apples, peeled, cored and sliced	1 lb
75 g	sugar	3 oz
1	lemon, rind grated, juice strained	1

Apricot filling (optional)

200 g	dried apricots	8 oz
150 g	honey	5 oz
2 tsp	grated orange rind	2 tsp
$\frac{1}{2}$	orange, juice strained	$\frac{1}{2}$

Prune filling (optional)

200 g	prunes	8 oz
75 g	raisins	3 oz
50 g	walnuts	2 oz
1	lemon, rind grated, juice strained	1
100 g	sugar	4 oz

To make the apple filling, butter a pan and put in the apples, sugar and lemon rind and juice in layers. Cover the pan and cook gently until the apples are tender. Uncover the pan and continue to cook the apples to drive off any excess liquid. Cool the apple filling before using.

To make the apricot filling, soak the apricots overnight in enough water to cover them. Next day, drain the apricots well and put them through the coarse blade of a food mill. Add the honey, orange rind and orange juice.

To make the prune filling, soak the prunes and raisins overnight. Remove the stones from the prunes. Chop the fruit with the walnuts, lemon rind, lemon juice and sugar, or alternatively use a food mill.

Reserve a little beaten egg for gilding the *Hamantaschen*. Whisk the sugar, oil and flavourings into the eggs. Finally, stir in enough flour to make a rollable dough. On a floured board, roll the dough out 5 mm ($\frac{1}{4}$ inch) thick and cut it into 7.5 cm (3 inch) rounds. Place a spoonful of your chosen filling in the centre of each round, then draw up the sides to form a pyramid, and pinch the edges firmly together. Brush the tops with the reserved beaten egg. Bake the *Hamantaschen* in a preheated 180°C (350°F or Mark 4) oven for 30 minutes.

EVELYN ROSE
THE COMPLETE INTERNATIONAL JEWISH COOKBOOK

Date-Walnut Turnovers

To make about 15 turnovers

175 g	stoned dates, finely cut	6 oz
30 g	walnuts, chopped	1 oz
$\frac{1}{8}$ tsp	salt	$\frac{1}{8}$ tsp
$\frac{1}{2}$ tsp	grated orange rind	$\frac{1}{2}$ tsp
4 tbsp	orange juice	4 tbsp
500 g	shortcrust dough (*page 163*)	1 lb
	Orange glaze	
150 g	icing sugar, sifted	5 oz
$\frac{1}{8}$ tsp	salt	$\frac{1}{8}$ tsp
1 tsp	grated orange rind	1 tsp
$1\frac{1}{2}$ to 2 tbsp	orange juice	$1\frac{1}{2}$ to 2 tbsp

Combine the dates, walnuts, salt, orange rind and juice; stir to blend. Roll the dough out 3 mm ($\frac{1}{8}$ inch) thick and cut it into 11 cm ($4\frac{1}{2}$ inch) circles. Place about a tablespoon of the date mixture on each dough circle. Fold over, seal the edges by pressing with a fork, and prick the tops. Bake the turnovers in a preheated 230°C (450°F or Mark 8) oven until they are brown, about 12 minutes.

For the glaze, combine the icing sugar, salt and orange rind in a bowl. Blend in orange juice until the mixture has the consistency of a glaze. Spread the glaze on the turnovers while they are still slightly warm.

NELL B. NICHOLS (EDITOR)
FARM JOURNAL'S COMPLETE PIE COOKBOOK

Little Cakes

Pastelitos

Pastelitos should be about as thick as the little finger. Any kind of dried fruit or combination of dried fruits can be used. Raisins may be added to the apricot pulp.

To make 25 to 30 cakes

500 g	dried apricots, soaked overnight	1 lb
100 g	granulated sugar	$3\frac{1}{2}$ oz
250 g	shortcrust dough (*page 163*)	8 oz
25 g	castor sugar	1 oz
1 tsp	ground cinnamon	1 tsp

Cook the apricots until they are soft enough to pass through a sieve; or mash them well. Add the granulated sugar to the pulp and cook again until very thick. Allow to cool.

Roll out half the dough and place it on a baking sheet. Spread the fruit mixture on this and cover with the rest of the

dough. Press the edges together. Sprinkle with a mixture of the castor sugar and cinnamon. Mark into small squares before baking, and prick each square with a fork. Bake in a preheated 220°C (425°F or Mark 7) oven for 20 minutes. Cool and cut as marked.

ANNA MACMIADHACHÁIN
SPANISH REGIONAL COOKERY

Moons

Lune

The original recipe for these famous pastries, made by the nuns of the Sanctissima Annunciata Convent, Paternò, was written in 1819. Another version substitutes sultanas for the crystallized fruit in the filling.

To make about 80 pastries

800 g	flour	1 lb 10 oz
250 g	sugar	8 oz
250 g	lard	8 oz
3	eggs	3
200 g	honey	7 oz
	Dried fruit filling	
75 g	raisins, finely chopped	$2\frac{1}{2}$ oz
75 g	dried figs, finely chopped	$2\frac{1}{2}$ oz
125 g	honey	4 oz
40 g	crystallized orange, lemon and tangerine peel, finely chopped	$1\frac{1}{2}$ oz
30 g	pine-nuts, chopped	1 oz
30 g	walnuts, chopped	1 oz
40 g	almonds, blanched and chopped	$1\frac{1}{2}$ oz
2 tsp	ground cinnamon	2 tsp

Mix together the flour, sugar, lard, eggs and honey to make a firm dough. Roll it out thinly and cut it into rounds with a biscuit cutter. Mix together the ingredients for the filling, and place a small mound of filling on one side of each round of dough. Fold over the other half of the dough and press the edges together firmly. Bake in a preheated 180°C (350°F or Mark 4) oven for 25 minutes or until the pastries are golden.

PINO CORRENTI
IL LIBRO D'ORO DELLA CUCINA E DEI VINI DI SICILIA

All Fruit Mazurka

Mazurek Bakaliowy

To steam raisins, place them in a vegetable steamer and put this, covered, over boiling water for 10 minutes.

To make 48 squares

150 g	butter, softened	5 oz
300 g	flour, sifted	10 oz
90 g	icing sugar	3 oz
2 tsp	baking powder	2 tsp
1	egg	1
1	egg yolk	1
3 tbsp	soured cream	3 tbsp

Dried fruit topping

90 g	candied orange peel, chopped	3 oz
90 g	dried figs, thinly sliced	3 oz
90 g	stoned dates, thinly sliced	3 oz
90 g	dried apricots, thinly sliced	3 oz
90 g	raisins, steamed	3 oz
60 g	walnuts, chopped	2 oz
90 g	almonds, blanched and chopped	3 oz
1	egg	1
1	egg yolk	1
75 g	icing sugar	2½ oz
1 tbsp	lemon juice	1 tbsp
1 tsp	vanilla extract	1 tsp
75 g	butter, melted	2½ oz
60 g	ground almonds	2 oz
2 tbsp	breadcrumbs	2 tbsp

To make the dough, cut the butter into the flour with a knife, then rub it in with your fingertips. Add the icing sugar and baking powder and mix. Add the rest of the ingredients and knead the dough. Place the dough in a covered dish and refrigerate it for 30 minutes.

Roll the dough out thinly and place it on a buttered 38 by 30 cm (15 by 12 inches) baking sheet. Spread the dough with your fingers to cover the sheet. Bake in a preheated 190°C (375°F or Mark 5) oven for 10 minutes. Remove from the oven and allow to cool slightly.

Mix together the fruits and nuts for the topping and arrange them over the pastry base. Beat the egg and the egg yolk with the icing sugar for 5 minutes. Add the rest of the ingredients. Mix well. Pour this mixture evenly over the cake and return it to the oven for another 15 minutes. Cool the cake and cut it into squares.

ALINA ZERANSKA
THE ART OF POLISH COOKING

Devonshire Mint Cakes

The author suggests substituting lard for half the quantity of butter in the rough-puff dough, and moistening the dough with a squeeze of lemon juice as well as a little cold water.

To make about 30 cakes

1½ tbsp	chopped fresh mint	1½ tbsp
850 g	rough-puff dough (*page 163*)	1¾ lb
60 g	candied peel, chopped	2 oz
60 g	butter	2 oz
350 g	currants	12 oz
150 g	castor sugar	5 oz
1	egg, yolk separated from white, white lightly beaten	1

Roll out the dough and cut it into rounds. Mix together the candied peel, butter, currants, 125 g (4 oz) of castor sugar, the mint and the egg yolk. Put a little of the mixture on to each dough circle, draw the edges together and roll into round flat cakes. Brush with white of egg, sprinkle with a little more castor sugar and bake in a preheated 220°C (425°F or Mark 7) oven for 15 minutes.

RIA SYSONBY
LADY SYSONBY'S COOK BOOK

Eccles Cakes

To make 12 cakes

500 g	rough-puff dough (*page 163*)	1 lb
125 g	currants	4 oz
150 g	castor sugar	5 oz
60 g	candied peel, chopped	2 oz
60 g	butter	2 oz
1	egg yolk	1
2 tbsp	milk	2 tbsp

Roll out the dough and cut it into 10 cm (4 inch) rounds. Mix the currants, 125 g (4 oz) of the castor sugar and the candied peel in a basin. Divide this mixture evenly on the rounds, and put a small lump of butter on top of each. Take hold of the dough all round the edges and close in the centre, being very careful to seal the dough so that the filling cannot get out. Roll with a rolling pin gently; turn over and roll again. Beat together the egg yolk, the remaining sugar and the milk and brush over the cakes with this mixture. Bake on the top shelf of a preheated 200°C (400°F or Mark 6) oven for about 15 minutes or until golden.

MRS. H. G. HALDANE (EDITOR)
A PRACTICAL COOKERY BOOK

Curd Cheese Cakes

You can substitute 250 g (8 oz) of commercially made curd cheese for the curds made by the method described here.

To make 36 cakes

1.25 litres	milk	2 pints
15 cl	buttermilk or 2 tsp lemon juice	$\frac{1}{4}$ pint
125 g	butter, softened	4 oz
125 g	sugar	4 oz
4	egg yolks	4
1	egg white, stiffly beaten	1
$\frac{1}{4}$ tsp	nutmeg, grated	$\frac{1}{4}$ tsp
60 g	currants	2 oz
1	lemon, rind grated	1
500 g	shortcrust dough (*page 163*)	1 lb

Put the milk into a pan and heat it. When it is quite hot, remove the pan from the heat, add the buttermilk or lemon juice and stir the mixture slowly, cutting it across with the spoon. When it begins to turn, stop stirring; strain when the whey is quite clear, and allow the curds to become firm. They should weigh 250 g (8 oz).

Put the curds into a basin and add the butter; mix well. Add the sugar and mix well, then add the egg yolks and white. Stir in the nutmeg, currants and lemon rind. Beat all thoroughly.

Roll out the dough and use it to line patty tins. Put a teaspoonful of curd mixture into each. Bake in a preheated 180°C (350°F or Mark 4) oven for about 15 minutes.

MRS. H. G. HALDANE (EDITOR)
A PRACTICAL COOKERY BOOK

Jam Turnovers

Ravioli di Marmellata

To make 12 turnovers

20 cl	jam	7 fl oz
250 g	flour	8 oz
125 g	sugar	4 oz
	salt	
125 g	butter	4 oz
3	eggs, beaten	3
$\frac{1}{2}$	lemon, juice strained	$\frac{1}{2}$
	icing sugar, sifted	

To prepare the pastry dough, sift the flour, sugar and a pinch of salt into a bowl. Rub in the butter until the mixture resembles coarse crumbs. Add two of the beaten eggs and the lemon juice and mix with a fork until the mixture coheres.

Gather into a ball and chill in the refrigerator for 15 minutes. Roll the dough out to a thickness of 5 mm ($\frac{1}{4}$ inch).

With a biscuit cutter, cut the dough into rounds 8 cm (3 inches) in diameter. Put a good spoonful of jam on half of each round and fold the other half over, pressing down on the edges. Place the turnovers on a buttered and floured baking sheet and brush with the remaining egg. Bake in a preheated 200°C (400°F or Mark 6) oven for 15 minutes or until browned. Serve hot or cold, sprinkled with icing sugar.

LEONE BOSI (EDITOR)
DOLCI PER UN ANNO

Rich Jam Slices

To make 8 squares or 16 triangles

3 tbsp	jam or marmalade	3 tbsp
250 g	flour	8 oz
	salt	
1 tsp	baking powder	1 tsp
60 g	sugar	2 oz
60 g	lard	2 oz
60 g	butter	2 oz
1	egg, beaten	1
	milk	

Sift the flour, a pinch of salt, the baking powder and the sugar together; then rub in the fats lightly, and mix to a stiff paste with the beaten egg. Add a little milk, if necessary, to make the dough cohere. Divide into two parts; roll out thinly, both to the same size, about 20 by 10 cm (8 by 4 inches).

Cover one piece of dough with the jam or marmalade. Place the other piece on top and nip the edges together with your fingers or a fork. Place the filled rectangles of dough on a greased baking sheet and bake in a preheated 180°C (350°F or Mark 4) oven for 15 to 20 minutes or until browned. When cool, cut into dainty squares or triangles.

MRS. H. G. HALDANE (EDITOR)
A PRACTICAL COOKERY BOOK

Lemon Curd Tarts

The technique of blind-baking is shown on page 52.

If an even richer curd is desired, use all egg yolks—but 16 in all will be required for these ingredients.

To make about 48 tarts

500 g	shortcrust dough (*page 163*)	1 lb

Lemon curd		
6	lemons, rind grated, juice strained	6
150 g	butter	5 oz
500 g	sugar	1 lb
6	large eggs	6

Make some small pastry cases in buttered individual tartlet tins. Bake these blind in a preheated 190°C (375°F or Mark 5) oven for about 10 minutes. Allow them to cool.

Meanwhile prepare the curd. Put the lemon rind in a jar and stand it in a pan of water, or use the top of a double boiler with water in the bottom. Add the lemon juice, butter and sugar and stir, heating gently, until the sugar has melted. Then let the mixture cool slightly before adding the eggs. Place over a gentle heat and cook slowly, stirring well, until the mixture will coat the back of the wooden spoon lightly. Take care to stir the mixture very thoroughly and to heat it very gently until it thickens, otherwise the egg will scramble and make the mixture curdled and lumpy.

Fill the cold pastry cases with the curd.

SHEILA HUTCHINS
ENGLISH RECIPES AND OTHERS FROM SCOTLAND, WALES AND IRELAND

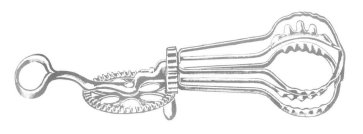

Lemon and Honey Pasties

Pastisets

These pasties are a speciality of Cherta, near Tarragona.

To make 80 to 90 pasties		
1 litre	olive oil	1¾ pints
¼ litre	sweet white wine	8 fl oz
15 cl	eau-de-vie or brandy	¼ pint
About 2 kg	flour	About 4 lb
	sugar	
Lemon and honey filling		
12	lemons, rind grated	12
1 kg	thick honey	2 to 2½ lb

To make the lemon and honey filling, soak the lemon rind in cold water for two to three days, changing the water several times. When the rind no longer tastes bitter, drain it and mix it with the honey. Place in a heavy saucepan and simmer the mixture slowly for 1½ hours.

Prepare the dough as follows: mix the oil, wine and *eau-de-vie* or brandy and add enough flour to make a compact dough. Knead the dough a little and let it rest for 15 minutes. Take pieces of the dough and shape them into small rounds, about 8 cm (3 inches) in diameter and 1 cm (½ inch) thick. Put a teaspoonful of lemon and honey filling in the centre of each round and fold it to make a half-moon shape. Bake these pasties in a preheated 180°C (350°F or Mark 4) oven for 35 minutes or until they are golden, then take them from the oven and sprinkle them with sugar.

COCINA REGIONAL ESPAÑOLA

Honey Ring-Cakes

Kaghak Tal-Ghasel

This is a Maltese recipe. Honey ring-cakes are made all the year round, but they are especially associated with Christmas.

To make 4 cakes		
30 g	butter	1 oz
250 g	flour	8 oz
	salt	
125 g	semolina	4 oz
About 17.5 cl	water	About 6 fl oz
Honey filling		
250 g	honey	8 oz
15 cl	water	¼ pint
1	orange or lemon, rind grated	1
	ground cloves	
250 g	semolina	8 oz

To make the pastry dough, rub the butter into the flour. Add a pinch of salt, the semolina and enough water to make a firm dough. Leave the dough to rest in the refrigerator.

To make the filling, put the honey, water, grated rind and a pinch of ground cloves into a saucepan. Cook, stirring all the while, until almost boiling. Add the semolina, continue to stir and cook until the mixture is thick.

Cut the dough into four pieces and roll each piece into a strip 25 by 10 cm (10 by 4 inches). Spread some filling along one long side of each piece of dough. Fold the other side over to cover the filling. Join the edges and shape into a ring. After shaping, cut a slit on the top of each ring-cake so that, during baking, the filling will rise, burst through the slit and decorate the cake. Bake in a preheated 180°C (350°F or Mark 4) oven for 30 minutes or until brown.

ROBIN HOWE
COOKING FROM THE COMMONWEALTH

Little Dukes

Petits Ducs

To make 16 cakes

25 g	flour	1 oz
60 g	ground almonds	2 oz
1 tsp	vanilla sugar	1 tsp
	salt	
45 g	butter	1½ oz
1	egg yolk	1
	granulated sugar	

Cake batter

125 g	sugar	4 oz
4	eggs	4
125 g	flour	4 oz
125 g	butter, melted	4 oz

Chocolate cream

250 g	plain chocolate	8 oz
30 g	butter	1¼ oz
12.5 cl	single cream	4 fl oz

To make the pastry, sift the flour, ground almonds, the vanilla sugar and a pinch of salt on to a work surface or into a large bowl. Add the butter and rub it in. Knead it all into a firm dough with the egg yolk. Roll out the dough 7 to 8 mm (⅓ inch) thick and cut it into 32 rounds, 7.5 cm (3 inches) in diameter. Place the rounds on a floured baking sheet and cook them in a preheated 180°C (350°F or Mark 4) oven for 10 minutes, or until firm but not coloured. Leave them to get completely cold before removing them from the baking sheet.

To make the cake batter, put the sugar and eggs into a copper bowl and place the bowl over a pan of gently simmering water. Whisk them together until the volume has increased by one-third, and until the mixture falls in a thick ribbon from the whisk and is lukewarm. Remove the bowl from the saucepan and continue to whisk the batter until it is completely cold. Sift the flour over the batter and stir it in by cutting through the mixture with the edge of a spatula, then add the melted butter and fold it in. Butter and flour 16 small straight-sided individual cake moulds, 7.5 cm (3 inches) in diameter and half fill them with batter. Bake the cakes in a preheated 180°C (350°F or Mark 4) oven for 20 to 25 minutes.

Melt the chocolate gently over hot water, then pour it into a bowl. Stir in the butter and then the cream. Leave the mixture to cool a little before using it.

To assemble the cakes, lightly spread some chocolate cream over half the pastry rounds. Place a little sponge cake on top of each one and spread more chocolate cream over its top. Put a second pastry round on top of the sponge cake. Lightly cover the sides of the assembly with chocolate cream

and roll each cake in granulated sugar so that the sugar crystals stick to the sides. Pipe rosettes of chocolate cream on top, using a piping bag with a fluted nozzle.

ACADÉMIE DES GASTRONOMES, ACADÉMIE CULINAIRE DE FRANCE
LA HAUTE CUISINE FRANÇAISE

Chocolate Mazurka

Mazurek Czekoladowy

To make 48 squares

150 g	butter, softened	5 oz
300 g	flour, sifted	10 oz
90 g	icing sugar	3 oz
2 tsp	baking powder	2 tsp
1	egg	1
1	egg yolk	1
3 tbsp	soured cream	3 tbsp

Chocolate spread

250 g	chocolate	8 oz
4 tbsp	single cream	4 tbsp
4	egg yolks	4
300 g	sugar	10 oz
1 tbsp	flour	1 tbsp
12	almonds, blanched and chopped	12

To make the dough, cut the butter into the flour with a knife, then rub it in with your fingertips. Add the icing sugar and baking powder and mix. Add the rest of the ingredients and knead the dough. Place the dough in a covered dish and refrigerate it for 30 minutes.

Roll the dough out thinly, and place it on a buttered 38 by 30 cm (15 by 12 inch) baking sheet. Spread the dough with your fingers to cover the baking sheet. Bake in a preheated 190°C (375°F or Mark 5) oven for 15 minutes. Remove from the oven and allow to cool for a little. Reduce the oven heat to 150°C (300°F or Mark 2).

To make the chocolate spread, melt the chocolate with the cream in a warm oven or in a bowl over a pan of hot water. Beat the egg yolks with the sugar until fluffy, then stir in the flour. Mix the melted chocolate with the egg mixture and add the almonds. Spread the chocolate mixture over the slightly cooled pastry. Return the baking sheet to the oven and bake for 10 minutes. Cool the cake, then cut it into small squares and remove the squares from the baking sheet with a knife.

ALINA ZERAŃSKA
THE ART OF POLISH COOKING

Linser Cream Tarts

Fine Linser

To make 12 tarts

250 g	flour	8 oz
90 g	sugar	3 oz
½ tsp	salt	½ tsp
2	egg yolks	2
1 tsp	vanilla extract	1 tsp
175 g	butter, cut into pieces	6 oz
½ litre	vanilla-flavoured pastry cream (*page 166*), made with double cream, chilled	16 fl oz

Sift the flour, sugar and salt together into a bowl or on to a pastry board. Make a well in the middle. Place the egg yolks, vanilla and butter pieces in the well. With your hands, work all the ingredients together until the mixture is smooth and thoroughly blended. Wrap it in greaseproof paper and chill in the refrigerator for 1 hour.

Roll out two-thirds of the dough 3 mm (⅛ inch) thick and use it to line small buttered individual moulds or buttered tartlet tins. With floured hands, press the dough into the moulds or tins, lining them completely. Trim off excess dough and roll again to the same thickness. (If the dough is difficult to handle, chill again; also place the tins in the refrigerator while the excess dough is chilling. All the dough must be kept as cold as possible.)

Place a little of the chilled pastry cream filling into each dough-lined tin. Roll out the remaining dough and use it to cover the tarts. Crimp the edges together. Bake in a preheated 200°C (400°F or Mark 6) oven for 8 to 10 minutes, or until golden-brown. Cool the tarts in their tins for about 5 minutes, remove them carefully and then allow them to cool completely before serving.

NIKA STANDEN HAZELTON
THE ART OF DANISH COOKING

Pont-Neufs

The technique of making pont-neufs *is shown on page 62.*

To make 20 to 25 tartlets

250 g	shortcrust dough enriched with eggs (*page 163*)	8 oz
125 g	pastry cream (*page 166*)	4 oz
125 g	choux dough (*page 162*)	4 oz
	icing sugar	
	redcurrant jelly	

Roll out the shortcrust dough and use it to line small tartlet tins; prick the bottoms with a fork. Fill them up to the top with a well-blended mixture of the pastry cream and the choux dough. Roll out the shortcrust dough scraps and cut them into thin strips. Lay two of these strips on top of each tart in the shape of a cross. Bake the tartlets in a preheated 220°C (425°F or Mark 7) oven for 10 to 12 minutes, then dust them with icing sugar. Brush two opposite segments between the crossed strips of pastry with redcurrant jelly.

PIERRE MENGELATTE, WALTER BICKEL AND ALBIN ABÉLANET
BUFFETS AND RECEPTIONS

Polkas

The technique of making polkas is shown on page 62 where a larger version is demonstrated. A liqueur such as cointreau may be used instead of vanilla in the pastry cream.

To make 20 to 25 pastries

250 g	shortcrust dough enriched with eggs (*page 163*)	8 oz
125 g	choux dough (*page 162*)	4 oz
1	egg, beaten	1
200 g	vanilla-flavoured pastry cream (*page 166*)	7 oz
	icing sugar	

Roll out the pastry dough to a thickness of 2 to 3 mm (about ⅛ inch). Cut out rounds with a fluted cutter, 2 to 3 cm (about 1 inch) in diameter. Place the rounds of pastry on a greased baking sheet and prick them with a fork. Using a piping bag fitted with a small, plain nozzle, pipe a ring of choux dough round the edge of each one. Brush the pastries with the beaten egg. Bake in a preheated 220°C (425°F or Mark 7) oven for 10 to 12 minutes. Allow the pastries to cool, then fill the centres with the vanilla-flavoured pastry cream. Dust the tops with icing sugar and caramelize the sugar with a red-hot skewer.

PIERRE MENGELATTE, WALTER BICKEL AND ALBIN ABÉLANET
BUFFETS AND RECEPTIONS

Praline-Flavoured Choux with Cherry Sauce

Choux Pralinés Montmorency

The technique of making praline is shown on page 12. To poach morello cherries, bring 15 cl (¼ pint) of medium sugar syrup (page 6) to a simmer. Gently tip the cherries into the syrup and cook them for about 5 minutes, or until tender.

To make about 30 choux balls

4 tbsp	praline	4 tbsp
350 g	choux dough (*page 162*)	12 oz
1	egg, beaten	1
125 g	almonds, blanched and chopped	4 oz
30 cl	double cream	½ pint
	icing sugar	
	Cherry sauce	
250 g	tinned or poached morello cherries, drained and stoned, juice reserved	8 oz
2 tsp	arrowroot	2 tsp
17.5 cl	red wine	6 fl oz
3 tbsp	redcurrant jelly	3 tbsp
1	orange, rind grated	1

To prepare the cherry sauce, stir a little cherry juice into the arrowroot to make a thin, smooth cream. Pour this into the remaining juice and stir together over a gentle heat until the juice thickens. Allow it to cool. Meantime, heat the red wine to reduce it to half its quantity, add the redcurrant jelly and dissolve it slowly. Add this to the thickened cherry juice and, when it is quite cold, stir in the cherries and the orange rind.

Pipe or spoon out mounds (about 2 teaspoonfuls each) of the choux dough on to dampened baking sheets. Brush them lightly with the beaten egg and sprinkle them with the chopped almonds. Bake in a preheated 190°C (375°F or Mark 5) oven, increasing the heat to 200°C (400°F or Mark 6) after about 10 minutes, once the dough has started to "puff" well. Bake for a total of 25 to 30 minutes, or until the choux balls are brown and crisp. Prick the side of each ball and leave them to cool on a rack. Whip the cream and fold in 2 tablespoons of the praline. Fill the balls with this. Pile the balls up in a dish for serving, dust them with icing sugar and sprinkle them with the rest of the praline. Serve them with the cherry sauce.

ROSEMARY HUME AND MURIEL DOWNES
CORDON BLEU DESSERTS AND PUDDINGS

Orange Cream Salambos

Salambos à l'Orange

The technique of making caramel is shown on page 7.

To make about 20 salambos

350 g	choux dough (*page 162*)	12 oz
175 g	castor sugar	6 oz
1	orange	1
6 to 8	sugar lumps	6 to 8
	rum or brandy (optional)	
30 cl	double cream	½ pint

Pipe out the choux dough in mounds the size of a golf ball on to a dampened baking sheet, using a piping bag with a small plain nozzle. Place the choux balls in a preheated 190°C (375°F or Mark 5) oven and, once the dough has started to puff well, after about 10 minutes, increase the heat to 200°C (400°F or Mark 6). Bake until the balls are brown and crisp, about 25 to 30 minutes in all. Prick the side of each one to release the steam and cool them on a rack.

When they are cold, prepare the caramel topping. Place the castor sugar in a small heavy pan and cook it slowly over a very low heat to a rich brown colour; then dip the top of each choux ball in the caramel.

Rub the lumps of sugar over the orange to remove all the zest. Squeeze a little of the juice out of the orange and pound or crush the sugar lumps with it to give a rich syrup. A little rum or brandy can be added if liked. Whip the cream lightly, adding the orange syrup by degrees, until the cream holds its shape. Fill the salambos with the orange cream and serve.

ROSEMARY HUME AND MURIEL DOWNES
CORDON BLEU DESSERTS AND PUDDINGS

Othello Buns with Egg-Snow

Othellokager med Ràcreme

One or two drops of vanilla extract can be used in the egg-snow in place of the vanilla seeds. The technique of piping a filling into choux buns is shown on page 60.

To make about 20 buns

125 g	butter	4 oz
30 g	sugar	1 oz
	salt	
30 cl	water	½ pint
150 g	flour	5 oz
4	eggs	4
	chocolate-flavoured fondant icing (*page 165*)	

	Egg-snow	
2	egg yolks	2
1 tbsp	icing sugar	1 tbsp
$\frac{1}{2}$	vanilla pod, seeds scraped out	$\frac{1}{2}$
30 cl	double cream, stiffly whipped	$\frac{1}{2}$ pint

Boil up the butter, sugar, a pinch of salt and the water in a small saucepan, sprinkle the flour in and beat up the dough until it is smooth and firm and slides easily from the whisk and the sides of the saucepan. Let the dough cool slightly before beating in the eggs, one at a time. Beat well between each addition so as to make the dough light and fluffy. Place the dough in a piping bag and squirt small portions out on to a greased baking sheet. Put the sheet in a preheated 220°C (425°F or Mark 7) oven and bake for 10 minutes; then reduce the heat to 170°C (325°F or Mark 3) and bake for another 20 minutes or until the buns are completely dry and light.

For the egg-snow, beat the egg yolks with the icing sugar until the mixture is very thick. Beat in the vanilla seeds. Stir in the whipped cream. Fill the cooled pastries with egg-snow and glaze them with chocolate icing.

GRETE GRUMME
DANISH FOOD

German Choux Puffs

Windbeutel

Instead of using a piping bag, you can form these puffs with a tablespoon. Dip the spoon in cold water each time you take a mound of dough and place it on the baking sheet.

	To make about 70 puffs	
$\frac{1}{4}$ litre	water	8 fl oz
80 g	butter	$2\frac{1}{2}$ oz
$\frac{1}{2}$	lemon, rind grated	$\frac{1}{2}$
	salt	
200 g	flour	7 oz
4	eggs	4
$\frac{1}{2}$ litre	double cream	16 fl oz
60 g	castor sugar	2 oz
	icing sugar	

Place the water, butter, lemon rind and a pinch of salt in a saucepan and bring to the boil. Sift the flour on to a piece of paper. Pour the flour, all at once, into the boiling mixture, and immediately beat the mixture vigorously until the dough comes away from the sides of the pan. Off the heat, beat in the eggs one by one.

Put the dough in a piping bag with a large rosette-shaped nozzle and pipe small puffs of dough on to an ungreased baking sheet. Put the sheet into a preheated 230°C (450°F or Mark 8) oven. To make the puffs even lighter, pour about 10 cl (3½ fl oz) of water into the oven when you put in the puffs, and close the door very quickly. Do not open the oven door for the first 10 minutes of baking, so that you do not let out the steam. Bake the puffs for 15 to 20 minutes, until they are risen and golden-brown.

Let the baked puffs cool, and cut them in half with a sharp knife. Whip the double cream together with the castor sugar until stiff and place a large spoonful of whipped cream on the bottom half of each puff. Replace the tops and sprinkle them with icing sugar.

ARNE KRÜGER AND ANNETTE WOLTER
KOCHEN HEUTE

Small Cherry Rings

Kirschkränzchen

To poach fresh cherries, cook them gently in sugar syrup made from 15 cl (¼ pint) of water and 125 g (4 oz) of sugar for about 5 minutes, or until they are soft but not disintegrating.

	To make 24 rings	
500 g	poached fresh cherries, or preserved cherries, drained, halved and stoned	1 lb
$\frac{1}{4}$ litre	double cream, whipped with $\frac{1}{2}$ tbsp castor sugar	8 fl oz
	icing sugar	
	Choux dough	
$\frac{1}{4}$ litre	water	8 fl oz
50 g	butter	2 oz
	salt	
150 g	flour	5 oz
4 or 5	eggs	4 or 5

To make the dough, bring the water, butter and a pinch of salt to the boil, and pour in the flour all at once. Stir the mixture over the heat until it comes away from the bottom of the pan; remove from the heat and beat in the eggs, one by one. Allow the dough to cool slightly, then place it in a piping bag with a large nozzle. Make small rings of the dough on greased and floured baking sheets. Bake in a preheated 180°C (350°F or Mark 4) oven for about 30 minutes or until puffed and golden-brown. The door should not be opened for the first 20 minutes of baking. Cool the rings on a rack.

Slice the cooled rings open. Fold the cherries into the sweetened whipped cream and use this to fill the rings. Sprinkle with icing sugar before serving.

ROTRAUD DEGNER
DAS SCHNELLKOCHBUCH FÜR FEINSCHMECKER

Yeast-Leavened Cakes

Rum Babas

Babas au Rhum

The technique of making rum babas is demonstrated on page 72, where raisins are used as an alternative to currants. Rum babas can be brushed with warm apricot glaze and decorated with angelica and glacé cherries if desired. If you do not wish to serve extra syrup with the babas, add the rum to the syrup before the cakes are soaked in it.

Babas can be baked up to two weeks before serving and kept in an airtight container, or they can be frozen. The drier they are, the more rum syrup they absorb. Once the babas have been soaked in syrup, they can be kept for up to 24 hours, tightly covered.

To make 8 babas

12.5 cl	rum	4 fl oz
15 g	fresh yeast or 2 tsp dried yeast	$\frac{1}{2}$ oz
3 tbsp	lukewarm water	3 tbsp
225 g	flour	$7\frac{1}{2}$ oz
3	eggs, lightly beaten	3
1 tsp	salt	1 tsp
1 tbsp	sugar	1 tbsp
125 g	butter, softened	4 oz
75 g	currants	$2\frac{1}{2}$ oz
4 tbsp	water	4 tbsp
	Syrup	
500 g	sugar	1 lb
1 litre	water	$1\frac{3}{4}$ pints

Sprinkle or crumble the yeast over the lukewarm water and let it stand for 5 minutes or until dissolved. Sift the flour into a warm bowl, make a well in the centre and add the yeast mixture, eggs, salt and sugar. Work to a smooth dough with your hand. Knead by lifting the dough with your fingers and throwing it back into the bowl for 5 minutes or until it is smooth and elastic. Put the softened butter in pieces on top of the dough. Cover the bowl with a damp cloth and leave the dough to rise in a warm place for 45 minutes to 1 hour or until it has doubled in bulk.

Soak the dried currants in half the rum and the water.

Butter eight dariole or small deep moulds, chill them in the freezer and then butter them again.

Beat the softened butter into the risen dough until smooth; then drain the currants and add them. Drop the dough from a spoon into the moulds, to fill them by one-third. Set them on a baking sheet, cover with a cloth and let rise in a warm place for 50 minutes to 1 hour, or until the moulds are almost full. Check to make sure the dough does not stick to the cloth. Bake the babas in a preheated 200°C (400°F or Mark 6) oven for 20 minutes or until they begin to shrink from the sides of the moulds. Unmould and let cool.

Heat the sugar and water for the syrup over a low heat until the sugar dissolves, then boil for 2 to 3 minutes or until the syrup is clear. Take the pan from the heat and add the babas. Carefully turn them over several times to make sure they absorb as much syrup as possible. They will swell and be very shiny. Using a large slotted spoon, carefully transfer them to a rack. Reserve the remaining syrup for serving.

Just before serving, sprinkle some of the remaining rum over the babas. Add the rest of the rum to the reserved syrup and serve separately.

FAYE LEVY
LA VARENNE TOUR BOOK

Brioche Peaches

Pêches

For a demonstration of making brioche peaches, see page 76.

To make 16 peaches

500 g	brioche dough (*page 161*)	1 lb
150 g	castor sugar	5 oz
10 cl	water	$3\frac{1}{2}$ fl oz
$4\frac{1}{2}$ tbsp	rum	$4\frac{1}{2}$ tbsp
20 cl	pastry cream (*page 166*)	7 fl oz
150 g	apricot jam, sieved and warmed	5 oz
50 g	redcurrant jelly, warmed	2 oz
50 g	marzipan (*page 166*), coloured with spinach extract	2 oz
	crystallized angelica (optional)	

Make the brioche dough, cover it with a cloth, and leave it to rise in the refrigerator. When it has risen, take it from the refrigerator and place it on a floured surface. Punch down the dough, gather it into a ball, then roll it with your hands into a smooth sausage shape about 30 cm (12 inches) long.

Divide the sausage into 32 equal parts by the following method: find the centre of the sausage and mark it with a knife; then mark the centres of each half, then the centres of each quarter, and so on until you have 32 parts. Cut the sausage into pieces as marked, checking that they are equal.

Flour the pieces and roll them carefully into smooth, even balls. Place the balls, one by one, in staggered rows on a dampened baking sheet. Flour the palm of your hand and press firmly on each ball to flatten it. You should obtain regular discs of dough about 5 mm ($\frac{1}{4}$ inch) thick. Cover the dough and leave it in a warm place until the discs have risen to twice their original size or more. Bake them in a preheated 230°C (450°F or Mark 8) oven for about 15 minutes. Remove them from the oven and leave them to cool on a wire rack.

Dissolve 50 g (2 oz) of the sugar in the water over a low heat, then raise the heat and boil the syrup for about 1 minute. Add 3 tablespoonfuls of the rum. When the half peaches are cold, hollow them out from the flat side, using the point of a small knife. Brush the brioche with rum-flavoured syrup. Flavour the pastry cream with the remaining rum and fill the cavities in the brioche with this pastry cream, using a small metal spatula. Stick the half peaches together in twos. Brush them again with rum syrup.

Brush each peach all over with warmed apricot jam, then "blush" the middle of each side of the peach with a brush dipped in redcurrant jelly. Roll the peaches in the remaining castor sugar, or shake sugar over them from a sieve. Brush off any surplus sugar, then place them in paper cake cases.

Roll out the green marzipan and cut out leaf shapes with a small oval cutter. Place a leaf in the middle of the top of each peach. If you like, cut 16 tiny lozenge-shaped pieces from a stick of crystallized angelica and press a lozenge into each peach, just where the base of the leaf is, to form a stalk.

B. DESCHAMPS AND J. CL. DESCHAINTRE
PÂTISSERIE, CONFISERIE, GLACERIE

Mrs. Tashis' Little Puddings

This is an adaptation of a recipe from the *Receipt Book of Mrs. Anne Blencowe 1694*. These "little puddings" are quite delicious and turn out rather like a lemon-flavoured brioche. Ordinary household flour instead of strong bread flour can be used for this batter, but the volume of the little puddings will be smaller, and the texture not quite so open and light.

To make 8 little puddings

250 g	strong plain flour	8 oz
90 g	castor sugar	3 oz
15 g	fresh yeast or 2 tsp dried yeast	$\frac{1}{2}$ oz
4 to 6 tbsp	double cream	4 to 6 tbsp
3	eggs	3
1	lemon, rind grated	1

Put the flour and sugar in a bowl. Cream the yeast to a paste with warm water, add it to the flour, then put in the cream and the eggs. Add the lemon rind. Mix lightly to the consistency of a batter. Cover it and leave to rise for approximately 1 hour, or until it is very light and spongy.

Butter eight dariole moulds, approximately 7.5 cm (3 inches) high and 7.5 cm in diameter at the top. Spoon the batter into them until they are just about half full. Place the moulds on a baking sheet, cover them with plastic film and leave them for approximately 45 minutes, until the batter has risen just to the top of the tins. Put them in the centre of a preheated 190° to 200°C (375° to 400°F or Mark 5 or 6) oven and bake for about 15 minutes. Leave them to cool a little before turning them out of the tins on to a wire rack.

The shape of the little puddings or brioches will be rather like that of babas, with a mushroom-like head, beautifully golden-brown in colour.

ELIZABETH DAVID
ENGLISH BREAD AND YEAST COOKERY

Honey Cakes

Nonnettes

To make about 18 cakes

500 g	clear honey	1 lb
200 g	rye flour	7 oz
30 g	fresh yeast or 1 tbsp dried yeast	1 oz
12.5 cl	milk	4 fl oz
15 g	ground aniseeds	$\frac{1}{2}$ oz
15 g	ground cinnamon	$\frac{1}{2}$ oz
15 g	ground cloves	$\frac{1}{2}$ oz
4 tbsp	rum	4 tbsp
1	egg white, stiffly beaten	1
4 tbsp	icing sugar	4 tbsp

Heat the honey to boiling in the upper part of a double boiler over boiling water. Remove any scum. Pour the honey into a mixing bowl and stir the flour into it to form a thick paste. There should be enough flour to make a dough stiff enough to roll. Roll it out in a thick layer on a lightly floured board. Leave it to stand for 30 minutes.

Dissolve the yeast in the milk. Pound together the aniseeds, cinnamon and cloves, mix with the rum and add to the yeast. Work this mixture into the dough and knead well for 15 minutes. Pull off pieces, shape them into rounds and place them in well-greased muffin tins or individual cake moulds. Bake them in a preheated 180°C (350°F or Mark 4) oven for about 10 minutes or until they are risen, delicately browned and light. Set the cake tins on the drop door of the oven if you have one, or somewhere close at hand. Mix the beaten egg white with the icing sugar and brush the tops of the cakes with this mixture. Put the cakes back in the oven for 1 to 2 minutes to dry the icing.

GERMAINE CARTER
THE HOME BOOK OF FRENCH COOKERY

Wigs

Wigs were eaten extensively in 17th-century England, and were mentioned by Samuel Pepys in his diary. The author recommends serving them with hot spiced cider, or with steaming coffee and raspberry jam.

To make about 24 wigs

30 g	fresh yeast or 1 tbsp dried yeast	1 oz
15 cl	lukewarm water	$\frac{1}{4}$ pint
135 g	sugar	$4\frac{1}{2}$ oz
45 cl	cream or milk	$\frac{3}{4}$ pint
125 g	butter	4 oz
1 kg	flour	2 lb
2 tsp	salt	2 tsp
1 tsp	grated nutmeg	1 tsp
$\frac{1}{8}$ tsp each	ground cloves and ground mace	$\frac{1}{8}$ tsp each
2 tsp	caraway seeds (optional)	2 tsp
1	egg, beaten	1

Crumble the yeast into a bowl with the lukewarm water and 2 tablespoons of the sugar. Set the mixture aside in a warm place for about 15 minutes.

Bring the cream or milk just to boiling point, remove from the heat and add the butter and the remaining sugar. Set aside to cool to lukewarm. Sift the flour with the salt and spices. Combine the yeast mixture with the cooled cream, butter and sugar mixture. Gradually add the flour, combining the mixture thoroughly. Add the caraway seeds if desired. Knead the dough until it is smooth and set it aside to rise in a covered, greased bowl in a warm place for about 2 hours or until the dough has doubled in bulk.

Form the dough into rather large round flat buns. Place them on a greased baking sheet, brush over the tops with the beaten egg and cut a deep cross on each bun with a knife blade, so that, when baked, the wigs may be broken easily into triangular pieces. Set the wigs to rise again in a warm place for about 30 minutes.

Bake the wigs in a preheated 200°C (400°F or Mark 6) oven for 10 minutes. Then reduce the heat to 190°C (375°F or Mark 5) and bake for 10 to 15 minutes, or until they are brown.

DOROTHY GLADYS SPICER
FROM AN ENGLISH OVEN

Banbury Cakes

Modern versions of Banbury cakes are usually made with rough-puff pastry enclosing a filling of currants and spices. If you use dried yeast, you should dissolve the sugar in the warm milk and cream, then whisk in the yeast and leave it for 10 to 15 minutes or until it is frothy.

A recipe "To make very good Banbury cakes" is given by Gervase Markham in his *English Hus-wife* (1615) but it is so involved that although interesting as a record of cakes made in Elizabethan days it is useless in its original form. The following has therefore been extracted for modern use without destroying its character.

To make about 16 cakes

60 g	butter	2 oz
1 kg	flour	2 lb
30 g	fresh yeast or 1 tbsp dried yeast	1 oz
250 g	sugar	8 oz
1 tsp	salt	1 tsp
30 cl	milk	$\frac{1}{2}$ pint
8 cl	cream	3 fl oz
1	egg, well beaten	1
500 g	currants	1 lb
2 tsp	mixed ground cloves, mace and cinnamon and grated nutmeg	2 tsp

Rub the butter into the flour. Cream the yeast with a little of the sugar and add the remainder of the sugar to the flour with the salt. Mix well.

Heat the milk and cream together until lukewarm (they must not be too hot). Mix them with the creamed yeast and the beaten egg and use them to make the flour and butter into a dough. Knead the dough very well.

Divide the dough into two. Put one half to rise in a warm place for about 1 hour. Mix the currants and spices well in with the other. Then put the currant dough to rise. Roll out the plain dough very thin. Now roll out the currant dough about 1 cm ($\frac{1}{2}$ inch) thick and cut circles with a biscuit cutter. Cover each one with a circle of the thinly rolled plain dough. Slash each cake across the top and bake in a preheated 200°C (400°F or Mark 6) oven for 20 minutes or until browned.

FLORENCE WHITE (EDITOR)
GOOD THINGS IN ENGLAND

Shrove Tuesday Buns

Semlor

The technique of grinding almonds is shown on page 13.

Tradition is deep-rooted in Sweden, therefore many eating habits go back several generations. One of them is to serve these buns on Shrove Tuesday night and all through Lent; they are traditionally accompanied by hot milk and cinnamon. These buns are very popular and you will see them in many coffee shop windows in Sweden. The almond paste can be made ahead of time, wrapped in wax paper and stored at room temperature in a covered container.

To make 10 buns

1	egg, lightly beaten	1
17.5 cl	cream or milk, warmed	6 fl oz
30 g	fresh yeast or 1 tbsp dried yeast dissolved in 4 tbsp warm water	1 oz
60 g	sugar	2 oz
$\frac{1}{4}$ tsp	salt	$\frac{1}{4}$ tsp
$\frac{1}{2}$ tsp	ground cinnamon	$\frac{1}{2}$ tsp
125 g	butter, softened	4 oz
350 to 400 g	flour	12 to 14 oz
12.5 cl	double cream, whipped	4 fl oz
	icing sugar	

Almond paste

75 g	almonds, blanched and ground	$2\frac{1}{2}$ oz
$\frac{1}{2}$ tsp	almond extract	$\frac{1}{2}$ tsp
150 g	icing sugar, sifted	5 oz
1	egg white, lightly beaten	1

Mix half of the beaten egg with the cream or milk and add the yeast; then add the sugar, salt, cinnamon, butter and some of the flour. Add more flour, a little at a time, beating with a wooden spoon until you have a soft dough.

Turn the dough on to a floured board and knead it until it is smooth and elastic, about 10 minutes. Place the dough in a lightly buttered bowl. Turn once to grease the surface all over, then cover and let the dough rise in a warm place until it has doubled in bulk, about $1\frac{1}{2}$ hours. When it is well risen, punch it down, turn it out on to a floured board and knead it lightly until it is smooth. Shape into 10 round buns.

Place the buns on a buttered baking sheet. Leave them to rise until almost double in size, then brush them with the remaining beaten egg and bake them in a preheated 200°C (400°F or Mark 6) oven for 10 to 12 minutes, until golden-brown. Cool on a rack.

To make the almond paste, place the ground almonds in a mixing bowl and sprinkle with the almond extract and icing sugar. Toss with a fork and gradually add the egg white. Work the paste until it is smooth, then shape it into a cylinder.

When the buns are cold, cut off a slice from the top of each one with a sharp knife. Insert a slice of almond paste into the bun, garnish with a generous tablespoonful of whipped cream, replace the top and sprinkle with icing sugar.

MARIANNE GRÖNWALL VAN DER TUUK
SWEDISH BAKING AT ITS BEST

Chelsea Buns

To shape the buns more quickly, roll out the dough on a floured board. Brush the dough with melted lard, sprinkle it with currants and candied peel and roll it up. Cut the roll into slices, and lay the slices on a greased baking sheet.

To make 20 buns

1 kg	flour	2 to $2\frac{1}{2}$ lb
	salt	
90 g	butter	3 oz
175 g	castor sugar	6 oz
2	eggs, beaten	2
60 g	lard, melted	2 oz
90 g	currants	3 oz
60 g	candied peel, chopped	2 oz

Yeast leaven

15 g	fresh yeast or 2 tsp dried yeast	$\frac{1}{2}$ oz
60 cl	skimmed milk, warmed	1 pint
1 tbsp	castor sugar	1 tbsp
2 tbsp	flour	2 tbsp

To make the leaven, put the yeast in a basin. Add a little milk, then the sugar, the flour and the remainder of the milk. Cover the basin and set it in a warm place for about 10 minutes, or until the leaven is frothy.

Sift the flour and a pinch of salt into a basin, rub in the butter and add 125 g (4 oz) of the sugar. Make a well in the centre of the flour. When the ferment is ready, pour it in, and mix to a smooth dough, adding the eggs. Cover the basin and put it in a warm place for about $1\frac{1}{2}$ hours, when the dough should have doubled in size.

Turn out the dough on to a floured board and cut it into small pieces. Roll these out to thin strips, 5 mm ($\frac{1}{4}$ inch) in thickness. Brush them over with the lard and sprinkle them with currants and peel. Roll them round in a ring, tucking the tail end under to keep them from unwinding. Put them on a greased baking sheet over a basin of boiling water. Let them prove in a warm place for 5 minutes. Dredge them with the remaining sugar and bake them in a preheated 200°C (400°F or Mark 6) oven for about 20 minutes, or until browned.

MABEL I. RIVERS
TIPS FOR TEA

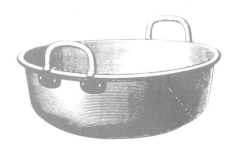

Fruity Buns

To make 12 large buns

12.5 cl	milk, scalded	4 fl oz
4 tbsp	oil or 60 g (2 oz) melted butter	4 tbsp
1 tbsp	honey	1 tbsp
1 tsp	salt	1 tsp
12.5 cl	cold water	4 fl oz
1 tbsp	dried yeast	1 tbsp
1	egg	1
350 g	wholemeal flour	12 oz
	Topping	
60 g	wholemeal breadcrumbs	2 oz
2 tbsp	honey	2 tbsp
¼ tsp	cinnamon	¼ tsp
1	egg white, slightly beaten	1
90 g	chopped cooked fruit (apricots, prunes, raisins, etc.)	3 oz

Combine the milk, oil or butter, honey and salt. Cool to lukewarm by adding the water. Stir in the yeast, then beat in the egg. Cover the mixture and leave it in a warm place for 10 to 15 minutes until frothy. Add the flour and work all the ingredients together until the dough is well blended and soft. Shape it into 12 buns.

For the topping, combine the breadcrumbs, honey and cinnamon. Dip each bun first in egg white, then in the crumb mixture; place the buns on a greased baking sheet, cover them with a cloth, and leave them to rise in a warm place until they are light (about 45 minutes).

Press a deep indentation in the centre of each bun. Place about 1 teaspoon of fruit in each indentation. Bake the buns in a preheated 190°C (375°F or Mark 5) oven for 25 minutes.

FAYE MARTIN
RODALE'S NATURALLY DELICIOUS DESSERTS AND SNACKS

Philadelphia Sticky Buns

In the 19th century, sticky buns—a Philadelphia speciality— were sold fresh every day, and were eaten at breakfast, teatime and dinner.

To make 12 buns

¼ litre	milk, scalded, then cooled to lukewarm	8 fl oz
15 g	fresh yeast or 2 tsp dried yeast, dissolved in 4 tbsp lukewarm water	½ oz
550 g	flour	1 lb 2 oz
150 g	butter, melted	5 oz
6 tbsp	sugar	6 tbsp
2	egg yolks, well beaten	2
1 tsp	salt	1 tsp
1	lemon, rind grated	1
1 tsp	ground cinnamon	1 tsp
75 g	currants	2½ oz
175 g	soft brown sugar	6 oz

In a bowl, combine the milk, yeast solution and 175 g (6 oz) of the flour and beat vigorously until the mixture is smooth. Cover it with a tea towel and leave it to stand in a warm place, away from draughts, until the mixture is light or has big dimples on the surface, about 1 hour. Now add 4 tablespoons of the melted butter, 4 tablespoons of the sugar, the egg yolks, salt, lemon rind and the remaining flour. Knead the mixture until it is smooth and springy. Cover the dough with a tea towel and leave it to rise in a warm place until doubled in size—this takes several hours.

Transfer the dough to a floured board and roll it out about 2 cm (¾ inch) thick in a long rectangular shape (the dough is elastic and springs back, but persevere). Brush the surface with 2 tablespoons of the melted butter and sprinkle with the remaining sugar, the cinnamon and the currants. Roll it up tightly and cut it in 2.5 cm (1 inch) slices. Work the brown sugar with the remaining butter and spread it over the bottom of a heavy baking tin. Place the swirls of dough on top of the sugar mixture, spacing them out evenly, and let them rise again, in a warm place, until doubled in size. Bake in a preheated 180°C (350°F or Mark 4) oven for 30 minutes, or until well browned on top. Turn the buns out on to a wire rack to cool, with their sticky sides uppermost.

THE EDITORS OF AMERICAN HERITAGE
THE AMERICAN HERITAGE COOKBOOK

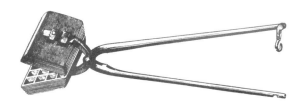

Curd Pie

Túrós Iepény

This pie may also be made without the top layer of pastry, as shown in the demonstration on page 68. In that case, you will need only half the quantities for the yeast dough given here. Before baking, brush the curd filling with beaten egg.

To make about 24 slices

1 kg	curd cheese, sieved	2 lb
400 g	sugar	13 oz
60 g	butter	2 oz
4	eggs, yolks separated from whites, whites stiffly beaten	4
60 g	sultanas	2 oz
$\frac{1}{2}$	lemon, rind grated	$\frac{1}{2}$
	salt	
15 cl	soured cream	$\frac{1}{4}$ pint
3 tbsp	semolina	3 tbsp

Yeast dough

20 g	fresh yeast or 2 tsp dried yeast	$\frac{3}{4}$ oz
30 cl	milk, warmed	$\frac{1}{2}$ pint
60 g	sugar	2 oz
500 g	flour, sifted	1 lb
2	egg yolks	2
	salt	
100 g	butter, melted	$3\frac{1}{2}$ oz
1 or 2	eggs, beaten	1 or 2

For the dough, crumble the yeast into 6 tablespoons of the milk and add 1 teaspoon of the sugar. When the yeast has dissolved, pour into the flour. Add the egg yolks, the remaining sugar, a pinch of salt and then gradually add the rest of the milk. Finally work in the butter. Work the dough thoroughly with a wooden spoon and leave to rest for 10 to 15 minutes.

Divide the dough into two, roll out one piece and line a greased baking tin with it. Roll out the other half and leave it to rest on the board. Cover both sheets of dough with a cloth.

For the filling, cream the sugar and butter until white and fluffy. Add the egg yolks singly and beat them in well. Mix in the sultanas, the grated lemon rind, a pinch of salt, the soured cream and 2 tablespoons of the semolina. Add the curd cheese. Fold in the egg whites very carefully.

Sprinkle the dough already in the tin with the remaining semolina and spread the filling over it evenly. Cover with the other sheet of dough and brush the top with a little beaten egg.

Bake for 35 to 40 minutes in a preheated 180°C (350°F or Mark 4) oven. Cut into slices to serve.

FRED MACNICOL
HUNGARIAN COOKERY

German Yeast Cake with Crumble Topping

Streusel Kuchen

The author suggests that, as a variation, you can assemble the dough with a jam filling. Roll out half the dough and spread it on the baking sheet, then spread it with a home-made jam such as damson. Sprinkle on ground cinnamon and cover with the remaining dough, then the streusel crumble topping. Bake in the same way, allowing a slightly longer cooking time.

To make about 30 squares

15 g	fresh yeast or 2 tsp dried yeast	$\frac{1}{2}$ oz
15 cl	milk, warmed	$\frac{1}{4}$ pint
250 g	flour	8 oz
75 g	butter	$2\frac{1}{2}$ oz
60 g	sugar	2 oz
1	egg	1

Crumble topping

90 g	butter, melted	3 oz
90 g	sugar	3 oz
175 g	flour	6 oz
1 tsp	ground cinnamon	1 tsp

Dissolve the yeast in the warm milk and add one-third of the flour. Cover and leave in a warm place to rise, about 30 minutes. Cream together 60 g (2 oz) of the butter and the sugar, add the egg and the rest of the flour. Beat briskly, then add the yeast batter. Work the mixture to a dough and knead with your hands until the dough no longer sticks to your hands or to the sides of the mixing bowl. Cover the bowl and leave the dough to rise for 1 hour or until doubled in bulk.

When the dough has risen, roll it out thinly and spread it on a greased baking sheet. Leave it to rise again, for about 30 minutes. Melt the remaining 15 g ($\frac{1}{2}$ oz) of butter and brush this over the surface of the dough.

While the dough is rising, prepare the *streusel* crumble topping. While the melted butter is still hot, mix in the sugar, flour and cinnamon. Cut this paste with a knife, and then crumble it up to resemble breadcrumbs. Sprinkle the mixture over the rolled-out dough and bake in a preheated 220°C (425°F or Mark 7) oven for 35 to 45 minutes. Leave the cake to cool, then cut it into squares and serve.

MARIA FLORIS
BAKERY

Chestnut Purée Rings from Hungary

The rings can be served plain, or they can be decorated, when they are cool, with apricot glaze and thin glacé icing, as in the demonstration on page 70.

To make 15 rings

20 g	fresh yeast or 1 tbsp dried yeast	$\frac{2}{3}$ oz
2 tbsp	milk, warmed	2 tbsp
275 g	flour	9 oz
75 g	sugar	$2\frac{1}{2}$ oz
275 g	butter, melted	9 oz
1	egg yolk	1
About 12.5 cl	single cream	About 4 fl oz
	milk or beaten egg yolk	

Chestnut filling

500 g	cooked chestnuts, sieved	1 lb
30 g	butter, softened	1 oz
60 g	sugar	2 oz
1 tbsp	rum	1 tbsp
1 tbsp	single cream	1 tbsp

Mix the yeast with the warm milk, 1 tablespoon of the flour and a pinch of the sugar; let it rise in a warm place. When it has risen, add the remaining flour and sugar, the butter, egg yolk, and as much cream as it takes to make a dough soft enough to manipulate easily. Mix well together until it becomes very smooth. Then put it on a pastry board and let it rest for 30 minutes or so.

While you wait for the dough to rise, make the filling. Add the butter, sugar, rum and cream to the chestnuts. Mix all these well together. Now roll out the rested dough as thin as a matchstick. Cut it into rectangles 7.5 cm (3 inches) long and about 4 cm (1½ inches) wide. Pipe or spoon a good tablespoonful of the chestnut cream on to each strip. Roll them up like cigarettes and shape them into rings. Arrange them on a greased and floured baking sheet, brush them over with milk or beaten egg yolk and leave to rise again for 15 minutes. Bake in a preheated 200°C (400°F or Mark 6) oven for 16 to 18 minutes, or until golden-brown.

MARIA FLORIS
BAKERY

Poppy Seed Horseshoes

Mákos Patkó

To make the tiny crescents shown on page 70, roll the dough out thinly and use an oval pastry cutter to stamp out small ovals of dough which are shaped round the filling to form crescents. The quantities given here will make about 18 crescents. They can be glazed with lemon glacé icing (recipe, page 166) and sprinkled with chopped nuts if desired.

To make 2 large or 4 small horseshoes

20 g	fresh yeast or 2 tsp dried yeast	$\frac{3}{4}$ oz
50 g	castor sugar	2 oz
About 15 cl	milk, warmed	About $\frac{1}{4}$ pint
500 g	flour	1 lb
250 g	butter	8 oz
2	eggs, well beaten	2
	salt	
1	egg white, lightly beaten	1

Poppy seed filling

300 g	poppy seeds, finely ground	10 oz
60 g	semolina	2 oz
45 cl	milk	$\frac{3}{4}$ pint
200 g	sugar	7 oz
125 g	sultanas (optional)	4 oz
1 tsp	grated lemon rind	1 tsp

Start the yeast working with 1 teaspoon of the sugar in about 4 tablespoons of the milk. Rub the flour and butter together and add the beaten whole eggs, reserving 1 tablespoon of egg. Add the yeast mixture and the remaining sugar. Add a pinch of salt with just enough of the remaining milk to give a fairly firm dough. Work it together quickly, and then leave the dough to rest for 2 hours.

For the filling, mix the poppy seeds with the semolina. Bring the milk to the boil and pour in the poppy-seed mixture. Add the sugar and sultanas, if using. Mix very well, cool the mixture and work in a little grated lemon rind.

Divide the dough into two larger or four smaller lumps. Roll each out to an oval shape about 8 mm (⅓ inch) in thickness. Leaving 2.5 cm (1 inch) round the edge of each oval quite free, spread on the filling and roll up each piece. Then shape each of the rolls into horseshoe form, with the joins underneath. Place the horseshoes on a lightly greased baking sheet, brush them with the reserved beaten egg and leave them to rise in a warm place for about 1 hour.

Once the horseshoes have risen, brush them with the egg white and leave them in a cool place for 30 minutes—this helps to marble the surface of the dough. Before baking the horseshoes, pierce the sides here and there with a fork. Bake them in a preheated 220°C (425°F or Mark 7) oven for 10 minutes, then lower the heat to 190°C (375°F or Mark 5) and bake for 15 to 20 minutes more, or until golden-brown. Avoid opening the oven door during the baking.

FRED MACNICOL
HUNGARIAN COOKERY

Maundy Thursday Spirals

Gründonnerstag-Kringel

To make about 40 cakes

500 g	flour	1 lb
40 g	fresh yeast or 1 tbsp dried yeast dissolved in ¼ litre (8 fl oz) tepid milk	1½ oz
100 g	sugar	3½ oz
2	egg yolks, lightly beaten	2
	salt	
1	lemon, rind grated	1
150 g	butter, chilled and cut into small, thin slices	5 oz
200 g	marzipan (*page 166*), cut into small, thin slices	7 oz
	Topping	
2	egg yolks, lightly beaten	2
100 g	almonds, coarsely chopped	3½ oz
150 g	sultanas	5 oz
100 g	candied lemon peel, coarsely chopped	3½ oz
75 g	icing sugar	2½ oz

Sift the flour into a bowl, make a well in the centre and pour in the yeast and milk mixture. Mix in a little of the flour to make a thin batter. On the flour round the edge, sprinkle the sugar, egg yolks, a pinch of salt and the lemon rind. Cover the bowl and place it in a warm place until the batter has doubled in bulk. Then knead the batter and the surrounding flour together to make a dry dough. Place on a floured plate, cover and allow to rise again until doubled in bulk, about 1 hour.

On a floured board, roll the dough out to a thickness of 1 cm (½ inch), cover it with the small slices of butter and marzipan, fold it in half and roll it out again. Repeat this operation once or twice more. Finally, roll the dough out to a thickness of 8 mm (⅓ inch) and cut it into 12 by 3 cm (5 by 1¼ inch) strips. Form the strips into spirals and place on a floured baking sheet.

Brush the spirals with beaten egg yolk and sprinkle them with the chopped almonds, sultanas, candied peel and icing sugar. Bake in a preheated 180°C (350°F or Mark 4) oven on the middle shelf for 30 to 40 minutes or until golden-brown.

FRITZ BECKER
DAS KOCHBUCH AUS MECKLENBURG, POMMERN UND OSTPREUSSEN

Syrup Balls

Stroopbolussen

Marmalade balls and ginger balls can be made in the same way, replacing the syrup and cinnamon with either 250 g (8 oz) of orange marmalade or 200 g (7 oz) of finely chopped preserved ginger and 4 tablespoons of ginger syrup.

To make 5 syrup balls

20 g	fresh yeast or 2 tsp dried yeast	¾ oz
10 cl	milk, warmed	3½ fl oz
250 g	flour	8 oz
1 tsp	salt	1 tsp
15 g	soft brown sugar	½ oz
½	egg	½
65 g	butter, melted	2¼ oz
	Syrup filling	
150 g	butter	5 oz
200 g	golden syrup	7 oz
1 tsp	ground cinnamon	1 tsp

Soften the yeast in the lukewarm milk. Sift the flour, salt and sugar together into a bowl and make a well in the middle. Put the egg, yeast and milk mixture and melted butter into the well and mix together, gradually incorporating the flour and kneading to make a pliable dough. Leave the dough to rise in a fairly warm and moist place, free of draughts, for 30 to 45 minutes. Roll out the dough, on a floured board, to a thickness of 5 mm (¼ inch), and cut into 2 cm (¾ inch) wide strips.

Butter tartlet moulds, about 10 cm (4 inches) in diameter. Cover the bottoms with strips of dough, starting in the centre and circling towards the outer edge. Make sure that each successive turn partly overlaps the previous one. Moisten the end of each strip to attach it to the next.

To make the syrup filling, cream the butter, then stir in the syrup and the cinnamon. Spread a little more than half of this filling over the bottom layer of dough in the moulds. Make a second layer with the remaining strips of dough, this time beginning the circle at the outer edge and working towards the centre. Cover with the remaining filling and leave for 30 to 45 minutes for the dough to rise once more. Place the tartlet moulds in a preheated 230°C (450°F or Mark 8) oven and bake for about 20 minutes or until the cakes are brown. Remove them from the oven and leave them to cool.

H. H. F. HENDERSON, H. TOORS AND H. M. CALLENBACH
HET NIEUWE KOOKBOEK

Cream Cheese Pastries

Topfengolatschen

If you use dried yeast, you should dissolve the sugar in the tepid milk, then whisk in the yeast.

To make 12 pastries

250 g	flour	8 oz
	salt	
125 g	butter	4 oz
30 g	fresh yeast or 1 tbsp dried yeast	1 oz
15 g	sugar	$\frac{1}{2}$ oz
About 12.5 cl	tepid milk	About 4 fl oz
1	egg yolk	1
1	egg, lightly beaten	1

Cream cheese filling

250 g	cream cheese	8 oz
30 g	raisins	1 oz
90 g	sugar	3 oz
2	egg yolks or 1 egg	2
About 4 tbsp	cream	About 4 tbsp
$\frac{1}{2}$	lemon, rind grated	$\frac{1}{2}$

To make the pastry dough, sift the flour and salt and divide into two equal parts of 125 g (4 oz) each. Cut the butter into one half of the flour, knead a little, shape into a brick and chill.

Cream the yeast with the sugar, add the tepid milk and one teaspoonful of flour, and put in a warm place to prove. Sift the remaining flour into a warmed bowl, make a well in the centre and drop in the egg yolk. When the yeast begins to throw light bubbles, stir the egg yolk into the flour, add the yeast mixture and knead to a smooth dough. (A little more tepid milk may have to be added. This depends entirely on the size of the egg yolk and the quality of the flour.) Pat the yeast dough into a round, cover with a cloth and set to rise for 15 minutes in a warm place. After that time, place the dough on a floured pastry board and leave to cool for a little.

Roll out the yeast dough to about three times the size of the brick of butter and flour. Place the butter brick in the centre and fold the yeast dough over it. Beat with a rolling pin, then roll out to original size. Fold the dough into three again, beat with a rolling pin, then roll out. Repeat this once more, then place the pastry in a cool place for half an hour before using.

To prepare the filling, wash and dry the raisins. Beat the cream cheese with the sugar and egg yolks (or egg). Stir in sufficient cream to give a thick, creamy consistency. Add the raisins and the lemon rind.

Roll the dough out about 3 mm ($\frac{1}{8}$ inch) thick. Cut it into squares and place a spoonful of the cream cheese filling in the

centre of each square. Fold all four corners of each square to the middle so that the filling is completely encased. Secure with a very small round of dough on top (use trimmings). Place the pastries on a buttered and floured baking sheet and leave to rise in a warm place. When well risen, brush the pastries with the beaten egg and bake in a preheated 190° to 200°C (375° to 400°F or Mark 5 to 6) oven until golden-brown, about 30 minutes. Sprinkle with sugar before serving.

GRETEL BEER
AUSTRIAN COOKING

Light Coffee Cakes

Ensaimadas

To make about 20 cakes

About 500 g	flour	About 1 lb
10 g	fresh yeast or 1 tsp dried yeast	$\frac{1}{3}$ oz
15 cl	tepid water	$\frac{1}{4}$ pint
2	eggs	2
1 tsp	salt	1 tsp
75 g	sugar	$2\frac{1}{2}$ oz
2 tbsp	olive oil	2 tbsp
50 g	lard, melted and cooled	2 oz
	icing sugar	

Mix together 100 g ($3\frac{1}{2}$ oz) of the flour, the yeast and 3 tablespoons of the tepid water. Allow this leaven to rise until it is very spongy.

Place the remaining flour on a board and make a well in the centre. Put the eggs, the remaining water, the salt and sugar into the well; mix them together without incorporating the flour. Mix in the leaven and, little by little, work in the flour from round the edges, adding more if necessary to make a fairly firm dough. Mix in the oil.

Divide the dough into 40 g ($1\frac{1}{2}$ oz) pieces. Place the pieces on an oiled marble slab, and roll them out with an oiled rolling pin until they are wafer thin. Brush melted lard on each wafer. Fold the wafers and roll them out again. Brush with lard, fold and roll again. Roll the wafers up into cylinders, and curl each cylinder into a snail or spiral shape. Place them on a greased baking sheet, well apart, and leave them to rise in a warm place, covered, for about 12 hours or until they have doubled in volume.

Spray or sprinkle the cakes with water and bake them in a preheated 200°C (400°F or Mark 6) oven for 10 to 15 minutes or until golden. Sprinkle them generously with icing sugar.

MARIA MESTAYER DE ECHAGÜE (MARQUESA DE PARABERE)
CONFITERÍA Y REPOSTERÍA

Poached and Fried Cakes

Plum Dumplings

Served with soured cream, these dumplings make a very nice and unusual late Sunday breakfast. Apricots, cherries or peaches may be used instead of plums. Hungarians substitute 300 g (10 oz) of mashed potatoes for half the quantity of flour.

To make 16 dumplings

16	blue plums, stoned and sprinkled with lemon juice	16
350 g	flour	12 oz
1 tsp	salt	1 tsp
2	eggs, lightly beaten	2
60 g	butter, softened to room temperature	2 oz
12.5 to 17.5 cl	milk	4 to 6 fl oz
60 g	sugar	2 oz
1 tsp	ground cinnamon	1 tsp
$\frac{1}{8}$ tsp	grated nutmeg	$\frac{1}{8}$ tsp
	Topping	
40 g	finely chopped walnuts or 60 g (2 oz) dry breadcrumbs, fried for a few minutes in 60 g (2 oz) of butter	$1\frac{1}{2}$ oz

Sift together the flour and salt into a medium-sized bowl. Beat the eggs into the softened butter until they are well blended. Then stir into the flour, adding just enough milk to form a stiff dough. Remove the dough to a well-floured board and knead it for about 10 minutes, or until it feels smooth and satiny. Roll the dough into a ball, cover it and allow it to rest for 30 minutes.

Combine the sugar, cinnamon and nutmeg in a small bowl. Divide the dough in half and roll each section out to a thickness of about 3 mm ($\frac{1}{8}$ inch). Using a 7.5 cm (3 inch) round biscuit cutter, cut out 16 rounds from each section of dough.

Place each plum (two halves) in centre of 16 rounds. Sprinkle with the cinnamon sugar and cover each one with another round of dough. Seal the edges firmly by pressing down all round with the prongs of a fork. Bring about 7 litres (12 pints) of salted water to the boil and drop in eight to 10 dumplings. Simmer for 12 minutes.

Remove the dumplings with a slotted spoon and place them in a well-buttered ovenproof dish. Repeat until all are done.

Top the dumplings with buttered walnuts or breadcrumbs and sprinkle with any remaining cinnamon sugar. Serve the dumplings while still warm.

MARIA POLUSHKIN
THE DUMPLING COOKBOOK

Plum-Curd Dumplings

Zwetschen-Quark-Knödel

The technique of making fruit dumplings is shown on page 80.

To make 16 dumplings

16	blue plums, stoned	16
250 g	curd cheese, sieved	8 oz
2	eggs, yolks separated from whites, whites stiffly beaten	2
90 g	butter	3 oz
250 g	flour	8 oz
	salt	
16	sugar cubes	16
2 tbsp	castor sugar	2 tbsp
1 tsp	ground cinnamon	1 tsp

Work the cheese with the egg yolks, 30 g (1 oz) of the butter, the flour and a pinch of salt into a dough. Fold in the egg whites. Leave the dough to rest for 1 hour. Roll it out fairly thickly on a floured board, cut out rounds with a glass, put a plum on each round and place a cube of sugar inside each plum. Roll up the fruit in the dough to form small dumplings. Cook the dumplings in boiling salted water over a low heat until they rise to the surface. Drain them well.

Brown the remaining butter in a small saucepan over a low heat. Mix the castor sugar and the cinnamon together. When all the dumplings are cooked, trickle browned butter over them and sprinkle them with the cinnamon sugar.

LILO AUREDEN
WAS MÄNNERN SO GUT SCHMECKT

Bohemian Plum Dumplings
Zwetschgenknödl

Plum dumplings, along with apricot dumplings (*Marillenknödl*), cherry dumplings (*Kirschknödl*) and plum jam dumplings (*Powidlknödl*) all come from Bohemia and were traditionally made from potato dough, though sometimes yeast dough was used. In Vienna, especially good fruit dumplings were made from choux dough or curd dough. A stoned apricot with a sugar cube in the centre, or 3 or 4 glacé cherries, or 1 teaspoon of very thick plum purée may be substituted for the plum in each dumpling.

There are two things to know about potato dough: it should not rest otherwise it will soften, and potato dumplings are always cooked in an open pot.

To make about 20 dumplings

500 to 750 g	blue plums, stoned	1 to 1½ lb
1	egg	1
1	egg yolk	1
	salt	
2 tbsp	semolina	2 tbsp
500 g	potatoes, cooked the day before and sieved	1 lb
About 250 g	flour	About 8 oz
About 20	sugar cubes	About 20
100 g	butter	3½ oz
3 tbsp	breadcrumbs, toasted	3 tbsp
30 g	castor sugar mixed with 2 tsp ground cinnamon	1 oz

Add the egg and the egg yolk, a pinch of salt and the semolina to the potatoes. Stir well and add enough flour to make a stiff dough. Form the dough into a sausage shape 7.5 cm (3 inches) thick and cut it into slices about 1 cm (½ inch) thick. Flatten the slices to make thin cakes. Put a small cube of sugar in place of the stone into each plum. Place a plum in the middle of each piece of dough and fold the dough round to enclose the plum completely. Roll the dumplings between your hands to give them a round shape.

Place the dumplings carefully in an open pan of boiling salted water and cook them for about 8 minutes, or until they rise to the surface. Remove the dumplings from the pan with a slotted spoon and drain them.

Cook the butter in a small pan over a low heat until it browns. Turn the cooked dumplings in the butter, roll them in toasted breadcrumbs and sprinkle them with the cinnamon sugar. Serve immediately.

GRETE WILLINSKY
KULINARISCHE WELTREISE

Cherry Vareniki

Blackcurrant jam, bilberries or well-drained cottage cheese worked into a stiff paste with an egg and sugar can also be used as fillings for *vareniki*.

To make about 20 vareniki

500 g	morello cherries, stoned	1 lb
125 g	sugar	4 oz
250 g	flour, sifted	8 oz
1	egg	1
	salt	

Mix the stoned cherries with the sugar and leave them to macerate for 1 to 2 hours.

Into the sifted flour mix the egg and a pinch of salt, gradually adding 1 to 2 tablespoons of water to form a stiff dough. Knead the dough to ensure it is absolutely smooth. Roll it out as thinly as possible on a floured board and cut it into small rounds, about 6 cm (2½ inches) in diameter.

On each round of dough place one or two cherries, leaving the juice and sugar in the basin. Join the edges of the dough very firmly over the fruit, and drop the *vareniki*, a few at a time, into a large pan of boiling water. When they float up to the surface, remove them with a perforated spoon.

Make a syrup of the sugar and the cherry juice, adding a little water and boiling it for 5 minutes. Serve the syrup hot with the *vareniki*.

SOFKA SKIPWITH
EAT RUSSIAN

Cheese Dumplings
Túrós Gombóc

To make about 20 dumplings

500 g	cottage cheese or curd cheese	1 lb
3	eggs, beaten	3
45 g	butter	1½ oz
100 g	semolina	3½ oz
2 tbsp	flour	2 tbsp
	salt	
12.5 cl	soured cream	4 fl oz
75 g	vanilla icing sugar	2½ oz

	Coating	
90 g	butter	3 oz
60 g	breadcrumbs	2 oz

Force the cheese through a sieve. Mix well with the eggs and butter. Add the semolina, the flour and a pinch of salt. Let the mixture rest for a couple of hours.

Put 3 litres (5 pints) of water in a 4 litre (7 pint) pan and add 1 tablespoon of salt. Bring to a slow boil. Put cold water in a dish large enough to dip your hands into.

Wet your hands. Take a mounded tablespoon of the cheese mixture and roll it into a round dumpling. Test cook the first dumpling. Drop it into the boiling water and cook it for 5 minutes. Then cut it in half to see if the centre is cooked. Adjust the cooking time according to the test dumpling.

Form the rest of the mixture into dumplings; dip your hands into cold water before forming each dumpling. When all the dumplings are cooked, rinse them with cold water.

To make the coating, melt the butter in a frying pan. Add the breadcrumbs and sauté over a low heat until golden brown. Roll the rinsed dumplings in the butter and crumb coating and place them on a serving platter. Spoon soured cream on top and shake enough vanilla icing sugar over all to make the dumplings look snowy.

GEORGE LANG
THE CUISINE OF HUNGARY

Small Indonesian Rice Cakes

Ondé-Ondé

The technique of grating fresh coconut is shown on page 12. Glutinous rice flour is available from Oriental delicatessens. In Indonesia, ondé-ondé *are always a fresh green colour since they are made with a fragrant leaf called* daun pandan. *As green food colouring is not a satisfactory substitute, the author suggests using cocoa powder to give colour and a mild chocolate flavour to the rice cakes.*

To make about 45 cakes

250 g	glutinous rice flour	8 oz
2 tbsp	cocoa powder (optional)	2 tbsp
	salt	
$\frac{1}{4}$ litre	water	8 fl oz
90 g	Demerara sugar	3 oz
$\frac{1}{2}$	coconut, grated	$\frac{1}{2}$

Sift the rice flour and the cocoa, if using, into a mixing bowl, with a pinch of salt. Add the water, a little at a time, mixing and then kneading the dough until it is soft and smooth. Take a knob of dough about as big as a small marble, flatten it on a pastry board and fill it with a third of a teaspoonful of

Demerara sugar. Shape the dough into a ball, with the sugar inside. Repeat until all the dough is used up.

Half-fill a large saucepan with water, and add a pinch of salt. Bring to the boil, and drop in the *ondé-ondé*, one by one, until there are 10 to 12 in the pan. Boil them for 10 to 15 minutes, or until they float on the surface. Take them out very carefully and drain them in a colander. When cooking is completed, mix three-quarters of a teaspoon of salt with the grated coconut and roll the *ondé-ondé* in the gratings until they are well covered. Arrange on a serving dish and sprinkle any remaining coconut on top. Serve warm or cold.

SRI OWEN
INDONESIAN FOOD AND COOKERY

Marvels

Merveilles

To make about 40 fritters

500 g	flour	1 lb
15 g	baking powder	$\frac{1}{2}$ oz
About 300 g	castor sugar	About 10 oz
	salt	
5	eggs	5
4 tbsp	rum or 1 tsp orange-flower water	4 tbsp
100 g	fat (oil, melted lard or butter)	$3\frac{1}{2}$ oz
	oil for deep frying	

Sift the flour into a large bowl and sprinkle the baking powder over it. Add 200 g (7 oz) of the sugar and a pinch of salt. Stir with a wooden spatula and make a well in the centre. Break the eggs into the well. Add the rum or orange-flower water and the fat. Mix all the ingredients together thoroughly, at first with a wooden spatula and then with your hands until you have a smooth dough. Cover the bowl with a clean cloth and leave the dough to rest. Spread a large clean cloth on the kitchen table and sprinkle it with flour. Place the dough on the towel and roll it out in a sheet about 5 mm ($\frac{1}{4}$ inch) thick. Using a pastry wheel, cut the dough into vertical strips, then cut each strip diagonally into lozenges.

Heat the oil in a deep pan and when it is very hot, drop in four or five lozenges. Fry them until golden-brown, turning so that they brown on both sides. They should brown very quickly (in less than 2 minutes for each side). Remove the fritters with a slotted spoon and place them on a cloth or kitchen paper to drain. Continue until all the dough is used up. Sprinkle the fritters with plenty of castor sugar.

HENRI PHILIPPON
CUISINE DU QUERCY ET DU PÉRIGORD

Messelmen

To make about 16 pastries

500 g	fine semolina	1 lb
1 tsp	salt	1 tsp
	water	
	oil for deep frying	
200 g	honey, hot	7 oz

Mix the semolina, salt and 30 cl ($\frac{1}{2}$ pint) of water to a stiff dough in a basin. Knead the dough and moisten it with a little more water until the mixture becomes supple and elastic.

Oil your hands and a board and, with your fingers, shape the dough into balls about 5 cm (2 inches) in diameter. Arrange these on the board and leave to rest for 10 minutes.

Take one ball and flatten it. Stretch it in all directions to make a very thin, transparent rectangle. Fold it in four. Plunge it into deep hot oil. When the pastry is golden on both sides, drain it and sprinkle it with some hot honey. Continue the procedure with each ball of dough.

Messelmen are eaten hot, as soon as they are cooked.

IRÈNE AND LUCIENNE KARSENTY
CUISINE PIED-NOIR

Sweet Potato Puri

Patata Puri

Sweet potatoes are available from good greengrocers. They should be peeled and cooked exactly as ordinary potatoes.

These are delicious with coffee if eaten hot; they keep well if stored in a tin.

To make about 20 puris

250 g	mashed boiled sweet potatoes	8 oz
30 g	butter	1 oz
1 tsp	baking powder	1 tsp
$\frac{1}{4}$ tsp	salt	$\frac{1}{4}$ tsp
60 g	sugar	2 oz
About 100 g	flour	About $3\frac{1}{2}$ oz
	oil for deep frying	

Carefully drain off any moisture from the mashed sweet potatoes, otherwise the dough will be sticky. Add the butter, baking powder, salt and sugar. Mix lightly and add enough of the flour to form a fairly stiff and rollable dough. Roll the dough out 5 mm ($\frac{1}{4}$ inch) thick, cut it with biscuit cutters to desired shapes and fry the shapes in hot oil. Drain well.

ZULEIKHA MAYAT
INDIAN DELIGHTS

Tea Crowns

Couronnes pour le Thé

To make about 30 crowns

1 tsp	aniseeds	1 tsp
4 tbsp	hot water	4 tbsp
20 g	fresh yeast or 2 tsp dried yeast	$\frac{3}{4}$ oz
250 g	castor sugar	8 oz
4	eggs, yolks separated from whites, whites stiffly beaten	4
4 tbsp	olive oil	4 tbsp
400 g	flour	14 oz
	oil for deep frying	
100 g	sugar crystals	$3\frac{1}{2}$ oz

Infuse the aniseeds in the hot water. Cool the water until it is barely lukewarm, then dissolve the yeast in it.

Add the castor sugar to the beaten egg whites then, beating continuously, add the egg yolks, one by one. Pour in the olive oil, the flour and the yeast solution. Leave the dough to rest for 1 hour so that it stiffens.

Flour your hands and shape the dough into small rings. Place them on a tray and leave them to rest for another hour. Deep fry the rings in hot oil, a few at a time, for about 10 minutes, or until they are golden-brown. While they are still hot, roll them in the sugar crystals.

IRÈNE AND LUCIENNE KARSENTY
CUISINE PIED-NOIR

Smalls

Klejner

To make about 16 pastries

4	egg yolks	4
90 g	icing sugar	3 oz
60 g	butter, melted	2 oz
2 tbsp	double cream	2 tbsp
2 tbsp	brandy	2 tbsp
$\frac{1}{2}$ tbsp	grated lemon rind	$\frac{1}{2}$ tbsp
250 g	flour	8 oz
	lard or oil for deep frying	

Stir the egg yolks together with the sugar and the melted butter, add the cream, brandy and grated rind and stir in the flour. Knead the dough until it is firm and elastic. Roll it out thinly and cut with a pastry wheel or knife into strips about 2.5 cm (1 inch) wide, then cut the strips into 15 cm (6 inch) lengths. Make a slit in the middle of each length and pull one end of the pastry through the slit to make a loop. Bring the lard or oil to the boil in a pan and deep fry the pastries until golden. Remove them from the pan with a slotted spoon and place them on kitchen paper until cold.

GRETE GRUMME
DANISH FOOD

Sweet Sticks

Strúfele

To make about 50 sticks

1 kg	flour	2 to 2½ lb
300 g	sugar	10 oz
4	eggs	4
2 tbsp	vanilla sugar	2 tbsp
	salt	
About ¼ litre	warm water	About 8 fl oz
	olive oil for deep frying	
	honey or sugar crystals (optional)	

Sift the flour into a bowl and make a well in the middle. Put the sugar, eggs, vanilla sugar and a pinch of salt into the well and combine the ingredients. Gradually blend in enough warm water to make a smooth dough. Pull off pieces of the dough and roll them into cylinders, each approximately the length of a finger.

Fry the cylinders for 5 to 6 minutes in plenty of very hot olive oil, drain them and place them on a baking sheet. Bake them in a preheated 150°C (300°F or Mark 2) oven until they have dried out, about 20 minutes. When the sticks are cooked, they may be soaked in honey or sprinkled with sugar crystals.

OTTAVIO CAVALCANTI
IL LIBRO D'ORO DELLA CUCINA E DEI VINI DI CALABRIA E BASILICATA

Syrup-Dipped Cakes

Narenjak

To make about 20 fritters

75 g	butter	2½ oz
17.5 cl	water	6 fl oz
125 g	flour	4 oz
5	eggs	5
	oil for deep frying	

Syrup

250 g	sugar	8 oz
2 tbsp	water	2 tbsp

Melt the butter in a saucepan. Add the water and bring it to the boil. Add the flour all at once and stir with a wire whisk until the mixture thickens. Allow it to cool. Add the eggs one at a time, beating well after each addition. Heat the oil in a deep saucepan to 190°C (375°F). Place the dough in a piping bag with a large plain nozzle. Pipe out a piece of dough, the length of a finger, into the hot oil. Fry until lightly golden (about 30 seconds). Lift it out with a slotted spoon and drain it on kitchen paper. Continue until all the dough is used up.

To make the syrup, dissolve the sugar over a medium heat with the water. Bring to the boil and cook until the syrup is a light golden caramel colour. When the fritters are cool, dip each one in the hot caramel syrup until it is well coated.

NESTA RAMAZANI
PERSIAN COOKING

Anise-Flavoured Honey Cakes

Cicirata o Cicirchiata

To make about 50 cakes

750 g	honey, heated	1½ lb
1 kg	flour	2 to 2½ lb
12	egg yolks	12
6 tbsp	olive oil	6 tbsp
3 tbsp	anise-flavoured liqueur	3 tbsp
4 tbsp	sugar	4 tbsp
6	egg whites, stiffly beaten	6
	oil for deep frying	
175 g	almonds, toasted and chopped	6 oz
125 g	crystallized fruit, chopped	4 oz

Sift the flour and make a well in the middle. Place the egg yolks, olive oil, liqueur and sugar in the well, stir together and then gradually amalgamate the flour. When all the ingredients are blended, add the egg whites and mix to form a fairly soft dough. Divide the dough into little balls and roll them out by hand into little sticks. Then cut these up into 1 cm (½ inch) pieces. Fry the pieces in very hot oil until golden, then drain them on kitchen paper before soaking them in the hot honey. Mix the honeyed pastry pieces with the almonds and crystallized fruit and press the whole mass together with your hand into a slab about 1 cm (½ inch) thick. When it has got completely cold, cut the slab across into slices.

OTTAVIO CAVALCANTI
IL LIBRO D'ORO DELLA CUCINA E DEI VINI DI CALABRIA E BASILICATA

Colombina's Choux Fritters

Bignè di Colombina

To make about 30 fritters

100 g	butter	3½ oz
20 cl	water	7 fl oz
30 g	castor sugar	1 oz
	salt	
200 g	flour	7 oz
6	eggs	6
	oil for deep frying	

Put the butter in a saucepan and add the water, 20 g (⅔ oz) of the sugar and a pinch of salt. Heat and, when nearly boiling, remove from the heat and add all the flour; stir vigorously. Reheat and cook over a medium heat, stirring constantly, until smooth and creamy. When the mixture comes away from the sides of the pan, remove the pan from the heat and leave it to cool. Now add the eggs, one by one, stirring them in well. Leave the mixture to settle for 1½ hours. Heat the oil to 190°C (375°F) and fry a few tablespoonfuls of the mixture at a time, removing each fritter from the oil when it is brown and risen. Drain the fritters well on kitchen paper and serve them hot, covered with the remaining sugar.

LEONE BOSI (EDITOR)
DOLCI PER UN ANNO

Sausage-Shaped Choux Fritters

Churros

To make about 70 fritters

1 litre	milk	1¾ pints
40 g	salt	1½ oz
800 g	flour, sifted	1¾ lb
4	eggs	4
	oil for deep frying	
	sugar	

Pour the milk and salt into a large saucepan and place on the heat. When it begins to boil, add the flour and beat well with a wooden spoon. When the mixture comes away from the sides of the pan, remove from the heat. Add the eggs and work well until everything is thoroughly mixed. Place the dough in a piping bag with a 1 cm (½ inch) star nozzle.

Heat a pan of oil to 190°C (375°F); squeeze in 7.5 cm (3 inch) long pieces of the dough. Fry until the *churros* are crisp and golden. Remove from the pan, drain and sprinkle with sugar. Serve immediately, as they are better eaten hot.

ANA MARIA CALERA
COCINA CASTELLANA

Sicilian Ricotta-Filled Pastries

Cannoli

For a demonstration of making cannoli, *see page 88. The cocoa powder and coffee can be omitted. The recipe for pastry cream is on page 166; to flavour pastry cream with chocolate, substitute 125 g (4 oz) of plain chocolate for the vanilla pod.*

The traditional filling for *cannoli* is the sweet ricotta mixture given here, but plain or chocolate-flavoured pastry cream may be used instead. Some Sicilian patisseries and restaurants fill their *cannoli* with two differently flavoured fillings, so that one half of each *cannolo* is filled with chocolate and vanilla-flavoured ricotta and the other half with cocoa.

To make 12 pastries

150 g	flour	5 oz
10 g	sugar	⅓ oz
½ tbsp each	cocoa powder and finely ground coffee	½ tbsp each
	salt	
10 g	lard	⅓ oz
1 tbsp	Marsala	1 tbsp
1 tbsp	brandy	1 tbsp
1	egg white, lightly beaten	1
	oil or lard for deep frying	
	Ricotta filling	
250 g	fresh ricotta, sieved	8 oz
About 175 g	icing sugar	About 6 oz
20 g	crystallized fruit, chopped small	¾ oz
20 g	bitter chocolate, chopped small	¾ oz
12	glacé cherries	12
12	pieces crystallized orange peel	12
30 g	pistachio nuts, chopped	1 oz

Sift the flour into a bowl and add the sugar, cocoa and coffee and a pinch of salt. Rub in the lard. Add the Marsala and brandy and work all the ingredients together to make a dough of a fairly firm consistency. Gather it into a ball, wrap it in a tea towel and leave it for 2 hours.

Roll the dough out thinly and cut 12 discs or ovals approximately 10 cm (4 inches) wide, using a biscuit cutter or the rim of a glass. Wrap each piece of dough round a greased tube and brush the edges of the dough with egg white to make them stick together.

Fry the *cannoli* in plenty of very hot oil or lard until they are golden. Drain them on kitchen paper until they are cool enough to handle. Take the *cannoli* from the tubes and allow them to cool completely.

For the filling, mix the ricotta with 125 g (4 oz) of the icing sugar, the crystallized fruit and the chocolate. Use a metal spatula or a piping bag to fill the *cannoli* with the ricotta mixture. Garnish one end of each *cannoli* with a cherry and the other end with a piece of crystallized orange peel. Sprinkle both ends with the chopped pistachio nuts to give a contrast of colour. Sift the remaining icing sugar over the *cannoli*.

PINO CORRENTI
IL LIBRO D'ORO DELLA CUCINA E DEI VINI DI SICILIA

Date-Filled Pastries

Makroutes

For a demonstration of making makroutes, *with a slightly different method of assembling the pastries, see page 88.*

To make about 32 pastries

1 kg	semolina	2 to 2½ lb
15 cl	oil, heated	¼ pint
About 15 cl	water, warmed	About ¼ pint
	oil for deep frying	
500 g	honey, warmed	1 lb
	Date filling	
1 kg	peeled and stoned fresh dates, puréed	2 to 2½ lb
1	orange, rind thinly pared and finely chopped	1

Place the semolina in a bowl. Add the hot oil, a little at a time, and work the semolina with a fork until the oil has been completely absorbed. Add sufficient water to make a firm dough. Place the dough on the table and roll it out to a thickness of 1 cm (½ inch). Cut it into strips 8 cm (3¼ inches) wide. Mix together the dates and orange rind. Cover half of each strip of dough with the date mixture, fold over the other half and press the edges firmly together. Cut each sealed package into pieces, slantwise. Fry the pieces in very hot oil, drain them and immerse them in tepid honey. Remove them from the honey and serve them hot or cold.

LÉON ISNARD
LA GASTRONOMIE AFRICAINE

Fried Fruit Pies

This recipe comes from North Carolina. Schoolchildren took these pies to school as snacks.

To make 12 pies

275 g	flour	9 oz
½ tsp	salt	½ tsp
175 g	butter or 125 g (4 oz) butter and 50 g (2 oz) lard	6 oz
8 cl	iced water	3 fl oz
	oil or lard for deep frying	
	Dried fruit filling	
250 g	dried fruit (apples, peaches, apricots or a mixture)	8 oz
½ litre	water	16 fl oz
125 g	sugar	4 oz

To make the filling, combine the fruit and the water in a heavy saucepan. Simmer, covered, over a low heat for 20 minutes. Add the sugar and continue cooking for 10 to 15 minutes more. Mash the fruit (do not purée it) to a thick consistency. If the fruit is still too moist, return it to the heat and cook, stirring constantly to avoid scorching, for 3 to 6 more minutes, or until dried out. Cool and reserve.

To make the pastry dough, sift the flour and salt together into a bowl. With two knives or a pastry blender, cut in the butter, or butter and lard, only until the pieces of mixture are about pea-sized. (Bits of unincorporated fat make a flakier crust.) Add the water all at once. With a fork, stir only until the mixture forms a loose ball. Leave the dough to rest in the refrigerator for about an hour. Place the dough on a large piece of waxed paper. Cover with a matching piece of waxed paper. Pat the dough into a flat round. With a rolling pin or bottle, roll the dough out to a thickness of 3 mm (⅛ inch). Cut into rounds about 10 to 11 cm (4 to 4½ inches) in diameter. Place about 1 tablespoon of cooked fruit in the centre of each round. Wet the edges with water and fold over to enclose the filling completely, making a half-moon shape. Seal the edges by pressing down on them with the prongs of a fork.

Heat the lard or oil in a deep-fryer to a temperature of 190°C (375°F) on a frying thermometer. Fry a few pies at a time (they must not touch) for 3 to 4 minutes. Turn and fry on the other side for a further 3 to 4 minutes or until golden. Drain on kitchen paper and serve hot or cold.

NIKA HAZELTON
AMERICAN HOME COOKING

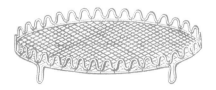

Pear Turnovers

Rezules aux Poires

The author suggests that you bake the turnovers in a preheated 200°C (400°F or Mark 6) oven for 15 minutes as an alternative to deep frying them.

In Savoie, these turnovers are traditionally eaten in winter, from Christmas until the middle of Lent.

To make about 16 turnovers

2 kg	hard cooking pears, peeled, cored and cut into quarters	4 lb
400 g	granulated sugar	14 oz
35 cl	water	12 fl oz
½	stick cinnamon	½
400 g	rough-puff dough (*page 163*)	14 oz
	oil for deep frying	
	icing sugar (optional)	

Place the pears in a casserole with the sugar, the water and the cinnamon stick. Cook, covered, over a low heat for 1½ to 2 hours, then uncover the casserole and leave it to cool.

Roll out the rough-puff dough to a thickness of 5 mm (¦ inch) and cut it into circles the size of a saucer. Place a spoonful of stewed pears on half of each circle, fold the other half over and stick the edges together well by pressing them with your fingers, moistened with a little water.

Deep fry the turnovers in very hot oil for 6 to 8 minutes or until browned. If you like, you can dust them with a little icing sugar before serving.

CHARLOTTE VANEL
LA BONNE CUISINE DES MONTAGNES SAVOIE-DAUPHINE

Almond-Filled Cakes

Ghotab

To make about 20 cakes

2	egg yolks	2
125 g	butter	4 oz
12.5 cl	yogurt	4 fl oz
175 g	flour	6 oz
½ litre	vegetable oil for deep frying	16 fl oz
150 g	icing sugar	5 oz

Almond filling

50 g	ground almonds	2 oz
40 g	icing sugar	1½ oz
1 tsp	ground cardamom	1 tsp

Beat the egg yolks, butter and yogurt until creamy. Gradually stir in the flour and knead well with your hands. If the dough is sticky, add more flour. Place the dough in a plastic bag and keep it at room temperature for 2 to 3 hours. Mix together the ingredients for the filling.

Place the dough on a floured board and roll it out to a thickness of 5 mm (¦ inch). Cut it into circles with a floured biscuit cutter. Place a small amount of filling in the middle of each circle. Fold up the edges, pinch them together and roll each cake into the shape of an egg in the palms of your hands. Heat the vegetable oil to 190°C (375°F) in a deep saucepan. Drop the cakes in and deep fry them for 3 to 5 minutes until they are golden-brown. Drain them on kitchen paper. While the cakes are still warm, roll them in the icing sugar. When they are cool, roll them again in the icing sugar.

NESTA RAMAZANI
PERSIAN COOKING

Fried Walnut Dumplings

Samsa

These sweet walnut dumplings come from central Asia.

To make 72 dumplings

175 g	shelled walnuts, pulverized in a blender or food processor	6 oz
30 g	butter, softened	1 oz
1½ tbsp	granulated sugar	1½ tbsp
	vegetable oil for deep frying	
	icing sugar	

Dough

175 g	flour	6 oz
8 cl	warm water	3 fl oz
½ tsp	salt	½ tsp
60 g	butter, softened	2 oz

To prepare the dough, mix together the flour, water, salt and 30 g (1 oz) of the butter in a medium-sized bowl. Beat with a wooden spoon to make a firm dough. Gather the dough into a ball. Cover and leave it to rest for 30 minutes.

For the filling, mix together the walnuts, butter and granulated sugar in another bowl.

Roll the dough into a rectangle approximately 45 by 40 cm (18 by 16 inches) and smear the remaining butter over the dough. Fold the rectangle into quarters and roll it out again as thin as possible. Cut it into 5 cm (2 inch) squares.

Place about a teaspoon of filling in the centre of each square and bring the four corners up to meet in the middle. Pinch the edges and corners together to seal completely. Moisten your fingers with water if necessary. Heat the vegetable oil to 190°C (375°F). Drop about six *samsa* at a time into the hot oil and fry for 3 minutes or until golden-brown. Remove with a slotted spoon and drain on kitchen paper. Repeat until all are done. Sprinkle with icing sugar and serve.

MARIA POLUSHKIN
THE DUMPLING COOKBOOK

Madrid Tarts

Bartolillos de Madrid

To make 32 tarts

500 g	flour	1 lb
100 g	granulated sugar	3½ oz
100 g	butter, cut into pieces	3½ oz
20 g	baking powder	⅔ oz
¼ litre	cold milk	8 fl oz
250 g	pastry cream (*page 166*)	8 oz
	oil for deep frying	
	castor sugar	

Mix together the flour, granulated sugar, butter and baking powder, working with your fingertips until the mixture is crumbly. Reserve 2 tablespoons of the milk and stir in the rest to make a dough. Roll out the dough on a floured surface into a rectangle about 20 cm (8 inches) wide. With a brush, paint half the rectangle with milk. Fill a piping bag with the pastry cream and put dabs of pastry cream on the painted half of the dough, leaving some space between the dabs. Fold over the unpainted half of the dough, making sure that the edges meet. Cut the filled dough into small squares with a knife or ravioli cutter, making sure that a dab of cream is in the centre of each square. Set aside for 15 minutes, then heat up the oil in a large pan and fry the squares until golden. Sprinkle with castor sugar.

ANA MARIA CALERA
COCINA CASTELLANA

Moroccan Tea Cakes

Braewats

Braewats can also be made with almonds which have been blanched but not toasted.

To make 8 tea cakes

125 g	almonds, blanched and toasted	4 oz
125 g	sugar	4 oz
250 g	shortcrust dough (*page 163*)	8 oz
45 g	butter, melted, or 4 tbsp olive oil	1½ oz
250 g	honey	8 oz
	oil for deep frying	

Add the almonds to the sugar and grind this mixture together using a pestle and mortar, a blender or a food processor. Roll out the shortcrust dough and cut it into rectangles, about 15 by 10 cm (6 by 4 inches). Grease each rectangle with the butter or olive oil. Spread each thinly with the almond and sugar mixture. Fold over a tiny bit of dough at each end, then roll up, like a Swiss roll.

Deep fry the pastries in the oil until they are light brown. Then bring the honey to the boil, lay each *braewat* in the boiling honey and leave them to soak for 5 to 10 minutes.

Serve the *braewats* cold, with tea or as a dessert.

IRENE F. DAY
KITCHEN IN THE KASBAH

Curd Puffs

This recipe for curd puffs dates from the 17th century.

To make about 20 puffs

250 g	curd cheese	8 oz
2	eggs, yolks separated from whites, yolks well beaten, whites stiffly beaten	2
2 tbsp	rose-water	2 tbsp
½ tsp	ground cinnamon	½ tsp
¼	nutmeg, grated	¼
250 g	flour, sifted	8 oz
60 g	butter	2 oz

Add the egg yolks to the curd cheese and mix well together. Then fold in the egg whites. Put in the rose-water, cinnamon and nutmeg, and enough flour to make a fairly stiff mixture which will not spread too much in the frying pan. Fry tablespoonfuls of the curd cheese mixture in the butter so that they brown on both sides.

ALISON REVELL (EDITOR)
A KENTISH COOKERY COLLECTION

Dutch Oat Cakes

Havermoutkoekjes

To make about 30 cakes

150 g	rolled oats	5 oz
30 cl	water	½ pint
150 g	flour	5 oz
	salt	
4 tsp	sugar	4 tsp
2 or 3	eggs, beaten	2 or 3
1 tsp	ground cinnamon or 2 tsp grated lemon rind	1 tsp
About 150 g	butter	About 5 oz
	brown sugar	

Soak the oats in the water for about 1 hour. Add the flour, a pinch of salt, the sugar, eggs, flavouring and enough extra water, if necessary, to make a fairly stiff mixture. Form the mixture into small round cakes, about 6 cm (2½ inches) in diameter. Melt the butter in a frying pan and fry the cakes over a medium heat until they are golden-brown and cooked through. Serve them warm, sprinkled with brown sugar.

C. J. WANNÉE
KOOKBOEK VAN DE AMSTERDAMSE HUISHOUDSCHOOL

Semolina Fritters

Frittelle Semola

To make about 80 fritters

300 g	semolina	10 oz
1.5 litres	milk	2½ pints
4	egg whites, stiffly beaten	4
1	lemon, rind grated	1
	salt	
	flour (optional)	
	oil for deep frying	

Bring the milk to the boil, stir in the semolina, and cook, stirring, until thickened. Remove from the heat and allow to cool. Add the egg whites, lemon rind and a pinch of salt and mix well, adding flour if necessary to make a firm dough.

Heat the oil in a large pan. Drop tablespoonfuls of the mixture into the oil and fry the fritters until they are golden-brown on both sides.

FERRUCCIO BOTTI (MASTRO PRESCIUTTO)
GASTRONOMIA PARMENSE

Mexican Fritters

Buñuelos

These deep-fried puffs of batter, sprinkled with cinnamon and sugar, are delicious any time, especially for breakfast.

To make about 48 fritters

500 g	flour	1 lb
1 tbsp	granulated sugar	1 tbsp
1 tsp	baking powder	1 tsp
1 tsp	salt	1 tsp
2	eggs, lightly beaten	2
¼ litre	milk	8 fl oz
60 g	butter, melted	2 oz
	oil for deep frying	
	castor sugar	
	ground cinnamon	

Into a medium-sized bowl, sift together the flour, granulated sugar, baking powder and salt. Add the eggs, milk and butter. Mix to form a soft dough. Remove the dough to a floured board and knead it until it feels smooth and satiny. Divide the dough into walnut-sized pieces. Cover them with a cloth and leave them to stand for 30 minutes.

Heat the oil to 190°C (375°F). Flatten each ball into a flat pancake between the palms of your hands and drop about four at a time into the hot oil. Fry them for 4 to 5 minutes, or until they are puffed and brown. Remove them with a slotted spoon and drain them on kitchen paper. Repeat until all the puffs are cooked. Sprinkle them with castor sugar and ground cinnamon and serve.

MARIA POLUSHKIN
THE DUMPLING COOKBOOK

Pumpkin Fritters

Beignets de Potiron

In Bonifacio, grated raw pumpkin is added to the batter. You can also add raisins soaked in brandy or rum.

To make about 40 fritters

500 g	section of pumpkin, seeded, peeled and cut into cubes	1 lb
	oil for deep frying	
	castor sugar	

	Fritter batter	
20 g	fresh yeast or 2 tsp dried yeast	$\frac{3}{4}$ oz
4 tbsp	warm salted water	4 tbsp
500 g	flour	1 lb
2 tbsp	olive oil	2 tbsp
2	eggs	2

To make the fritter batter, dissolve the yeast in the warm salted water. Stir in 100 g ($3\frac{1}{2}$ oz) of flour, form the mixture into a ball and leave it for at least 1 hour in a warm place until it has doubled in volume. In a large bowl, mix together the rest of the flour with the olive oil and eggs. Add the risen leaven and mix everything together well to form a smooth dough. Leave the dough for another hour.

Cook the pumpkin in lightly salted boiling water, until it is tender, about 15 minutes. Drain it carefully and press it in a cloth to extract all the water. Mash the pumpkin with a fork or put it through a food mill. Mix the purée into the fritter batter.

Shape the fritters with a spoon and drop them into the oil, heated to 190°C (375°F). Fry each fritter for about 5 minutes or until golden, then drain them and sprinkle with sugar.

MARIE CECCALDI
CUISINE DE CORSE

Fried Rice Cakes

Rijstkoekjes

To make about 30 cakes

600 g	boiled rice	$1\frac{1}{4}$ lb
2	eggs, yolks separated from whites, whites stiffly beaten	2
100 g	castor sugar	$3\frac{1}{2}$ oz
100 g	flour	$3\frac{1}{2}$ oz
1	vanilla pod, seeds scraped out and reserved, or 1 lemon, rind grated, or 2 tsp ground cinnamon	1
	milk (optional)	
100 g	butter or 6 tbsp oil	$3\frac{1}{2}$ oz
	icing sugar or castor sugar	

Whisk the egg yolks with the sugar until smooth and creamy. Add the flour, the flavouring and the rice. Fold the egg whites lightly into the mixture and, if necessary, add a little milk to make a batter of a soft, dropping consistency.

Heat the butter or oil in a frying pan over a moderate heat. Drop tablespoons of the batter into the hot fat and fry the cakes until golden-brown on all sides. Remove from the pan, sprinkle with icing sugar or castor sugar, and serve.

C. J. WANNÉE
KOOKBOEK VAN DE AMSTERDAMSE HUISHOUDSCHOOL

Fritters in Anise-Flavoured Syrup

Buñuelos

These can be cooked several hours ahead and doused with syrup just before serving, but they do not keep successfully from one day to another.

To make 12 fritters

$\frac{1}{4}$ litre	water	8 fl oz
$\frac{1}{4}$ tsp	salt	$\frac{1}{4}$ tsp
$\frac{1}{4}$ tsp	aniseeds	$\frac{1}{4}$ tsp
45 g	lard	$1\frac{1}{2}$ oz
125 g	flour, sifted	4 oz
3	eggs	3
	baking powder	
	oil for deep frying	
	Anise syrup	
$\frac{3}{4}$ litre	water	$1\frac{1}{4}$ pints
350 g	dark brown sugar	12 oz
$\frac{1}{4}$ tsp	aniseeds	$\frac{1}{4}$ tsp

Put all the ingredients for the syrup together into a saucepan. Set the pan over a medium heat until the sugar has melted, and then bring it quickly to the boil. Let the syrup boil for about 20 minutes; by then it should have reduced to about 30 cl ($\frac{1}{2}$ pint). Set the syrup aside to cool.

Put the water, salt, aniseeds and lard into a saucepan and bring to the boil. When the lard has completely melted and the mixture is still boiling, stir the flour into it quickly. Beat the mixture, while continuing to cook it, until it shrinks away from the sides of the pan. Set the dough aside to cool.

When the dough is cool enough to handle, knead it until it is quite smooth. Beat the eggs lightly and stir them into the mixture, a little at a time, reserving some of the egg until you have tested the dough. You should be able to roll it into a soft ball that will just hold its shape. Add the rest of the egg if necessary. Mix a pinch of baking powder into the dough.

Heat 1 cm ($\frac{1}{2}$ inch) of oil in a frying pan until it smokes. Wet your hands well, take a piece of the dough and roll it into a ball about 4 cm ($1\frac{1}{2}$ inches) in diameter. Place the ball on your fingers—not on your palm—and flatten it to make a cake about 2 cm ($\frac{3}{4}$ inch) thick. Make a large hole in the centre of the dough and drop it into the hot fat. Cook it on both sides until it is a golden-brown and well puffed up.

Remove the fritter from the fat with a slotted spoon and drain it on kitchen paper. Shape and dry the rest of the dough in the same way. Pour 4 tablespoons of the syrup over each serving of two *buñuelos* and serve immediately.

DIANA KENNEDY
CUISINES OF MEXICO

Jallebis

To make about 50 jallebis

350 g	flour, sifted	12 oz
15 cl	yogurt	$\frac{1}{4}$ pint
30 g	dried yeast	1 oz
About $\frac{3}{4}$ litre	water	About 1$\frac{1}{2}$ pints
500 g	sugar	1 lb
$\frac{1}{8}$ tsp	powdered saffron or turmeric	$\frac{1}{8}$ tsp
6	cardamom pods	6
6	cloves	6
	oil for deep frying	
	icing sugar	

Place the flour in a large bowl. Add the yogurt, yeast and sufficient water to form a batter the consistency of double cream. Cover and stand in a warm place for about 4 hours.

Prepare a syrup by boiling the sugar and 60 cl (1 pint) of water together with the spices for 15 minutes.

Place the batter in a piping bag, or a plastic bag with one corner cut away to make a small hole. Pipe the mixture into the hot oil in figures-of-eight or double circle shapes. Cook for about 1 minute, turning frequently, until the *jallebis* are lightly browned. Drain, and put the *jallebis* into the sugar syrup for 5 minutes. Drain again, sprinkle the *jallebis* with icing sugar and serve them hot or cold.

ANNABEL SHAXSON, PAT DICKSON AND JUNE WALKER
THE MALAWI COOKBOOK

Raised Doughnuts

The technique of shaping doughnuts by hand is demonstrated on page 84.

To make 24 doughnuts

17.5 cl	milk, scalded	6 fl oz
75 g	sugar	2$\frac{1}{2}$ oz
1 tsp	salt	1 tsp
30 g	fresh yeast or 1 tbsp dried yeast	1 oz
4 tbsp	warm water	4 tbsp
500 g	flour, sifted	1 lb
1 tsp	grated nutmeg	1 tsp
75 g	lard, melted and cooled	2$\frac{1}{2}$ oz
2	eggs	2
	fat for deep frying	

Mix the milk with the sugar and salt; cool the mixture to lukewarm. Mix the yeast with the warm water and stir until the yeast is dissolved. Add the milk mixture, half of the flour

and the nutmeg. Beat well. Stir in the lard, then the eggs. Add the remaining flour, kneading in the last portion on a lightly floured surface. Place the dough in a greased bowl, turning it once to grease the top. Let the dough rise in a warm place until it has doubled in bulk.

Turn the dough out on a lightly floured board. Roll it out 8 mm ($\frac{1}{3}$ inch) thick; cut rounds with a doughnut cutter. Remove the trimmings of dough and form them into a ball. Leave it to rise again. When it has doubled in bulk, roll the dough out and cut more doughnuts.

Let the cut doughnuts rise until they are very light (30 to 40 minutes). Leave them uncovered so that a crust will form. Pick them up on a wide, floured, spatula and ease them into deep hot fat. Fry them until golden-brown, about 2 minutes, turning once. Drain the doughnuts.

Sugared doughnuts: While the doughnuts are still warm, dip them into a bowl of sugar or a mixture of 125 g (4 oz) sugar and $\frac{1}{2}$ teaspoon of ground cinnamon. Or, when the doughnuts have cooled, shake them in a bag with icing sugar.

Glazed doughnuts: Mix 175 g (6 oz) of sifted icing sugar with enough boiling water to make a thin glaze (about 3 tablespoons). Dip the slightly cooled doughnuts into the warm glaze. Cool them on a wire rack covered with a piece of greaseproof paper.

Raised orange doughnuts: Proceed as for raised doughnuts: in place of milk use 12.5 cl (4 fl oz) of orange juice plus 4 tablespoons of boiling water. Use 2 tablespoons of finely grated orange rind in place of nutmeg.

NELL B. NICHOLS (EDITOR)
FARM JOURNAL'S COUNTRY COOKBOOK

Little Cream Cakes from Andalusia

Pastelillos de Crema

In Spain, the bread dough required for this recipe can be bought from bakeries. However, a suitable dough can easily be made at home: sift 250 g (8 oz) of strong plain flour with a pinch of salt into a bowl. Mix a teaspoonful of fresh yeast (or half a teaspoonful of dried yeast) with 15 cl ($\frac{1}{4}$ pint) of tepid water. (If you are using dried yeast, leave it to soften for about 15 minutes.) Pour the yeast mixture into the flour. Mix the flour and liquid together into a stiff, sticky dough. Put the dough on to a floured board and knead it thoroughly, until it is elastic and glossy—about 15 minutes.

To make about 24 cakes

250 g	bread dough	8 oz
1 tbsp	lard	1 tbsp
4 tbsp	Seville orange juice	4 tbsp
	oil for deep frying	
2 tsp	sugar mixed with 2 tsp ground cinnamon	2 tsp

	Filling	
2 tbsp	flour	2 tbsp
¼ litre	milk	8 fl oz
200 g	sugar	7 oz
1	egg, beaten	1

Prepare the filling beforehand so that it has cooled down before it is needed. Mix together the flour, milk and sugar in a heavy saucepan. Then add the egg and place the pan over a low heat. Stirring constantly, cook until everything has blended together, then turn out on to a plate to cool.

Put the bread dough in a bowl and add the lard and the orange juice. Knead together well and, when the dough is very smooth, roll it out to the thickness of a coin and cut into rounds with a biscuit cutter.

Place a little of the filling in the centre of half the number of dough rounds, then top each one with another circle, pressing the edges firmly together. Deep fry the cakes in very hot oil until they are golden. Remove from the pan and dust with the sugar and ground cinnamon.

ANA MARIA CALERA
COCINA ANDALUZA

Honey Puffs

Loucoumades

To make about 30 puffs

60 g	fresh yeast or 2 tbsp dried yeast	2 oz
About 30 cl	warm water	About ½ pint
250 g	flour	8 oz
½ tsp	salt	½ tsp
	olive oil for deep frying	
	ground cinnamon	
	Syrup	
300 g	honey	10 oz
12.5 cl	water	4 fl oz
1	lemon, juice strained	1

Dissolve the yeast in a basin with half the warm water. Add 2 tablespoons of the flour and leave it to rise in a warm place for 30 minutes. When the yeast has worked, add the rest of the flour, the salt and enough of the remaining warm water to make a thick batter of dropping consistency. Cover the basin with a cloth and let it stand for 2 to 3 hours until bubbles appear on the top. The batter is then ready for frying.

Heat at least 60 cl (1 pint) of olive oil in a deep pan and when it is really hot (190°C or 375°F on a cooking thermometer) drop the batter into it from a spoon. Dip the spoon into cold water each time before dipping it into the batter, so that the batter will not stick to the spoon. Cook the puffs until they are golden, about 5 minutes. Dry them on a sheet of greaseproof paper and pile them on a warmed plate for serving.

Bring the syrup ingredients to the boil together. Dust the puffs with cinnamon and pour on the syrup. Serve at once.

JOYCE M. STUBBS
THE HOME BOOK OF GREEK COOKERY

Mashed Potato Doughnuts

An alternative method of shaping ring doughnuts is demon-strated on page 84.

To make 36 doughnuts

250 g	hot mashed potatoes, seasoned	8 oz
60 g	butter, melted	2 oz
175 g	sugar	6 oz
2	eggs, beaten	2
500 g	flour, sifted	1 lb
5 tsp	baking powder	5 tsp
1 tsp	salt	1 tsp
1 tsp	grated nutmeg	1 tsp
12.5 cl	milk	4 fl oz
	fat for deep frying	
2 tbsp	icing sugar	2 tbsp

Cream together the butter and sugar. Blend in the mashed potatoes, then the eggs. Sift the dry ingredients together twice. Add them to the first mixture alternately with the milk. Chill the dough for 2 hours.

Roll out the dough 1 cm (½ inch) thick on a lightly floured surface and cut with a doughnut cutter. Fry the doughnuts in deep hot fat for about 1 minute on each side, until they are golden-brown, turning them once. Do not have more than one layer of doughnuts in the pan at one time. Drain them on kitchen paper and sprinkle with icing sugar while still warm.

NELL B. NICHOLS (EDITOR)
FARM JOURNAL'S COUNTRY COOKBOOK

Whole-Wheat Doughnuts

Eat these doughnuts within a day, or allow them to cool completely, then wrap them closely, seal them and freeze them. To reheat them, place the doughnuts on a baking sheet in a preheated 180°C (350°F or Mark 4) oven for 15 minutes.

To make about 18 doughnuts

125 g	medium or fine wholemeal flour	4 oz
1	egg	1
60 g	light brown sugar, sifted	2 oz
60 g	granulated sugar	2 oz
45 g	butter, melted and cooled	1½ oz
½ tsp	vanilla extract	½ tsp
150 g	flour	5 oz
1 tbsp	baking powder	1 tbsp
¼ tsp	salt	¼ tsp
¼ tsp	ground mace	¼ tsp
15 g	unprocessed coarse bran	½ oz
About ¼ litre	milk	About 8 fl oz
	fat or oil for deep frying	
2 tsp	ground cinnamon, mixed with 125 g (4 oz) sugar	2 tsp

Beat together the egg and the sugars until thick and light. Beat in the butter and vanilla. Sift together the flours, baking powder, salt and mace. Stir in the bran.

Add the flour mixture to the egg and sugar mixture, alternating it with the milk. Stir to combine the ingredients into a soft dough, adding as much milk as necessary to achieve this. Mix just until the dough is the proper consistency—smooth and not sticky; do not overbeat or the doughnuts will be tough. Form the dough into a rough rectangle, wrap it in floured plastic film and refrigerate it for at least 1 hour.

Over a medium heat, in a deep-fryer or saucepan, begin heating fat or oil to a depth of 7.5 cm (3 inches). Roll the dough out to a thickness of 1 cm (½ inch). Cut with a 6 cm (2½ inch) doughnut cutter, or use a plain round cutter and cut a centre hole with a bottle cap or small glass. Keep the centres. Continue cutting and rolling until all the dough is used.

When the fat shows 190°C (375°F) on a deep-frying thermometer, drop a few doughnuts into the fat, leaving plenty of room for them to swell. Fry them for about 2 minutes on each side, until golden-brown. The cut-out centres will take less time to fry. Remove the doughnuts with tongs to a rack covered with kitchen towels. Put the next batch in to fry.

Place the cinnamon and sugar mixture in a paper bag. Drop in the drained doughnuts, shake the bag vigorously to coat them, and return them to the rack. Continue until all the doughnuts and centres are fried and coated. Eat warm.

HELEN WITTY AND ELIZABETH SCHNEIDER COLCHIE
BETTER THAN STORE-BOUGHT

New Orleans Rice Fritters

Calas

Served with some good sausage and an assortment of honey, syrups and jams, *calas* make an unusual and delicious breakfast. Try them also with a good, home-made apple sauce. *Calas* can be reheated in the oven at 180°C (350°F or Mark 4) for 20 minutes, but are very good cold.

To make about 30 fritters

100 g	rice	3½ oz
15 g	butter	½ oz
1 tsp	salt	1 tsp
2 tsp	dried yeast	2 tsp
12.5 cl	warm water	4 fl oz
125 g	sugar	4 oz
3	eggs, lightly beaten	3
125 g	flour	4 oz
¼ tsp	vanilla extract	¼ tsp
¼ tsp	grated nutmeg	¼ tsp
	vegetable oil for deep frying	

Cook the rice in plenty of boiling water with the butter and salt for 45 minutes, or until very soft. Drain the rice and mash it with a potato masher or a wooden spoon. Allow it to cool until it is lukewarm.

Dissolve the yeast in the warm water with a pinch of sugar. Leave it to stand until the yeast begins to foam, about 5 minutes. Add this to the rice and beat well with a wooden spoon, for at least 2 minutes. Cover, and leave in a warm place to rise for at least 2 hours or, even better, overnight. Add the eggs, flour, the rest of the sugar, the vanilla and the nutmeg. Mix all the ingredients together well. Cover the bowl and put the batter in a warm place to rise for 30 minutes.

Heat the vegetable oil to 190°C (375°F). Drop tablespoonfuls of the batter into the hot oil, a few at a time. Fry the *calas* until they are a golden colour. Remove them with a slotted spoon and drain them on kitchen paper. Keep them warm in a preheated 130°C (250°F or Mark ½) oven until all are done.

MARIA POLUSHKIN
THE DUMPLING COOKBOOK

Corsican Rice Fritters

Panzarotti

These rice fritters are made particularly for religious festivals (Saint Joseph's Day, Good Friday), because rice is the symbol of purity, life, plenty and immortality. Good Friday *panzarotti* are little square pies, stuffed with chopped green leafy parts of Swiss chard (sometimes macerated in grape must) and sprinkled with sugar. In the Bastia region of Corsica potatoes replace the rice.

To make about 40 fritters

100 g	rice, boiled in a large quantity of milk or salted water for 20 minutes, then drained	3½ oz
300 g	flour	10 oz
	salt	
2 tbsp	*eau-de-vie* or brandy	2 tbsp
1 tbsp	olive oil	1 tbsp
20 g	fresh yeast or 2 tsp dried yeast, dissolved in 20 cl (7 fl oz) lukewarm water	¾ oz
4	eggs, yolks separated from whites, whites stiffly beaten	4
1	lemon, rind grated	1
	oil for deep frying	
	castor sugar	

Put the flour and a pinch of salt into a bowl. Pour in the *eau-de-vie* or brandy, the olive oil and the yeast solution. Mix into a smooth dough and leave it to rest for 1 hour.

Stir the egg yolks, the grated lemon rind and the rice into the batter. Fold in the egg whites. Shape the fritters with a spoon and deep fry them for 4 to 5 minutes each. Remove them from the pan when golden and drain. Serve the fritters hot, sprinkled with castor sugar.

MARIE CECCALDI
CUISINE DE CORSE

French Toast with Rum

Pain Doré au Rhum

To make 6 toasts

200 g	stale brioche loaf (*page 161*)	7 oz
3	eggs, beaten	3
¼ litre	milk or single cream, warmed	8 fl oz
110 g	sugar	3½ oz
10 cl	rum	3½ fl oz
125 g	butter	4 oz
1 tbsp	vanilla sugar or 1 tsp ground cinnamon	1 tbsp

Cut the brioche into 1 cm (½ inch) thick slices. Beat together the eggs, the warm milk or cream, 60 g (2 oz) of the sugar and the rum. Rapidly dip each slice of brioche in the mixture, then fry it in the butter until it is golden on both sides. Sprinkle the fried brioche with the remaining sugar, mixed with the vanilla sugar or cinnamon.

GINETTE MATHIOT
JE SAIS FAIRE LA PÂTISSERIE

St. Teresa's Toasts

Tostadas de Santa Teresa

To make about 30 toasts

3	large bread rolls	3
½ litre	milk	16 fl oz
2 tsp	ground cinnamon	2 tsp
	oil for deep frying	
2	eggs, beaten	2
	sugar	

Cut the bread rolls into slices 1 cm (½ inch) thick. Put the slices into a bowl and cover them with the milk. When they are well soaked, remove them and sprinkle them with the cinnamon. Heat up plenty of oil in a frying pan. When the oil is quite hot, soak the bread slices in the beaten egg and fry them on both sides. When the slices are brown, remove them from the oil and sprinkle them with sugar.

COCINA REGIONAL ESPAÑOLA

Sighs

Sospiri

To make 16 rounds

4	slices white bread, crusts removed	4
17.5 cl	oil for frying	6 fl oz
1 tbsp	potato flour	1 tbsp
3	egg yolks	3
100 g	sugar	3½ oz
17.5 cl	milk	6 fl oz

Using a biscuit cutter, cut each slice of bread into four rounds. Fry the bread rounds over a medium heat in the hot oil until they are golden, then drain them on kitchen paper. Meanwhile, put the potato flour, egg yolks, sugar and milk into a saucepan and cook over a moderate heat, stirring all the time, until the mixture thickens. Allow this custard to cool, then spread it on the bread rounds and serve them.

FIAMMA NICCOLINI ADIMARI
IL LIBRO DEL PANE

Pampurdy

Raw marrow can be extracted from a large beef bone with the help of a small knife. The bone should first be cut into sections by the butcher.

To make about 30 slices

12	egg yolks	12
6	egg whites	6
	grated nutmeg	
2 tbsp	rose-water	2 tbsp
30 cl	double cream	½ pint
60 g	beef marrow, finely shredded	2 oz
2	loaves white bread, crusts removed, sliced, lightly toasted	2
60 cl	sherry	1 pint
125 g	butter	4 oz
60 g	castor sugar	2 oz

Beat together the egg yolks and whites, a little nutmeg, the rose-water, cream and marrow.

Soak the toast in the sherry. When the sherry is absorbed, dip the slices of toast in the egg and marrow mixture. Fry them in the butter. Sprinkle with castor sugar and serve.

HAMISH WHYTE (EDITOR)
LADY CASTLEHILL'S RECEIPT BOOK

Poor Knights of Windsor

To make 4 slices

30 cl	sweet white wine or milk	½ pint
60 g	granulated sugar	2 oz
4 slices	stale bread, about 1 cm (½ inch) thick	4 slices
2	egg yolks, beaten	2
	butter or lard for frying	
4 tbsp	jam, or 2 tbsp castor sugar mixed with 1 tsp ground cinnamon	4 tbsp

Mix together the white wine or milk and the granulated sugar in a dish. Put the slices of bread into this mixture and turn them over so that both sides soak up some of the liquid. Take them up carefully, one by one, and dip them in the beaten egg yolk. Heat a little butter or lard until very hot in a frying pan, place the bread slices in it and fry them until they are a fine brown colour on both sides.

Drain the slices and serve them on a hot dish. Place a spoonful of jam on each or, if liked, strew on some castor sugar and ground cinnamon.

FLORENCE WHITE (EDITOR)
GOOD THINGS IN ENGLAND

Fried Pastry Cream Veneto-Style

Crema Fritta alla Veneta

The technique of making these creams is shown on page 90.

To make about 25 fried creams

½ litre	milk	16 fl oz
1 tsp	vanilla extract	1 tsp
125 g	sugar	4 oz
125 g	flour, sifted	4 oz
	salt	
4	eggs	4
4	egg yolks	4
75 g	butter	2½ oz
	dry breadcrumbs	
	fat or oil for deep frying	
	icing sugar	

Bring the milk to the boil, remove from the heat, add the vanilla and let it stand for 15 minutes.

In a saucepan, mix the sugar, flour, a pinch of salt, two of the whole eggs and the yolks. Mix well and gradually beat in the warm milk. Stir constantly over a moderate heat until smooth and very thick. Remove from the heat and beat in 30 g (1 oz) of the butter. Mix well and pour into a 20 cm (8 inch) square pan to make a layer 1 cm (½ inch) thick. Melt the remaining butter and pour it over the surface of the cream. Chill and then cut into 4 cm (1½ inch) squares or diamond-shaped pieces. Beat the remaining eggs in a bowl. Dip the custard pieces into the egg, then into the breadcrumbs. Heat the fat or oil to 182°C (360°F) and deep fry, turning the pieces to brown evenly on all sides. Drain them on absorbent paper and sprinkle with icing sugar. Serve very hot.

WAVERLEY ROOT
THE BEST OF ITALIAN COOKING

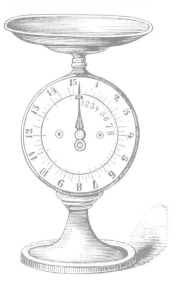

Chinese Fried Custard in Sesame Sugar

If necessary, the custard can be made an hour before serving and served at room temperature. However, do not make it the day before as it will taste stale.

To make about 100 strips

75 g	sesame seeds	2½ oz
125 g	sugar, tinted with 6 drops of red food colouring	4 oz
125 g	flour, sifted	4 oz
2 tbsp	cornflour	2 tbsp
¾ litre	cold water	1¼ pints
1	egg, lightly beaten	1
	oil for deep frying	

Roast the sesame seeds in an ungreased heavy frying pan over a medium heat, turning them constantly, until they are golden-brown. Crush them in a mortar with a pestle. Mix them with the coloured sugar and set aside.

Mix the sifted flour, the cornflour and ¼ litre (8 fl oz) of the cold water into a smooth paste. Add the beaten egg and mix again. Bring the remaining water to the boil. Add the flour and cornflour paste, stirring until the mixture thickens. Pour it into an oiled 30 by 23 cm (12 by 9 inch) rectangular baking tin and cool in the refrigerator until firm.

When the custard is cool, cut it into 5 by 1 by 1 cm (2 by ½ by ½ inch) strips. Heat oil to 180° to 190°C (350° to 375°F). Deep fry the custard strips, a few at a time, for about 1 minute each; drain, and roll them in the sesame seed and sugar mixture.

GRACE ZIA CHU
MADAME CHU'S CHINESE COOKING SCHOOL

Fried Semolina

Gonfietti alla Lombarda

To make about 40 cubes

60 g	semolina	2 oz
½ litre	milk	16 fl oz
30 g	butter	1 oz
	salt	
90 g	sugar	3 oz
2 or 3	egg yolks	2 or 3
	oil for deep frying	

Bring the milk to the boil and stir in the semolina. Add the butter and a pinch of salt, and cook over a low heat, stirring constantly, until the mixture is thick and comes away from the sides of the pan. Stir in half of the sugar and the egg yolks.

Pour on to a floured board, spread out to about 2.5 cm (1 inch) thick, and leave to cool completely.

Cut the cooled semolina into cubes. Heat the oil in a large pan and fry the cubes until golden-brown. Drain and serve hot, sprinkled with the remaining sugar.

FERRUCCIO BOTTI (MASTRO PRESCIUTTO)
GASTRONOMIA PARMENSE

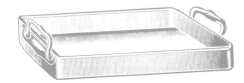

Fried Almond Cream

Li Bigñeta dé Péna

To make about 90 fritters

100 g	almonds, blanched and pounded	3½ oz
200 g	flour	7 oz
350 g	granulated sugar	12 oz
	salt	
6	eggs, beaten	6
10	egg yolks	10
1.25 litres	milk	2 pints
40 g	butter, melted	1½ oz
60 g	fine dry breadcrumbs	2 oz
	olive oil for deep frying	
	castor sugar	

Mix the flour, sugar and a small pinch of salt in a saucepan and add two-thirds of the beaten egg and then the egg yolks, mixing them in well. Combine the almonds with ¼ litre (8 fl oz) of the milk and stir in the flour and egg mixture. Bring the remaining milk to the boil and stir it slowly into the mixture with a wooden spoon. Place the saucepan on the heat and cook, stirring with a whisk. As soon as the mixture comes to the boil, pour it into a shallow buttered tin or dish. Spread the cream out into an even layer and brush the surface with the melted butter; allow it to cool.

Cut the cream into diamonds measuring 3 cm (1¼ inches) on each side. Dip the diamonds in the remaining beaten egg, roll them in the breadcrumbs and deep fry in the olive oil until golden-brown. Sprinkle the fritters with castor sugar and serve them on a napkin.

JACQUES MÉDECIN
LA CUISINE DU COMTÉ DE NICE

Cream Fritters

Buñuelos de Crema

To make about 50 fritters

225 g	flour	7½ oz
100 g	sugar	3½ oz
4	egg yolks	4
8	eggs, 2 beaten separately	8
1 litre	milk, boiled and cooled	1¾ pints
1	lemon, rind grated	1
½ tsp	vanilla extract	½ tsp
100 g	lard	3½ oz
½ tsp	salt	½ tsp
15 g	butter	½ oz
1 tbsp	sugar, flavoured with lemon peel and vanilla	1 tbsp
75 g	dry breadcrumbs	2½ oz
	oil for deep frying	
60 g	castor sugar	2 oz

Put the flour, sugar, egg yolks and six whole eggs into a saucepan. Stir in the milk, blending everything together. Pass the mixture through a sieve and then add the lemon rind, vanilla, lard and salt. Place over the heat and stir to bind the paste together. Remove from the heat immediately lumps start to form. Beat the mixture again with a spoon until it is smooth. Put it back over a low heat and stir constantly for a few minutes until it returns to the boil. Remove from the heat and stir in the butter and flavoured sugar. Pour the mixture into a greased tin that will hold a 1 cm (½ inch) layer of the paste. Cover it with greased paper and allow it to cool.

Once the paste is cool, cut it into rounds with a biscuit cutter. Coat the rounds with the two beaten eggs and breadcrumbs. Deep fry the rounds in the oil until they are golden-brown. Remove them from the oil with a slotted spoon and drain them on kitchen paper. Dust the fritters with castor sugar and serve them immediately.

MANUEL M. PUGA Y PARGA (PICADILLO)
LA COCINA PRÁCTICA

Waffles

Pâte à Gaufres

The technique of cooking waffles is shown on page 82.

To make about 15 waffles

200 g	flour	7 oz
	salt	
2 tsp	olive oil	2 tsp
2 tsp	rum	2 tsp
30 g	castor sugar	1 oz
3	eggs, yolks separated from whites, whites beaten to soft peaks	3
¼ litre	milk	8 fl oz

Place the flour in a bowl and add a little salt. Add the oil, rum, sugar and egg yolks. Gradually stir in the milk, being careful not to make lumps. Fold in the beaten egg whites. Cook the waffles in a buttered waffle iron for 2 to 3 minutes each side, or until crisp and golden.

GINETTE MATHIOT
JE SAIS FAIRE LA PÂTISSERIE

Flemish Gauffres

The technique of cooking waffles is shown on page 82.

In place of the orange rind rubbed on sugar, a vanilla pod pounded with 15 g (½ oz) of sugar may be substituted.

To make 36 waffles

350 g	flour	12 oz
30 g	fresh yeast or 1 tbsp dried yeast	1 oz
30 cl	milk	½ pint
175 g	butter, just melted	6 oz
	salt	
4	sugar cubes	4
2	oranges	2
6	eggs, 4 yolks separated from whites, whites stiffly beaten	6
30 cl	double cream, whipped	½ pint
	clarified butter, melted	
	orange, lemon or vanilla sugar	

Put the flour into a 5 litre (1 gallon) basin and spread it out in the centre; then dissolve the yeast in the milk over a low heat until the whole becomes tepid. Add this to the flour and mix these gradually and thoroughly; then take the spoon out, scrape the sides of the basin with a knife, cover with paper and set the batter to rise in a warm place.

When the sponge has increased to twice the original quantity, the butter should be added with a pinch of salt. Rub the sugar cubes on the orange rinds, crush the cubes and add them with the two whole eggs. Mix these in well with the sponge; then add the whipped cream, and the yolks of eggs. Lastly, mix the egg whites lightly in with the batter, and again set it to rise in a warm place, so that the mixture may rise to twice the original quantity.

While the batter is being prepared, leave the waffle iron on a low heat, and when sufficiently hot, run a little clarified butter through it with a pastry brush. Then fill one side of the iron with batter, handling it gently with a spoon. Close the iron, and then turn it upside down (that the batter may run into the opposite side). Set it over a low heat, and when done to a bright yellow colour on one side (about 3 minutes), turn the iron over, to let the gauffre cook on the other side.

The gauffre must then be turned out of the iron, and after the edges have been trimmed with a pair of scissors, set each one in the oven on a baking sheet, making a single layer, covered with paper. Repeat this until the whole of the batter is used up; then shake some orange, lemon or vanilla sugar over them, pile them up neatly on a napkin, and serve.

CHARLES ELMÉ FRANCATELLI
THE COOK'S GUIDE, AND HOUSEKEEPER'S AND BUTLER'S ASSISTANT

Delightful Waffles

The technique of cooking waffles is shown on page 82. You can substitute ordinary baking powder for the double-acting baking powder if you add 1 teaspoonful of tartaric acid.

To make about 36 waffles

250 g	butter, melted	8 oz
300 g	soft brown sugar	10 oz
4	eggs, yolks separated from whites, whites stiffly beaten	4
300 g	flour	10 oz
1½ tsp	double-acting baking powder	1½ tsp
½ tsp	rum or cognac	½ tsp
½ tsp	vanilla extract	½ tsp

Blend the butter with the sugar. Beat the egg yolks and stir them into the butter mixture. Sift the flour and baking powder together. Add the sifted ingredients, rum or cognac and vanilla to the yolk mixture. Fold the egg whites gently into the batter. Bake the waffles in a hot, oiled waffle iron for 4 minutes, or until they are crisp, turning them once.

DOMINIQUE D'ERMO
THE CHEF'S DESSERT COOKBOOK

Standard Preparations

Brioche Dough

To make 1 kg (2 to 2½ lb) brioche dough

20 g	fresh yeast or 2 tsp dried yeast	¾ oz
3 to 4 tbsp	tepid water	3 to 4 tbsp
500 g	strong plain flour	1 lb
60 g	sugar	2 oz
1 tsp	salt	1 tsp
6	eggs	6
300 g	butter, softened	10 oz

Mix the yeast in the tepid water and leave for 10 minutes to dissolve thoroughly. Put the flour, sugar and salt into a bowl. Add the yeast mixture and break in the eggs. Mix the eggs and yeast, gradually pulling flour from the sides of the well, until all the flour has been wetted.

Turn the dough out on to a cool working surface. It should be very soft and sticky. Using your hands and a dough scraper, knead the dough thoroughly until it loses its stickiness and becomes smooth and elastic, about 10 minutes.

Break off walnut-sized pieces of the butter and, using a dough scraper or spatula, fold them one at a time into the dough. When all the butter is incorporated, knead until the dough is smooth. Put the dough into a bowl, cover it with plastic film, and leave the bowl in a warm place until the dough has trebled in bulk, 3 to 4 hours.

Punch the dough down several times to expel gas. Cover the bowl with plastic film and leave the dough to rise again. For best results, the dough should be left in the refrigerator for 6 to 8 hours or overnight. Otherwise, leave the dough to rise at room temperature until doubled in bulk—3 to 4 hours—then chill it for at least 30 minutes before shaping.

To bake a brioche loaf: Place the dough in a well-buttered tin or mould. Cover the tin with a cloth or an inverted bowl and leave the dough to rise at room temperature until it has doubled in bulk, about 1½ to 2 hours. Glaze the top of the dough with egg yolk beaten with water. Bake the loaf in a preheated 220° C (425° F or Mark 7) oven for 10 minutes, then reduce the heat to 190° C (375° F or Mark 5) and bake for another 30 to 40 minutes. The bread is ready when a skewer inserted into the centre of the loaf comes out clean. Unmould the brioche loaf and leave it to cool on a wire rack.

Sweet Yeast Dough

This dough can be used to bake dough shapes such as those shown on page 66. It can also be deep fried to make ring-shaped or jam-filled doughnuts, such as those on page 84.

For the drop doughnuts demonstrated on page 85, a looser dough is made by increasing the amount of milk to ¼ litre (8 fl oz) and the amount of water to 12.5 cl (4 fl oz). As the initial yeast batter made with this increased quantity of liquid will be very runny, the remaining ingredients are then beaten in with a wooden spoon. For drop doughnuts, the amount of sugar in the dough can be decreased to 60 g (2 oz) because the doughnuts are soaked in honey after cooking, and the cinnamon in the dough may be omitted if the doughnuts are sprinkled with cinnamon after cooking.

To make about 800 g (1¾ lb) dough or about 25 shapes or doughnuts

125 g	plain flour	4 oz
350 g	strong plain flour	12 oz
1 tsp	salt	1 tsp
30 g	fresh yeast or 1 tbsp dried yeast	1 oz
15 cl	milk, warmed	¼ pint
2 tbsp	tepid water	2 tbsp
90 g	castor sugar	3 oz
90 g	butter, softened	3 oz
2	eggs, beaten	2
½ tsp	ground cinnamon	½ tsp
	ground cardamom	
	ground mace	
1	orange, rind grated	1

Sift the flours and the salt together. Dissolve the yeast in the milk and water. Put 150 g (5 oz) of the flour and a teaspoonful of castor sugar into a bowl and add the dissolved yeast. Mix to a smooth paste and leave to rise for about 20 minutes.

When the yeast batter is puffy and risen, start to incorporate small pieces of softened butter by hand. When all the butter has been added, add the eggs, one at a time, and work them in well. Then add the remaining flour and sugar, the cinnamon, a pinch of cardamom and of mace and the orange rind, and mix them together by hand. When all the flour has been combined, turn the dough out on to a floured surface and knead it vigorously by hand for about 20 minutes, until it is smooth and no longer sticky. Form the dough into a ball and place it in a bowl. Cover the bowl and leave the dough to rise in a warm place for about 2 hours or until it doubles in size.

Knock the dough down by kneading it lightly and shape it as required. Before they are baked, cover the dough shapes with a cloth and leave them to rise in a warm place for 30 to 40 minutes, or until they have doubled in size.

Sweet Noodle Dough

This dough, being very pliable, is suitable for making intricate deep-fried pastry shapes.

To make about 400 g (14 oz) dough

250 g	flour	8 oz
	salt	
2 tbsp	sugar	2 tbsp
½ tsp	ground spice (cardamom, cinnamon, nutmeg or a mixture)	½ tsp
1	egg	1
60 g	butter melted	2 oz
About 4 tbsp	tepid water	About 4 tbsp
1	orange or lemon, rind grated	1

Sift the flour, a pinch of salt, the sugar and spices into a bowl. Make a well in the centre and add the egg, melted butter, water and grated orange or lemon rind. Stir the ingredients together with a fork, working from the centre out, then knead the dough rapidly with your knuckles for about 2 minutes, until it is smooth. Form the dough into a ball, cover it with a cloth and leave it to rest for about 1 hour before rolling it out.

Choux Dough

To form choux buns, place the dough in a piping bag with a plain nozzle and pipe out small rounds of dough, about 2.5 cm (1 inch) in diameter, on to a baking sheet lined with silicon paper. To form éclairs, pipe out strips of dough about 6 cm (2½ inches) long on to the baking sheet. Bake the buns or éclairs in a preheated 220°C (425°F or Mark 7) oven for 20 minutes, or until the pastry is puffed and lightly browned. A few minutes before the end of the cooking time, remove them from the oven and use a knife tip to pierce the ends of each éclair, or the base of each bun, to release the steam; return them to the oven. Cool the pastries on a rack before filling and icing them.

To make 15 choux buns or 10 éclairs

12.5 cl	water	4 fl oz
60 g	butter	2 oz
75 g	flour	2½ oz
½ tsp	salt	½ tsp
2	eggs	2

Put the water in a heavy saucepan over a low heat. Add the butter. Sift the flour and salt on to greaseproof paper.

Increase the heat so that the butter melts and the liquid

comes to the boil simultaneously. Remove the pan from the heat and slide all the flour off the paper into the water, stirring all the time. Return the pan to a medium heat and beat the mixture constantly with a wooden spoon until it forms a solid mass that comes away cleanly from the sides of the pan. Remove the pan from the heat and cool the mixture for a few minutes.

Break one egg into a bowl and add it to the contents of the pan, beating with the wooden spoon to incorporate the egg thoroughly. Repeat with the other egg. Continue beating until all the ingredients are smoothly blended.

———◆———

Shortcrust Dough Enriched with Eggs and Sugar

This dough can be flavoured by stirring 100 g ($3\frac{1}{2}$ oz) of ground nuts, such as walnuts, almonds or hazelnuts, into the flour; the butter should then be rubbed, not cut, into the dry ingredients. The quantity below makes about 25 tartlet shells.

To make 500 g (1 lb) dough		
250 g	flour	8 oz
60 g	castor sugar or icing sugar	2 oz
	salt	
125 g	butter	4 oz
2	eggs	2

Sift the flour, sugar and a pinch of salt together into a bowl. Add the butter and rub it in lightly with your fingertips, or cut it into the dry ingredients with two knives, until the mixture resembles coarse breadcrumbs. Add the eggs and stir them in with a fork. When the mixture begins to cling together, press it into a ball with your hands, place it on a floured surface and knead it gently into a smooth and homogeneous mass. Wrap the dough in plastic film and refrigerate it for at least 30 minutes before rolling it out.

———◆———

Rough-Puff Dough

To make about 250 g (8 oz) dough		
125 g	flour	4 oz
	salt	
125 g	butter, chilled and cubed	4 oz
2 to 3 tbsp	cold water	2 to 3 tbsp

Sift the flour and a pinch of salt into a bowl. Add the butter and cut it into the flour rapidly, using two table knives, until the butter is in pieces the size of peas. Add half the water and, with a fork, quickly blend it into the flour and butter mixture.

Add just enough of the rest of the water to allow you to gather the dough together with your hands into a firm ball. Wrap the dough in plastic film or wax paper and refrigerate it for 30 minutes or put it in the freezer for about 15 minutes.

Take the ball of dough from the refrigerator or freezer and place it on a cool floured surface. Smack it flat with a rolling pin. Turn the dough over to make sure that both sides are lightly floured, and roll out the dough rapidly into a rectangle about 30 cm (12 inches) long and 12.5 to 15 cm (5 to 6 inches) wide. Fold the two ends to meet each other in the centre, then fold again to align the folded edges with each other. Give the dough a quarter turn and, following the direction of the fold lines, roll the dough into a rectangle again, fold again in the same way, wrap in plastic film and refrigerate for at least 30 minutes or put it in the freezer for 15 minutes. Repeat this process two or three more times before using the dough. Always let the dough rest in the refrigerator or freezer in between the times it is rolled out.

———◆———

Shortcrust Dough

The proportion of fat to flour in shortcrust dough can be varied according to the result required. For the standard shortcrust pastry consistency, use the smaller quantity of butter; for a richer and much crisper result, use the larger quantity of butter. The quantity of dough given here will line about 15 small tartlet moulds.

To make about 250 g (8 oz) dough		
125 g	flour	4 oz
	salt	
60 to 125 g	butter, chilled and cubed	2 to 4 oz
2 to 3 tbsp	cold water	2 to 3 tbsp

Sift the flour with a pinch of salt into a bowl. Add the butter. Rub the butter and flour together with your fingertips, or cut the butter into the flour with two knives, until the mixture has a coarse mealy texture. Add half the water and, with a fork, quickly blend it into the flour and butter mixture. Add just enough of the rest of the water to allow you to gather the dough together into a firm ball. Wrap the dough in plastic film and refrigerate it for 30 minutes, or put it into the freezer for about 15 minutes.

Remove the dough from the refrigerator or freezer and put it on a cool floured surface (a marble slab is ideal). Press the dough out partially with your hand, then give it a few gentle smacks with the rolling pin to flatten it and render it more supple. Roll the dough out from the centre until it is about 1 cm ($\frac{1}{2}$ inch) thick, then turn it over so that both sides are floured and continue rolling until the dough is about 3 mm ($\frac{1}{8}$ inch) thick. For small open pastries, cut out small rounds with a biscuit cutter to fit your tartlet tins. For *barquettes*, lay the sheet of dough over the tins and trim the excess from each tin.

Sponge Cake Batter

This batter is the basis for the sponge assemblies, the petits fours glacés and the decorated sponges shown on pages 40-47. It can be baked in a shallow 38 by 25 by 1 cm (15 by 10 by ½ inch) Swiss roll tin to provide a thin cake base to support thick layers of mousse or filling, or it can be baked in a deep 36 by 20 by 5 cm (12 by 8 by 2 inch) tin, so that the resulting cake can be split in half horizontally and sandwiched with a filling. A shallow cake should be baked only briefly in a hot oven, while a deep cake should be baked more slowly.

The batter can be flavoured in various ways. For example, 2 tablespoons of cocoa powder can be sifted with the flour before adding it to the eggs and sugar; alternatively, 2 to 3 tablespoons of a fruit purée such as raspberry or strawberry can be folded into the beaten eggs and sugar before the flour is added; or the flour quantity can be reduced to 90 g (3 oz), and 30 g (1 oz) of ground almonds or hazelnuts can be added to the mixture, with the flour.

To make one cake

4	eggs	4
125 g	sugar	4 oz
125 g	flour	4 oz
	salt	
60 g	butter, melted and cooled	2 oz

Whisk the eggs and sugar together in a large bowl. Place the bowl over a saucepan of hot water on a low heat, and whisk the mixture until it is thick and white and falls from the whisk in a thick ribbon, leaving a trail on the surface. This will take about 20 minutes by hand or 10 minutes with an electric beater. Sift the flour with a pinch of salt, then fold it into the mixture in two or three stages, adding it alternately with the butter. Continue to fold the mixture until all the ingredients are well blended.

Pour the cake batter into a deep rectangular cake tin or a shallow Swiss roll tin, lined with buttered greaseproof paper. Bake in a preheated 180°C (350°F or Mark 4) oven for 20 to 25 minutes for a deep cake, or in a 220°C (425°F or Mark 7) oven for 7 minutes for a shallow cake.

Place the tin on a wire rack to cool for about 5 minutes, then turn the cake out of the tin, peel off the greaseproof paper and leave the cake on the rack to cool completely.

Creamed Cake Batter

This batter is suitable for making the small moulded cakes shown on page 36. A stiffer mixture can be rolled out like a pastry dough, shaped with cutters and deep fried; the rosettes demonstrated on page 86 are made from this stiffened mixture. To stiffen the batter, increase the flour quantity to 250 g (8 oz) and add 125 g (4 oz) of ground hazelnuts with the flour.

To make about 20 individual cakes or one 25 by 38 cm (10 by 15 inch) cake

125 g	butter, softened	4 oz
125 g	sugar	4 oz
2	eggs	2
125 g	flour	4 oz
1 tsp	baking powder	1 tsp

Beat the butter with a wooden spoon until pale. Cream together the butter and sugar until the mixture is light in colour and fluffy. Add the eggs, one at a time, beating well after each addition. Sift the flour and baking powder together and gradually fold them in with a metal spoon. Butter and flour individual cake moulds or a 25 by 38 cm (10 by 15 inch) shallow baking tin, and fill two-thirds full with the batter. Bake in a preheated 190°C (375°F or Mark 5) oven for 10 to 15 minutes, until golden-brown. The top of the cake should feel springy and the edges shrink away slightly from the sides of the mould or tin. Allow to cool slightly in the moulds or tin before turning out on to wire racks to cool completely.

Swiss Meringue

As this mixture is very thick and stiff, it is particularly suitable for piping elaborate shapes, either for decoration or to make individual meringue shells. To make these, pipe out the desired shapes on a baking sheet lined with silicon paper. Bake the meringues at the lowest possible temperature in your oven for 3 to 4 hours, so that they dry out rather than bake and keep their white colour.

To make about 300 g (10 oz) meringue mixture or 20 individual meringues

4	egg whites, lightly beaten	4
250 g	castor sugar	8 oz

Place the egg whites and the sugar in a copper bowl and place the bowl over a pan of gently simmering water on a low heat. Beat the egg whites and sugar together by hand for about 30 minutes, or with an electric beater for 15 to 20 minutes, until the meringue mixture has greatly increased in volume and is very stiff, white and glossy.

French Meringue

French meringue is best used for simple constructions. To make individual meringue shells, pipe or spoon out small quantities of meringue on to a baking sheet lined with silicon paper. Bake the meringues at the lowest possible temperature for at least 3 hours so that they dry out and keep their white colour. Ways of assembling meringue shells with different fillings and coatings are shown on pages 26-31.

To make about 300 g (10 oz) meringue mixture or 20 individual meringues

4	egg whites	4
250 g	castor sugar	8 oz

Beat the egg whites until they form stiff peaks. Sprinkle on a little sugar and beat well. Continue to add small quantities of sugar, beating well after each addition, until all the sugar has been added and the mixture again holds stiff peaks.

Italian Meringue

This meringue is used for lightening fillings and mousses and for piped decorations—on the top of tarts, for example.

To make about 350 g (12 oz) meringue mixture

250 g	sugar	8 oz
10 cl	water	3½ fl oz
4	egg whites, stiffly beaten	4

Dissolve the sugar in the water in a heavy saucepan over a low heat. Bring to the boil and cook the syrup until it reaches the hard-ball stage (*page 6*). Pour the hot syrup in a thin stream on to the beaten egg whites, whisking all the time, and continue whisking until all the syrup has been incorporated and the meringue is very thick and glossy.

Chocolate Frosting

To make 500 g (1 lb) frosting

100 g	hard bitter chocolate	3½ oz
40 g	butter, cut into cubes	1½ oz
300 g	icing sugar, sifted	10 oz
	salt	
1 tsp	vanilla extract or 1 tbsp vanilla sugar	1 tsp
5 tbsp	milk	5 tbsp

Melt the chocolate and butter together in a pan over a low heat, stirring all the time. Keep the pan on the heat while you stir in the icing sugar, a pinch of salt and the vanilla extract or vanilla sugar. Pour in the milk and stir it in. Beat the mixture in the pan, over the heat, until it is smooth, then remove the pan from the heat and place it in a bowl of ice and water. Continue to beat the mixture until it becomes very thick.

Fondant Icing

Liquid glucose or cream of tartar incorporated into a sugar syrup prevents the formation of large crystals and thus produces a fine-textured fondant.

To flavour fondant icing with chocolate, stir in 60 g (2 oz) grated chocolate as the fondant is being melted before use; for a coffee flavour, add 1 tablespoon of strong black coffee. To colour fondant green, add about half a teaspoon of spinach extract; for yellow colouring, add powdered saffron dissolved in 1 to 3 teaspoons of hot water; for red colouring, add a few drops of cochineal. Stir the colouring in well.

To make 90 cl (1½ pints) icing

1 kg	sugar	2 lb
30 cl	water	½ pint
1½ to 2 tsp	liquid glucose or a pinch of cream of tartar	1½ to 2 tsp
About 2 tbsp	light sugar syrup (*page 6*)	About 2 tbsp

Put the sugar, water and glucose or cream of tartar into a pan over a low heat. Stir them together; dissolve the sugar completely. Raise the heat to bring the syrup to the boil; continue to cook the syrup until it reaches the soft-ball stage (*page 6*).

Sprinkle a little cold water on to a marble slab and pour the hot syrup on to it. Allow the syrup to cool a little. Using a metal scraper, work the syrup by repeatedly scooping it up from the edges and folding it into the middle. Continue to work the syrup in a figure-of-eight movement for about 10 minutes until it suddenly becomes grainy and opaque and is too stiff to be worked with the scraper. Knead it with your hands, folding and pressing it until it is smooth and supple. Work the fondant into a smooth ball, place it in a bowl and cover it with a damp cloth. Leave it to rest for at least 24 hours. It can be kept indefinitely in a tightly covered jar.

To prepare fondant icing, place the fondant in a bowl over a pan of hot water on a low heat. When the fondant begins to melt, stir in 2 tablespoons of light sugar syrup. Continue to stir the fondant over the heat, adding a little more syrup if necessary, until the fondant coats the back of the spoon and is the consistency of thick cream.

Royal Icing

To make about 30 cl (½ pint) icing

2	egg whites	2
500 g	icing sugar, sifted	1 lb
½	lemon, juice strained	½

Place the egg whites in a bowl and stir in a little of the icing sugar. Add the lemon juice. With a wooden spoon, beat the mixture vigorously until it is light and smooth. Add the remaining icing sugar, a little at a time, beating well after each addition. Continue beating until the mixture is very thick and white, a total of about 15 minutes by hand or 7 minutes with an electric beater. Use the icing immediately or keep it for up to 30 minutes, covered with a damp cloth to prevent it from drying out. Beat the icing again before use.

Glacé Icing

To flavour the icing, replace the water with strained orange or lemon juice, strong black coffee or other liquid flavouring as desired. If using the icing for piping, add more water to dilute it to a looser consistency.

To make 30 cl (½ pint) icing

250 g	icing sugar	8 oz
2 tbsp	warm water	2 tbsp

Sift the icing sugar into a bowl and make a well in the middle. Pour the water into the well and stir in the icing sugar. Continue stirring until all the icing sugar is incorporated and the mixture is very smooth. Use the icing at once.

Marzipan

To make 750 g (1½ lb) marzipan

350 g	ground almonds	12 oz
350 g	icing sugar, sifted	12 oz
½	lemon, juice strained	½
2	egg whites, lightly beaten	2

Mix together the ground almonds and icing sugar in a bowl. Make a well in the centre and add the lemon juice and some of the egg white. Mix them into the dry ingredients with a knife, then work the mixture by hand until it starts to come away from the sides of the bowl. Stir in enough of the remaining egg white to make a stiff paste. Turn the paste out on to a marble slab lightly sprinkled with icing sugar and knead it gently until smooth. Do not overwork the paste or it will become oily.

Buttercream

To make about 600 g (1¼ lb) buttercream

5	egg yolks	5
125 g	sugar	4 oz
10 cl	water	3½ fl oz
250 g	butter, softened	8 oz
1 tbsp	strong black coffee, praline powder, liqueur, lemon juice with a little grated rind, or 90 g (3 oz) chocolate melted over hot water	1 tbsp

Whisk the egg yolks until they are thick and foamy and light in colour (about 15 minutes by hand or 7 minutes with an electric beater). Over a medium heat, dissolve the sugar in the water and cook the syrup to the thread stage (*page 6*). Pour the hot syrup into the whisked egg yolks in a thin stream, beating all the time, and continue to beat until the mixture is cool. It will be pale, thick and fluffy.

Cream the butter in a bowl with a wooden spoon until it is smooth, then stir in the whisked egg mixture and beat it with the wooden spoon until all the egg is incorporated and the buttercream is smooth, light in texture and shiny. Stir in the coffee or other chosen flavouring.

Pastry Cream
Crème Pâtissière

To make ¾ litre (1¼ pints) pastry cream

45 g	flour	1½ oz
	salt	
125 g	sugar	4 oz
5 or 6	egg yolks	5 or 6
½ litre	milk	16 fl oz
5 cm	piece vanilla pod (optional)	2 inch

Sift the flour and a pinch of salt into a bowl. Mix the sugar and egg yolks together with a spoon, beating until the mixture is thick and cream-coloured. Gradually work in the flour.

Heat the milk with the vanilla pod, if using, to boiling point, then set aside until the milk is tepid. Remove the vanilla pod. Stirring constantly, pour the tepid milk into the egg mixture in a thin stream. Turn the pastry cream mixture into a saucepan and, stirring vigorously, cook over a medium heat until the mixture comes to boiling point. Cook for about 2 minutes. Strain the pastry cream and allow it to cool, stirring it occasionally to prevent a skin from forming. The cream may be stored, covered, in a refrigerator for two days.

Meringue Buttercream

To make about 600 g (1¼ lb) buttercream

350 g	Italian meringue mixture (*page 165*)	12 oz
250 g	butter, softened	8 oz

Cream the butter with a wooden spoon until it is smooth, then beat in the meringue mixture until it is completely incorporated and the buttercream is very smooth and light.

Fruit Mousse Filling

This mousse can be flavoured according to your taste. You can, for example, use strawberry, raspberry or blackberry purée. The technique of puréeing fruit is shown on page 14. The technique of making a fruit mousse is shown on page 17.

To make about 1.5 litres (2½ pints) mousse

½ litre	fruit purée or juice	16 fl oz
15 g	gelatine	½ oz
	Italian meringue mixture (*page 165*), made with 3 egg whites and 200 g (7 oz) sugar	
¾ litre	double cream, whipped to soft peaks	1¼ pints

Sprinkle the gelatine on to a little of the fruit purée or juice, and allow it to soften. Melt the softened gelatine over a very low heat. Remove the pan from the heat and add the rest of the fruit purée or juice, then fold this mixture into the meringue. Finally, fold in the whipped cream.

Chocolate Ganache

To make about ½ litre (16 fl oz) ganache

250 g	hard semi-sweet chocolate, chopped	8 oz
¼ litre	double cream	8 fl oz

Place the chopped chocolate and the cream in a heavy saucepan over a gentle heat and stir with a wooden spoon until the chocolate has completely melted. Continue to stir the cream on the heat for about 10 minutes, but do not allow it to boil. The colour will become an even dark brown and the texture will be smooth and thick. Pour the mixture into a large bowl and refrigerate it for at least 1 hour.

Remove the mixture from the refrigerator and whisk it by hand or with an electric beater until it has doubled in volume and is pale brown in colour and very light in consistency. This will take about 10 to 15 minutes by hand or 5 to 10 minutes with an electric beater.

Praline

To make 500 g (1 lb) praline powder

250 g	almonds, blanched	8 oz
250 g	sugar	8 oz
	almond oil	

Place the almonds and sugar in a heavy pan over a very low heat; stir continually until the nuts are toasted and the sugar has caramelized and is a pale amber. Pour the mixture on to a marble slab lightly oiled with almond oil, and spread it out to form a thin layer over the slab. Leave it to cool completely.

When the praline is cold and hard, break it into pieces and remove it from the slab. Place the pieces in a large plastic bag and pound them into coarse crumbs with a rolling pin. Sift the crumbs through a coarse-meshed sieve. Return any larger pieces that will not go through the sieve to the plastic bag and repeat until all the nut mixture is powdered.

White Praline

To make about 350 g (12 oz) praline powder

175 g	sugar	6 oz
5 tbsp	water	5 tbsp
175 g	ground almonds	6 oz
	almond oil	

In a heavy saucepan, dissolve the sugar in the water over a very low heat. Bring to the boil and cook the syrup until it reaches the hard-ball stage (*page 6*). Take the pan off the heat and thoroughly stir in the ground almonds. Oil a marble slab lightly with almond oil and pour the mixture out on to the slab. Spread it out to form a thin layer on the slab and allow it to cool completely. When it is cold and hard, break the praline into pieces and press it through a coarse-meshed metal sieve to make a fine powder.

Recipe Index

English recipe titles are listed by categories such as "Almonds", "Chocolate", "Doughnuts", "Icing", "Rough-Puff Pastries", "Tarts" and "Whisked Cakes", and within those categories alphabetically. Foreign recipe titles are listed alphabetically without regard to category.